KEYWORDS IN CREATIVE WRITING

KEYWORDS IN CREATIVE WRITING

WENDY BISHOP
DAVID STARKEY

UTAH STATE UNIVERSITY PRESS
Logan, Utah

Utah State University Press
Logan, Utah 84322

Printed on acid-free paper

Cover design by Barbara Yale-Read

Library of Congress Cataloging-in-Publication Data

Bishop, Wendy, 1953–2003
  Keywords in creative writing / Wendy Bishop, David Starkey.
    p. cm.
  Includes bibliographical references.
  ISBN 0-87421-629-X (pbk. : alk. paper)
  1. English language–Rhetoric–Study and teaching–Terminology. 2. Creative writing–Study and teach-
ing–Terminology. 3. English language–Rhetoric–Terminology. 4. Creative writing–Terminology. I.
Starkey, David, 1962- II. Title.

PE1404.B498 2005
808'.042'071–dc22

                                                      2005024616

CONTENTS (ALPHABETICAL)

CONTENTS (TOPIC CLUSTERS)

WRITING

THE WRITING LIFE

For DEAN *and for* SANDY

INTRODUCTION

The idea for this book occurred to me years ago. One afternoon I was daydreaming. I imagined a nineteen-year-old undergraduate thinking of majoring in English, with an emphasis in creative writing. Throughout her high school years, she has written poetry and short stories, and her friends and family have encouraged her dream of becoming a writer. Yet she's also been told, over and over, that very few people ever make it as writers. If only there were a concise, comprehensive guide to creative writing, she could begin to make an informed decision about her future plans.

Should that student decide to continue on in creative writing, she would face another decision in a few years: what to do after she graduates. Should she try to freelance, or should she go straight into the working world and write on the side? What about graduate programs? What's the difference between an MFA and a PhD with a creative dissertation? (And just what *is* a "creative dissertation"?) Supposing she completed one or even both of these degrees, what would be her chances of finding a job teaching creative writing? Where does she turn?

Then I envisioned that person thirty years older, looking at creative writing from the perspective of a middle-aged adult. Say she's been working and attained success in another field, yet she's always retained her dream of being a writer. Finally, circumstances will allow her to have a few years to herself. As a businessperson, she's used to investigating an opportunity before she makes a definite commitment to it. What are the potential rewards and drawbacks? Who controls the decision-making process and what are the details of that process? What will it take to make it?

And if a student like the one I was picturing would naturally have more questions than her instructors, that doesn't mean that faculty members don't have questions themselves. For the English department chair who specializes in medieval literature in a large midwestern university, creative writing might well be an entirely different discipline for all he knows about it, yet his position as chair would require him to regularly assess the work of the creative writing faculty and, ultimately, to make a recommendation for or against tenure. A handbook of some sort would be indispensable to him, just as it would be useful for the non-English faculty and administrators involved in a tenure decision.

The creative writer herself, even (and perhaps more so) if she is very much in the thick of the scene, will want to compare her own impressions with someone else's. Over time, creative writing instructors come to take certain things for granted. We assume everyone else has pretty much the same assumptions about our discipline, and when we find that's not the case, we're forced to resee the world from a different angle. Whether this re-visioning thrills us, disturbs us, or simply reconfirms what we've held to be true, it is a necessary process for any creative writing teacher who hopes to remain current in the field.

I imagined a book, which I began calling *Keywords in Creative Writing*, that would be useful both in the classroom *and* outside it. Because of its investment in the language and ideas of composition, professors might assign *Keywords* in advanced composition courses or in pedagogy seminars for new writing teachers. Yet readers would not need to encounter the book as part of an assigned curriculum. Picking up the book would be like sitting in on a conversation that was knowledgeable but friendly to newcomers. Ultimately, therefore, *Keywords in Creative Writing* would reach out to several different audiences that might, or might not, at times overlap. This would be a resource book; not every reader would find every entry necessary, but the book's diversity of subjects and approaches would be one of its chief strengths.

A little research uncovered the fact that I would be following on the heels of several similar books in other areas in English and academic studies: Paul Heilker and Peter Vandenberg's *Keywords in Composition Studies* (1996) and Cary Nelson and Stephen Watt's *Academic Keywords* (1999). These two books, each of which owes something to Raymond Williams's *Keywords: A Vocabulary of Culture and Society* (1976), touch on various areas of concern to creative writers. Heilker and Vandenberg's book, for instance, provides a great deal of useful information about expository writing theory, the sort of information creative writers who teach may find useful in their classes. And Nelson and Watt's book supplies a context for life in American colleges and universities that is especially useful to those in English studies, since both Nelson and Watt are English professors. Cocooned in their own insular world, as they too often are, creative writers are likely to be unaware of the history and structure of higher education in the United States.

Both of these are admirable volumes, yet it should be said that the writing theory in *Keywords in Composition Studies* is meant mainly for PhDs in rhetoric and composition, and that Cary Nelson, especially, is dismissive of the demiworld of semirespectability that most creative writers in the academy inhabit. In contrast, I imagined that *Keywords in Creative Writing* would both clarify and complicate the many issues that face American writers (and readers) of imaginative literature. Moreover, it would be written for a much wider audience, one that ranged from undergraduates who are interested in pursuing further study in creative writing to graduate students trying to locate themselves in the field to English faculty trying to situate creative writing within the larger discipline. In addition to the obvious academic audience, the book would also be useful to new writers outside the university: anyone who benefits from journals like *Writer's Digest* and *Poets and Writers Magazine* would also find *Keywords in Creative Writing* helpful in making sense of what can initially seem an overwhelming enterprise.

I puttered around with the idea for several months, then I realized what should have been obvious from the first: I couldn't do the book without turning to my friend Wendy Bishop, the supreme authority on all things creative writing, author of *Released into Language* (1988; second edition 1998), the first book to systematically use the insights of composition and rhetoric to inform the teaching of creative writing. In her usual tornadic fashion, Wendy jumped into the project, writing entries, suggesting new keywords, recommending further research. Soon, the original thirty entries I'd suggested had become sixty-one. However, as we wrote, we realized that terms such as "E-Zine" and "Hypertext" could be collapsed under a single heading, in this case, "Electronic Literature." Similarly, "Race," "Class," and "Gender" became "Identity Politics." On the other hand, some originally separate entries could more profitably be read together—"Image and Metaphor," "Style and Voice," and "Conferences, Colonies, and Residencies" became single chapters.

Our goal was to make each of the alphabetically listed entries concise and accessible (that is, relatively jargon-free), with extensive cross-referencing within the entries. Whenever we felt it was appropriate, we cited secondary sources, but the book was meant to be readable and reader-friendly, not a handbook of bland, faceless prose. Although we tried to be fair to our subjects, we made no claim to objectivity. There were times when we disagreed with one another on important issues, times when we felt the need to be outspoken advocates or critics—and rather than stifle our passion, we occasionally allowed it to rise to the surface.

In fact, we wanted to think that our voices would be recognizable to those who know them. *Keywords in Creative Writing* was not meant to represent a definitive attempt to define and categorize a continually developing discipline; such an effort would be quixotic anyway. Instead, the book would simply be the contribution of two participants among countless others in the centuries-long conversation among those who write, read, argue about, and love literature.

And so we wrote—off more than on—for the next four years. I left one job and started another. Other projects got in the way. In the spring of 2003, we finally seemed to have zeroed in on finishing the book. I would write three more entries; Wendy had ideas for another five. We promised ourselves that we would turn the manuscript over to our long-suffering editor, Michael Spooner, by August.

Then Wendy got sick.

In an e-mail dated 3 May, she complained of "a month of cold/pseudo-sars," but she believed that she was "finally knocking it out with antibiotics." Throughout June and July, she was writing furiously; we both were, with our eyes on the deadline. Then, on August 12, her husband sent a message saying that she was in the hospital, with what turned out to be adult acute lymphoblastic leukemia. He said that the recovery rate was 90 percent.

I was stunned. Two weeks later, Wendy wrote to me. She was brave, but she admitted that there were "scary hours and energy loss and a constant need to work up the courage to fight this." She concluded by saying, "one of my first when i come back to myself projects, of course, is ours. but right now that's a distant month or two away."

In the event, though, that turned out to be an overly optimistic prediction. On November 14, I wrote her an e-mail to ask how she was doing, to let her know how much she meant to her friends. She wrote back the next day, sounding tired but still optimistic, mentioning "our project" several times. "so i'm going to revise and plug on," she wrote, "and hope we still can come out somewhere first draft keyword-ish next year. i'm lucky i had 13 years of sick leave. and whether i can do any of this changes daily. i have more tired days than good days but in three months, almost four, i can see some forward progress. i get info on radiation this week. i think i'm facing some on weeks and off weeks to get strength. the steroids are the very worst—they make me crazy and unhappy but seem to complement the treatments. and i'm tired of these body reports so i'll stop. do think of our key words, poor things." She signed her message, as always, "l, w."

A week later she died of complications caused by the leukemia.

I was lost for a while, I admit, like all her friends. *She* had always been our guidepost, and now she was gone. As far as our book together went, I had two conflicting impulses. One of them, of course, was that I needed to finish it in Wendy's honor. That was certainly what she would have wanted. On the other hand, I wondered if it was really worth it. After all, in the face of death, what did one more academic book really mean? Shouldn't I turn my attention instead to plays and poems, to my own creative writing, instead of simply commenting on other writers' work and ideas?

I struggled to find focus, to stay on task. It took me six months to write my final two entries. It was a very un-Wendy-like performance. Nevertheless, I finally finished, in large measure out of a desire to see Wendy's intelligence and wit in print one more time. A few months later, the manuscript was returned as incomplete, but now I felt resolved to finish and I pushed on, writing another eighty-five pages, much of that material aimed at providing newcomers with the nuts-and-bolts information necessary to succeed as creative writers. I ended up writing 32 of the 43 entries, so—from page to page—the voice is more often mine than Wendy's. Yet her sense of the *mission* of creative writing remained an inspiration to me throughout the process, and *Keywords* is truly a collaborative project.

Ultimately, five main topic clusters emerged (these groupings can be found in the alternative table of contents). *Academia* covers questions of teaching. Readers will find information on graduate degrees in creative writing (both MFAs and PhDs), analyses of current and future job markets, and discussions of composition, reading and literary theory, and pedagogy as a whole. This is the section for beginning teachers seeking basic information and for their more experienced colleagues who want to refresh their memories. *Publishing* deals with everything from submitting one's work and dealing with the inevitable rejection slips to choosing the right agent and negotiating royalties and permission fees. Here one will find the nitty-gritty of creative writing as a business. *Literary Genres and Terms* contains entries on all four of the major genres—poetry, fiction, creative nonfiction, and drama (which is included under the heading "Scriptwriting"). This section also examines terms frequently mentioned in creative writing classes, such as "author," "image and metaphor," "postmodernism," and "style and voice." *Writing* discusses issues specific to the actual composition of a work of literature. How does one deal with writer's block and procrastination? What benefits can be derived from collaboration and writing groups? What does "creativity" really mean? Finally, *The Writing Life* looks at professional concerns that fall somewhere between teaching and publication. This grouping evaluates the relative merits of the Associated Writing Programs; it investigates conferences and colonies, residencies and grants; and it takes a lighthearted look at the necessity of schmoozing with one's peers. Taken altogether, this material provides both an entry into and a refresher course on the field of creative writing.

Of course, a book such as *Keywords in Creative Writing* can never truly be complete. The discipline is always changing and expanding, and throughout the writing and revising of the manuscript, new articles and ideas germane to our areas of interest kept coming across our desks. Sometimes we would incorporate them into our entries; other times we would have to let them go. Yet I offer up these keywords, the "poor things," as a tribute to Wendy Bishop, whose love and knowledge of creative writing were an inspiration to me, and to so many others. This is for you, Wendy.

l, d

ADJUNCT AND TEMPORARY FACULTY

The plight of adjunct (part-time) and temporary (nontenured) faculty has been well documented, particularly by contingent faculty themselves. The experience of Ben Satterfield, a former adjunct, is typical. While teaching at the University of Texas, Satterfield recalls that though they "were not shunned like pariahs, the temporary faculty were distinctly second-class citizens, tolerated but not encouraged" (1994, 130). When he moved from UT to Austin Community College, Satterfield's situation became even worse. He received even less respect from administrators and colleagues and was paid 60 percent less than full-time faculty for teaching the same courses: "Dozens of us shared one small office, occupying desks like shift workers; we were hired on a semester-to-semester basis and denied medical insurance coverage or any benefits that were standard for the regular faculty; we were disdained by the administration and treated like field workers with no rights whatever" (132).

The comparison of adjuncts with field workers—dislocated seasonal laborers who can be easily replaced—has been especially prevalent in English studies. As Cary Nelson and Michael Berube (1994) point out: "Tenure-track jobs in English regularly receive 800 to 1,000 applications. Even the most accomplished young scholars and teachers often remain unemployed. For in the 1990's, many colleges are finding that they lack the money even to replace retiring faculty members, and graduate programs that had expected boom times suddenly find that they are drastically overproducing Ph.D.'s."

Linda Ray Pratt, chair of an Association of University Professors committee on the status of nontenure-track faculty, predicted in 1997 that "if things continue unchecked, about 90 percent of the English Ph.D.'s on the market in the next few years will not find a tenure-track job" (265).

She was right. There are simply too many workers and not enough work to go around, with the result that aspiring academics who want to teach in a college or university nearly always settle for less than ideal jobs. Elizabeth Wallace notes: "Those who choose to settle [in a particular area] are often at disadvantage in their search for academic jobs, simply because they are already here: academia much prefers to interview exotic strangers from across the country." And potential teachers are at an even greater disadvantage if they are "following a spouse to a full-time job or coming to care for a sick relative or following children in the custody of a divorced partner . . . [these people] have automatically removed themselves from the national academic job market and have entered the local market with no choice in the matter" (1994, 29).

In *Gypsy Academics and Mother Teachers* (1997), Eileen Schell, one of the most prolific writers on the subject of contingent academic labor, examines the ways that the "feminization" of composition has turned it into an underrespected discipline, with no benefits or job security. Schell traces this situation in higher education back to the initial entry of women into the workforce, when many of them became elementary and secondary school teachers. Ironically, this "liberation" resulted in an entrenchment of women in the teaching force and led to lower pay and less respect for teaching in general. And it is not just those outside education who denigrate the work done by teachers of composition and other less-than-glamorous subjects. Both the authors of this book have heard tenured male professors refer to temporary writing faculty as "the little old ladies in the basement"; unfortunately, such noisome appellations coming from those in the upper echelons of academia are not uncommon.

Given the disregard and low wages adjunct faculty can expect to receive, one might wonder why *anyone* would take on the job of teaching writing part-time. Many adjuncts would answer that they love to teach, even if they are slighted by just about everyone. Some adjuncts take part-time work to gain enough experience to make themselves attractive as candidates for full-time jobs. Moreover, even if they are at the bottom of the pecking order *within* the college or university, some faculty receive outside validation, taking pride in being associated with an institution of higher learning. "I teach at the university," they can tell family and friends—without mentioning that their assignment is one course a semester for a few thousand dollars, or less. And since so few people can afford to live on a part-time instructor's salary, those who manage to do so have—de facto—solved the issue of working for low pay. Either they are single and frugal, or else they have another source of income to supplement their meager salaries.

Despite the fact that colleges and universities routinely disrespect their adjuncts, they nevertheless cannot live without them. According to former Conference of College Composition and Communication chair John Lovas, "Since the mid-1970s, California community colleges have been structurally dependent on the hiring of part-time faculty. The system could not function, its mission could not be carried out, if part-time

faculty work was limited to the original conception of it: some specialists from local industry would offer specialized courses in the evening"
(2001, 203). Nancy Sours, an instructor at San Francisco State University,
claims that in 2004, nontenured faculty taught "close to 100% of writing
classes offered by our English Department" and viewed themselves "as
career faculty" (2004, A7). And California colleges and universities are
hardly alone in relying on "temporary" labor. Linda Ray Pratt claims that
45 percent of all courses in higher education are taught by part-timers,
with the figure at 65 percent for community colleges (1997, 264). Ernst
Benjamin, secretary of the American Association of University Professors
(AAUP), found that "part-time faculty have grown four times (97%) faster
than full-time (25%). While the number of non-tenure-track faculty has
increased by 88%, the number of probationary [tenure-track] faculty has
actually declined by 9%" (Schell and Stock 2001, 4).

Nevertheless, until recently, the subject of adjunct exploitation hasn't
been of much interest to anyone other than adjuncts themselves. Now,
however, journals like *Adjunct Advocate* (and its companion Web site,
adjunctnation.com) and books like *The Adjunct Faculty Handbook* (Bianco-
Mathis and Chalofsky, 1996) give tips on how to strive for the best possible
outcome in any given situation. Jill Carroll, an adjunct at several Houston-
area universities, writes a column called "The Adjunct Track" for the
Chronicle of Higher Education, which shows adjuncts how to maximize their
profits and minimize their workload. Much of this advice is collected in
her books *Machiavelli for Adjuncts* (2004) and *How to Survive as an Adjunct
Lecturer* (2003). Carroll believes that it is most profitable—and least painful—for adjuncts to view themselves as independent contractors. If you
swim with the sharks, Carroll suggests, it's best to be a shark yourself.

A less individualist variation on this ethic of self-empowerment
has been promulgated by unions such as the American Federation of
Teachers, which must continually balance the interests of full-time and
part-time members. Granted, many adjuncts believe their most powerful
weapon is unionization and collective bargaining, but Schell discourages
creating an adversarial relationship between full- and part-time faculty.
Instead, she promotes the formation of a feminist "ethic of care" to trans-
form working conditions: "With a rhetoric that opposes binaries and
encourages agency and coalition building, we are in a good position to
articulate a broad educational agenda that acknowledges worker rights
and the fundamental need for a democratic, accessible, and diverse system of higher education" (2004, 110).

In part, the inroads made by nontenured faculty in spreading aware-ness of their plight has meant making their tenured colleagues conscious of the extent to which their fates are linked. Ruth Kiefson argues that most full-time faculty members "fail to see themselves as part of the work-ing class and that they are being assaulted by the same processes that are creating economic and social instability and misery for millions. In gener-al, the individualist training that [full-time faculty] received as profession-als . . . dominates their decision making and outlook" (2004, 148). Lovas argues that there are concrete steps full-time faculty can take to improve the working conditions of their adjunct colleagues. He suggests "sharing office space with a part-timer, offering informal mentoring, insisting that all departmental communications reach every faculty member, regardless of status, and arranging department support services convenient to part-time faculty" (2001, 216). Regrettably, while tenured faculty often agree in principle with gestures such as these, when it comes time to actually rearrange their schedules and work habits to accommodate contingent colleagues, very few follow through.

What does all this mean for creative writers? Despite the desperate job situation, most newly minted PhDs in literature still believe that they will be rewarded for their six to ten years of hard work with a permanent teaching position. In contrast, a creative writer emerging from a gradu-ate program in the twenty-first century probably doesn't expect much from her MFA. Yet, precisely because the MFA has generally failed to be a marketable terminal degree for tenure-track positions, many MFAs have turned to adjunct work to scratch out a living while they pursue their own creative writing. These degree holders may well consider themselves lucky to land a temporary job teaching freshmen composition. If there is an opportunity to teach creative writing—even if it pays poorly and offers no job security—they are more than happy to sign on.

Admittedly, it is just as odious to put the burden of contingent labor on creative writers as on their colleagues in literature and composition. Yet from one perspective, this is a reasonable matching of talents with needs. Creative writers are adept at careful reading of original writing, at offer-ing constructive criticism and shepherding work through multiple drafts. Moreover, if adjunct writing teachers have far less time to write than their tenured colleagues, they do still have relatively flexible schedules. Other than class meetings and office hours, their time is their own. If they are morning writers, they can ask for classes in the afternoon and do their grading at night. If they write best at night, they do the reverse.

Like it or not, though, unless the siren song of teaching suddenly diminishes, a stint as an adjunct or temporary instructor is probably in store for most writers who want to teach at the college level.

AGENTS

For many creative writers—poets, for instance, and writers of experimental literature—agents are largely a nonfactor in their writing careers. There simply isn't enough money to be made in these genres to warrant an agent's, or a publisher's, time and energy. There are exceptions, however. If a client also writes in another, more profitable area, his agent may be able to place his belletristic work. Thus, an author like Stephen Dobyns, whose poetry has been published by Penguin, probably owes his verse publications in trade paperbacks to the fact that he is also the writer of brisk-selling mystery novels. Some poets—Rita Dove, Billy Collins, Gary Snyder, W. S. Merwin, to name a few—become cottage industries in themselves. The fact that they can command five-figure fees for a single speaking engagement makes them attractive to literary agents.

However, agents are a significant feature of the current literary landscape in the world of novelists, writers of nonfiction, and screenwriters and playwrights. Dinty W. Moore, author of *The Accidental Buddhist*, believes agents are essential for this group of writers for several reasons. "A good agent understands which editors are likely to take on certain projects," he writes. "They understand contracts, and they understand how to negotiate better advances and better percentages for future rights. Never worry about the 15% your agent takes in commission—the agent more than earns it, and everyone is better off in the end" (2004).

Granted, Internet marketing and e-publishing may have made agents slightly less indispensable than they have been in the past. It's easier to locate and contact markets for one's work online. However, this ease of contact, and the inflation of self-promotion that goes along with it, makes many publishers and theatrical producers wary of unagented writers. From their standpoint, agents act as quality control managers, the guardians at the gate keeping out the many who are not yet ready for publication or production and letting in the few who are. Consequently, once writers in the "profitable genres" reach a certain level of craftsmanship (and often *before* that point), they are likely to spend a significant amount of time seeking literary representation. According to prominent agent Richard Curtis, "the overwhelming majority of new authors are focused on getting an agent. When I attend conferences, I see that how-to-get-an-agent panels are crowded to capacity, whereas the how-to-get-happily-self-published ones are more sparsely attended" (2001, 53).

Agents often start as writers themselves, which makes them—potentially at least—very sympathetic to the trials of writing and attempting to publish a manuscript. They can sympathize when things are going poorly and offer encouragement and advice that may have worked for their own writing. Peter Rubie observes, "As a writer, I try to be the sort of agent I would like to have" (Herman 2003, 663). Two other writer/agents, Michael Larsen and Elizabeth Pomada, list a number of essential services provided by authors' representatives. Agents are:

- mediators "between two realities": the author's and that of the marketplace
- scouts who know what publishers are looking for
- midwives in the birth of a manuscript
- matchmakers who help connect authors with good publishers and help them avoid the bad ones
- negotiators who "hammer out the most favorable possible contract"
- advocates who help solve problems
- mentors acting as "an oasis of encouragement" in a desert of rejection (2003)

At times, an agent may act as an editor, suggesting revision to a manuscript, even offering line-editing advice. More often, though, an agent's chief function is to get a manuscript into the hands of an editor she believes will publish it. In the past, conventional wisdom insisted that agents for fiction writers and playwrights had to live in New York, where many of the major publishing houses and theater companies are located. Film and television agents had to be based in Los Angeles. However, with the prevalence of electronic communications—fax and e-mail—representatives away from the two coasts argue that the location of an agent's office is less important than it once was. And most agents rely on the telephone as their primary method of communicating with both clients and potential sources of revenue. Nevertheless, a great deal of business continues to be conducted in person, and without personal contacts, an agent is essentially worthless to an author.

Perhaps the biggest point of contention in the agent-client arena revolves around the practice of charging fees for the reading of manuscripts. Granted, there *are* legitimate agents who charge a reading fee *and* place their clients' work. These agencies argue that such fees cover "the cost of additional readers or the time spent reading that could have been sent selling. This practice can save the agent time and open the agency to a larger number of submissions. Paying fees," they contend, "benefits writers because they at least know someone will look at their work" (Dickerson 2001, 17). In general, however, successful authors and agents avoid this practice. Dinty Moore advises: "Never pay an agent who wants money to read or edit your book. An agent reads works-in-progress for free, if she is interested, because she believes she will make money on the other end— when the book is sold to a publisher. The *only* agent you want working for you is one who feels confident that your work will sell, and make money for both of you" (2004). In fact, in order to be listed as an agent with the Writers Guild of America (WGA), agents *cannot* charge a reading fee.

Moreover, charging fees up front rather than waiting to collect the percentage of a sale obviously reduces an agent's incentive to get a contract for her author. If an agent is going to be paid one way or the other, what difference does it make what happens to the client's book or screenplay? Indeed, if an agent can lure enough unsuspecting authors to pay fees beforehand, it is to her benefit *not* to spend her time marketing their work. A far better use of the unscrupulous agent's energy is to *attract* clients, never mind how they fare. The Science Fiction and Fantasy Writers of America (2005) caution:

> Dishonest agents prey on writers by charging fees, promoting their own expensive editing services, engaging in kickback referral schemes, and misrepresenting their knowledge and expertise. These agents don't earn their income from selling manuscripts to publishers (many of them never bother to send anything out), but from charging money to their clients. Agents of this type may have hundreds of writers on their rosters, turning them over twice a year with a 6-month contract that requires $250 or more in up-front fees. Others are no more than fronts for editing services, offering editing to every writer who submits and charging thousands of dollars for "critiques" performed by unqualified minimum-wage employees. Still others run associated pay-to-publish operations, into which clients are funneled once they've racked up enough rejections to become desperate.

A useful online source for identifying, and avoiding, this group of deceitful agents is Preditors and Editors (www.anotherealm.com/prededitors/

pubagent.htm). This site lists well over a thousand agents, with "not recommended" notations next to the names of those accused of the transgressions described above.

Of course, just because an agent isn't dishonest, that doesn't mean that he's effective. The Science Fiction and Fantasy Writers of America (2005) calls agents of this type the "amateur, incompetent and marginal": "These [agents] are often drawn to agenting for odd reasons that don't have much to do with the profession (including the misapprehension that publishing is lucrative and agenting is an easy home business). Typically, they have no professional background in agenting or publishing, and lack the personal contacts that are essential for success, as well as important skills such as in-depth knowledge of the publishing industry and the ability to recognize a salable manuscript."

By checking to see if an agent is a member of a reputable organization like the WGA or the Association of Authors' Representatives (AAR), potential clients can begin to winnow the wheat from the chaff. The AAR's objectives include "keeping agents informed about conditions in publishing, the theater, the motion picture and television industries, and related fields; and assisting agents in representing their author-clients' interests." By also adhering to a policy of not charging their clients reading and other fees up front, member agents provide a reliable pool of authors' representatives. Contact information for many of these AAR and WGA agents can be found in Writers Digest Books' annual *Guide to Literary Agents.*

Unfortunately, once an author has identified agents that are both honest and effective, she is likely to have a difficult time convincing one of them to take her on as a client. Successful, legitimate agents are working so hard on their authors' behalf that they rarely have time to take on new writers. Where once the query letter with a sample from the manuscript was a staple of all agencies, many no longer consider unsolicited communications of any kind. Generally, the only new clients they take are by referral from authors already in their "stable." Even those writers who are lucky enough to become "pocket clients"—new, unproven writers—may find they have a limited shelf life if they don't quickly achieve success. Screenwriters are especially vulnerable to "the insidious, Dorian Gray time element [that] quickly creeps into this arrangement." As Michael Lent describes the process: "If a pocket client writes an undeniably marketable script . . . he or she becomes a full-fledged client entitled to more of the agent's time and attention. If not, there's a remote-control-operated trapdoor under the chair" (2004, 130).

Moreover, the current industry emphasis on sales means that long-term relationships between agents who love literature and are willing to gamble their time on unproven writers they think have talent are mostly a thing of the past. Lent recalls an agent who likened the process of taking on a new writer to "'pulling an engine up from the bottom of the ocean." He remarks that "most established agents opt out of this heavy lifting. 'Love your work; catch you at the next level,' they say" (2004, 130 131). Agents Larsen and Pomada note that in "the age of the mass-market hardcover, heavily discounted million-copy selling blockbusters," it has become "cheaper and more profitable for publishers to print 1,000,000 copies of one book than 10,000 copies of a hundred books. The advances lavished on bestsellers leave less money for new writers who need it, and the more publishers pay, the more they push" (2003).

Consequently, it can be extremely difficult for new writers to find a good agent. This problem is exacerbated for the unwary by the way agents advertise themselves. Shady agents often have the flashiest Web sites. Again, they spend their time marketing themselves rather than their authors. By contrast, it can be extremely difficult to find contact information for in-demand agents. Their e-mail addresses may be closely guarded secrets, and some agencies don't have Web sites at all. While there may not be a direct inverse relationship between the quality of the online presentation and the legitimacy of the agency, writers who shop for agents this way should heed the motto caveat emptor.

For those lucky and persistent enough to sign with an agent, questions will arise. What, a new author will want to know, should I be getting from my representative? According to Donya Dickerson, there are a number of questions an author who is about to sign with agent should consider asking. Among them: "Who are some other authors you represent and what are examples of recent sales you've made for those authors? What is your commission? Do you charge clients for office expenses? How often should I expect to be in touch with you? Will you consult with me before accepting an offer? What are your policies if, for whatever reason, we decide to part company?" (2001, 58).

For writers whose main focus is literary craft, an agent's emphasis on marketable *product* may seem loathsome. However, while university presses may prefer to read agented books, those publishers may not be particularly attractive to agents themselves. As Larsen and Pomada point out, "You have [many] options for getting your books published. . . . Large and medium-sized houses are only one of them, but they're the only way agents can make a living" (Herman 2003, 603). Larsen and Pomada also note, "The six conglomerates that dominate trade publishing want books that they can recycle in as many ways that they own as possible" (2003). They advise authors to "come up with ideas that you can profit from in as many forms, media and countries as possible."

Playwright Jon Tuttle warns those who retain a representative not to assume that the agent will now take care of every aspect of the writer's career. Instead, he believes that writers should think of the agent as one more weapon in their arsenal.

> It's a mistake to think of landing an agent as the key to the kingdom. Usually, it just means more rejections from new and different theatres. Occasionally, I'll hear a playwright complain that his agent hasn't "done her job" by landing him some plumb productions, and that's ridiculous, of course. On the other hand, I hear playwrights complain that their agents really aren't doing anything any more—they don't even read their scripts, or don't circulate them much—and that's a valid complaint. The most important thing to keep in mind if you're seeking an agent is that it *is* a business relationship. An agent doesn't ask, "Is this a good play?" He asks, "Will this make money?" And those are two very different things, whether or not we writers like to admit it. (2004)

Screenwriter Max Adams agrees: "I would not sit around saying, 'Whew! At last I have an agent, now I can drink ice tea and watch *Oprah* while the offers roll in.' I would stay out there and hustle" (2001, 143).

Writers having difficulty generating interest from an agent may opt instead for hiring a manager, sometimes called a literary manager. (Note: in theater, the term "literary manager" is also used as a synonym for a "dramaturg," the person responsible for administering a theater company's literary office.) Unlike an agent, whose focus is more often than not on selling a particular project by a writer, a literary manager is concerned with the overall arc of a writer's career. Indeed, he may well sink a good deal of his own money into producing the work of a screenwriter or playwright, believing that his investment will be returned manyfold. From a writer's point of view, the drawback is that a literary manager is likely to ask much more in return than an agent will. Rather than the standard 10 or 15 percent of a contract, he may demand 25 percent or even half, if he has invested heavily in the writer. This relationship may at times seem more like a marriage than the "serious dating" involved in an agent-client connection, so writers should know and feel very comfortable with the person they are hiring.

Ultimately, though finding appropriate representation may at times seem like a Sisyphean task, Dinty Moore does offer some encouragement for new writers seeking agents:

> The fact that one or two agents say no to your project doesn't mean the project isn't sound or the book isn't good. The trick to finding the right agent is two-fold: you have to find an agent who responds well to your work, but you also have to run across her at a time in her professional cycle when she is taking on new clients. Most agents are amazingly busy, all the time. So a 'no' sometimes only means, 'I don't have time to take this on right now.' It doesn't mean your idea is a loser. (2004)

ANTHOLOGY

A literary anthology is a collection of works by various authors in a single volume. In Greek, the word is a combination of *anthos* (flower) and *logia* (collecting). The Greeks used the word to describe a compilation of epigrams which, like a gathering of flowers, brings the loveliest specimens together in one place.

In the classroom, the advantages of anthologies are obvious. Teachers want to cover as many representative works as they can; students would like to spend as little money as possible. Anthologies offer a convenient, relatively inexpensive alternative to syllabi made up of a long costly list of books by single authors. Anthologies may attempt to cast a very wide net indeed—witness *The Norton Anthology of English Literature*—or they may focus on particular eras (the Beat Generation, nineteenth-century Ireland), groups (working-class writers, African American women), or specialized genres (science writing, travel essays). However, even when it has a limited scope, an anthology can still showcase a variety of writing within that field.

In four-year colleges and universities, creative writing students are often English majors. These students will have been exposed to canonical authors in other courses; however, they may not have read much contemporary writing. Anthologies featuring the best work published in the past year or years can move toward rectifying this situation. Scribner, for instance, publishes a *Best American* series in a variety of genres: fiction, poetry, creative nonfiction, and so on. Anchor publishes *The O. Henry*

Awards for fiction and the *Anchor Essay Annual. The Pushcart Prize: Best of the Small Presses* contains a sometimes more adventurous annual selection of poetry, fiction, and creative nonfiction. In addition to being conscientious editors, Robert Atwan, series editor of *Best American Essays*, and David Lehman, series editor of *Best American Poetry*, are also accomplished writers themselves in the genres they cover. They clearly take their missions seriously. Unless the reader is independently wealthy and has no time constraints (few college students or instructors fit this description), she can rest assured that an editor has read far more examples of a genre than she ever could herself.

And yet, even if they read hundreds of stories or thousands of poems a year, anthologists will miss plenty of good work. After all, there are thousands of literary *magazines* published each year. Moreover, every anthologist will have his or her bias. In his introduction to the 2001 edition of *The Best American Poetry*, Robert Hass, editor of that year's volume, notes his differences with Lehman: "Reading for a while, I was aware that David had, on the whole, favored a poetry of wit and that I, on the whole, had singled out poems that were a little spiky or raw, and intellectually demanding. He was drawn to charm and I was drawn away from it" (21). This variation in taste is all the more noteworthy because, seen from a distance, the work of Hass and Lehman is not strikingly dissimilar. When two poets who share a fairly common aesthetic disagree with each other, we can expect a much greater gap between writers from two distinct camps. And if these opposing anthologists should each publish anthologies, whose should we trust as the most characteristic of the age? Whose is the best? Whose should we be reading?

Perhaps the most (in)famous anthology war in America this century was the "confrontation" between *New Poets of America and England* (1957), edited by Donald Hall and Robert Pack, and *The New American Poetry: 1945 1960* (1960), edited by Donald Allen. The former book contained poets such as Anthony Hecht, John Hollander, and Howard Nemerov—all of them writing in traditional forms—while Allen's anthology featured the experimental work of Allen Ginsberg, Gregory Corso, and Frank O'Hara. Pack later claimed that "in marked contrast" to Allen's book, "which promoted the incandescent, brief revolt of the Beats," his and Hall's anthology "centered upon many of the most important and lasting poets of the last 40 years" (McWilliams, 2002). Writing from a distinctly different vantage, Paul Hoover, editor of *The Norton Anthology of Postmodern American Poetry*, calls the poems in *New Poets of America and England* "decorous and well made" (1994, xxix) by "contributors . . . not eager to reject the influence of British letters in favor of a home-grown idiom" (xxviii). Even in these polite summaries, made decades after the battle of the anthologies, one can hear condescension and disdain lurking just beneath the surface. How much less likely is an anthologist to be sympathetic to the opposing camp in the heat of an ideological war!

One of the most searing indictments of the anthology phenomenon appears in Jed Rasula's *The American Poetry Wax Museum*. In a chapter entitled "Anthologist's Ontologies," Rasula argues convincingly that anthologies breed uniformity, precluding "the appearance of an anthology that is at once eclectic and representative" (1996, 447). He notes how poems become established by appearing in one anthology after another, with editors apparently making their selections primarily by choosing from each other's anthologies. Whether it is for marketing purposes, or simply because the anthologist wants to make a clear aesthetic statement, work is selected with an eye to making disparate parts resolve into a unified whole. The result, Rasula says, is that poems, "like women on view in a Miss Universe pageant, look more like one another than like anybody around them. Any breach in this façade—this means of advertising coherence, unanimity of purpose, and 'universal' relevance—amounts to a disabling infraction" (466).

Finally, though, one suspects Rasula's judgment is too harsh, too sweeping—and too little cognizant of the mitigating effects of time. Adrienne Rich was one of the few women in either *New Poets of America and England* or *New American Poetry*. Her early formalist work fit nicely in Hall and Pack's anthology, yet in the 1960s she rejected what she saw as the patriarchal principles operating in traditional English verse. Had they published their book ten years later, it is doubtful they would have included Rich's poetry. And while Pack's aesthetic has not changed markedly over the years, when Donald Hall edited *The Best American Poetry* in 1989, he included several avant-garde poets who would never have made it into his earlier anthology. The right moves left and the left moves right. As Hoover notes, "The distinction between bohemia and academia was clear in 1960. Today that difference is harder to establish, as many avant-gardists make their living by university teaching" (1994, xxix). The simple fact that Norton anthologies of postmodern poetry and fiction even exist suggests the extensive transformation of the literary landscape. Things change, and even the most polemical anthology may one day find its authors in the canon.

Associated Writing Programs

If you are currently enrolled in a college or university creative writing degree program, you are probably also already a member of the Associated Writing Programs (AWP), "a national, nonprofit literary organization for teachers and writers. Founded in 1967, AWP is dedicated to serving writers, teachers and writing programs" (awpwriter.org/faq.htm). AWP provides members with a variety of services, including a subscription to the *Writer's Chronicle*, a journal published six times during the academic year, a job placement service, award contests leading to book publication, a catalog of writing programs, and an annual conference.

The association represents "approximately 18,000 individual writers, teachers, students and 300 college and university creative writing programs in the United States, Canada, and the United Kingdom" (awpwriter.org/history.html). The best way to find out about these services is to visit the AWP Web site, but the best way to experience the community represented by AWP is to attend the annual convention, where writers join to listen to panelists, attend readings, and visit the book exhibit. Here writers expect to connect, to share their work and interests, and to meet editors of literary journals and presses (see "Schmoozing").

AWP has long been an activist organization, taking up issues of government arts funding, censorship, human rights, quality of writing programs, support for adjunct teachers, and other issues. The association's growth from an original fifteen members representing thirteen programs to a program representing over three hundred programs parallels the growth of academic programs in creative writing (see "MFA," "Creative Dissertation"). The different "membership" categories in this organization also indicate this growth: individual members, affiliate members (literary colonies, literary magazines, small academic programs), institutional memberships (academic programs), writer's conferences and centers memberships. Particularly useful are the AWP site "Links to Other Resources" (including a listing of member programs) and *The AWP Official Guide to Writing Programs*, a more thorough, book-length version of these listings.

As a nonprofit, AWP is governed by a board of directors elected from a slate of Writing Program members who serve as regional representatives for the Pacific West, West, Midwest, Northeast, and Southeast. The annual conference rotates among these regions, returning periodically to the

Washington, D.C. area, where the program offices are located at George Mason University.

An undergraduate or unaffiliated writer's first and best way to get connected with the national creative writing scene is to get acquainted with this Web site and pursue the appropriate membership strategy, since the *Writer's Chronicle* includes AWP program-related news, articles of general interest to writers, and a listing of current contests and awards available to writers. Thus, a membership assures a quick introduction to the "profession" of creative writing.

AUTHOR

In his lecture to the Royal Society of Literature in April 1995, novelist Russell Celyn Jones (1995–96) captures both the surprise of British writers that authors should take up residence in institutional spaces and the U.S. construction of creative writer as wild and wooly outlaw of an identifiable sort:

> Americans do not look on institutionalized creativity as an oxymoron at all. The creative writing course is an industry there, with thousands of students attending poetry and fiction sections each year. . . . Anyone who has ever attended such a course can tell you that the American writers' workshop is a party. The problem sets in when the party never ends. . . . The writers' workshop was pioneered by Paul Engle at Iowa City in an attempt to replicate Parisian café society. I met Engle in 1983 whilst a student at Iowa. He asked me how my workshop was going and I complained it seemed a little over-polite. "Your prayers have been answered," he said. "We've got Barry Hannah coming next semester. He just got fired from Alabama for bringing a loaded revolver into class. Of course we snapped him up." The story that got about was that Hannah, a chronic alcoholic and native of Mississippi, turned up to teach class, drunk and with a Colt .45. He placed the weapon on the table, saying "This morning I got up and read a $50,000 tax demand from the IRS and a $20,000 alimony bill from my ex-wife. The third thing I read was this piece of shit that someone done turned in. I don't know which is worse."

British writers—who these days are also finally investing in academic creative writing programs—are not alone in imagining the only good writer is the bohemian iconoclast touched by madness and genius in bewildering mixtures and measures. Several sources feed this imagistic river. Linda Brodkey investigates the modernist scene of writing—"a solitary writer alone in a cold garret working into the small hours of the morning by the thin light of a candle . . . in which the writer is an Author and the writing is Literature" (1987, 396)—and outlines the many problems involved in this construction of authorship and writing, primarily, of course, all that it leaves out. For much of the last century, this author was not only solitary and literary but white and male. Equally, this version of writing process was one in which "solitude is at once inevitable and consequential, the irremediable human condition from which there is no escape . . . a vicarious narrative told by an outsider who observes rather than witnesses life" (398). In this image of writing, there is waiting (for inspiration) and arrival (at expert final product); there is no drafting, no collaborating, no circulation of text through an economic production system (publishing). When writing does happen, "the writer is an unwilling captive of language, which writes itself through the writer," or, as T. S. Eliot would have it, "The progress of an artist is a continual self-sacrifice, a continual extinction of personality" (1975, 8). What writer wouldn't, along with Barry Hannah, vault from the desk and roar into action in order to make up for his mad isolation, his raw deal with the muse?

For different reasons, film images of writers have contributed their share of dramatic failures, white male writers in search of a story. In all these images, due to the nature of film, writers are doing everything *but* writing alone. This is because the act of writing is eminently unfilmable: a relatively boring internal action, aside from a few voiceovers or papers ripped in tiredness from a typewriter platen. Instead, filmmakers substitute a new scene of nonauthorship, reporters buzzing after a story (*The Front Page*), writers on the road (*Almost Famous*), writers not writing Literature (*Barton Fink*), writers pursuing their demons during writer's block or as charismatic teachers (*Wonder Boys*), writers seeking admission to a writing program (*Orange County*), or being forced to write (*Misery*). In *Finding Forrester* we find a mentor and a writer of color; in *His Girl Friday* we find that a woman writes, but such sightings are few and far between.

If, as Katherine Haake argues, "before you can remember who you are [as a writer], you must identify your own private writing demons, and then dispense with them, one by one" (2000, 191), the writer who wants to challenge received images has a lot of work before him or her. First, if the modernist writer is always writing alone, living *la vie bohème* and working to join the literary tradition, she has to work against "the unexamined assumptions that this and only this moment counts as writing" (Brodkey 1987, 399) and that these and only these sorts of texts count as valuable. These writers must buck a long misreading of the romantic tradition that suggests that "[t]he romantics, of course, privileged emotions, imagination, synthesis, less linear forms of discourse and logic, and the importance of non-academic setting in which to learn—usually nature" (Gradin 1995, 92) while forgetting that they also were deeply concerned with educational processes. The "myth of the inspired writer," argues Gradin, has become "a negative romantic legacy" (93). Romantics, she continues, believed that both imagination and genius were innate and too often educated out of individuals, whereas Wordsworth and others were searching for a method to draw both forth (955).

If novice writers seek to become like the writers they admire, if they move into the profession of writing by seeking writers' identities, as argued by Robert Brooke, then the danger lies in what images of authorship and writer they are receiving. "Writers learn to write by imitating other writers," Brooke argues, "by trying to act like writers they respect" (1988, 23). If this is so, the inspiration for young writers is crucial. If they are offered film types—master writer, madman, writer who doesn't write, action hero, flustered female—certain responses to the scene of learning to write are predictable. If they are offered a walk in the dells or a garret in Paris, certain other responses are likely. At either pole of behavior—isolation or mad camaraderie—a number of questions are ignored. While T. S. Eliot suggests all successful authors learn from and join the tradition, Roland Barthes suggests—equally problematically—that the Author is more likely a site of contestation: "We know now that a text is not a line of words releasing a single 'theological' meaning (the 'message' of the Author-God) but a multi-dimensional space in which a variety of writings, none of them original, blend and clash. The text is a tissue of quotations drawn from the innumerable centers of culture" (1968, 149).

Given the choice of chaos or certainty, most writers would opt for the latter, but they do so by relying on received images that certainly leave a number of would-be authors out of the picture or forced to remake themselves into writer types that won't serve them well. Katharine Haake (2000, 191) reminds us that "we turn out the way we are by virtue of our experience in culture, in class, in gender, in race, in family, in history, in being" (see also "Identity Politics"), which predicts that novice writers—perhaps all writers—need two things: the chance to interrogate the scene(s) of writing that have been offered them and the encouragement to ask hard questions about the politics and economics and current cultural practices affecting authorship in the United States and in world cultures.

Robert Brooke argues, "Composition teaching works, in the modern sense, when it effectively models an identity for students which the students can in some way accept. It works when part of their identity becomes a writer's identity, when they come to see that being a writer in their own way is a valid and exciting way of acting in the world" (1988, 40). In creative writing, it has long been assumed that the modernist scene of writing is the scene we should be accessing, that the writer in graduate programs undergoes certain recognizable and necessary stages of education, acculturation, and identity formation. However, changing literary realities suggest that an interrogation of our assumptions may be in order. The challenge to dominant genres (see "Creative Nonfiction"), the consolidation of the power of publishing houses, the loss of funding for the arts and humanities, the threat to university presses, the proliferation of degree programs, the change in student demographics—all suggest writing programs and writers might do well to consider a by now fairly well-known set of theoretical questions: "'What are the modes of existence of this discourse? Where has it been used, how can it circulate, and who can appropriate it for himself? What are the places in it where there is room for possible subjects? Who can assume these various subject-functions?' And behind all these questions, we would hear hardly anything but the stirring of an indifference: 'What difference does it make who is speaking?'" (Foucault 1969, 187).

Who is an author? We are not arguing that we shouldn't attend our conferences in blue jeans or have a drink at the bar after the reading or that we don't want to write excellent texts and have them widely read, but we do want to consider where our field is going, whom it includes, how well it trains those new to the scene to do their work, and with what sorts of inclusivity or diversity. When we laugh at Grady Tripp's 2,000-page second novel blowing into the water (*Wonder Boys*), when we wince at Paul Sheldon forced to write another romance novel by Annie Wilkes (*Misery*), when we see Shaun trying to gain admission to Stanford's prestigious writing program despite his dysfunctional family (*Orange County*), when we long for a mother as humorous and supportive as William Miller's (*Almost Famous*) and pride ourselves on knowing the story behind *Finding Forrester*, we are tapping into the authors we have all been constructed to want to be as well as into the authors that some of us are or will be.

BLOCK AND PROCRASTINATION

Death and taxes. Writers and writing blocks. We aren't writing but we want to write. We hope to (or struggle to) move from one state to the other but we delay. We label those more disciplined than we are as plodders or hacks yet we chastise ourselves for our own procrastination. It's so easily characterized as either/or: we're blocked or we're in volcanic action, sitting down at a computer and rising hours later, dazed and (hopefully) delighted, product finally in hand. It's a manic-depressive sort of life, we think, though secretly we'd like to. . . if not plod . . . then progress, regularly, productively, daily closer to our writing goals. Because the stakes are high, the competition stiff, the activity relatively unnatural (sit in a room and write?), and the rewards distant *(possible* publication, *possible* readers, *possible* remuneration), to accomplish our demanding work—this activity we call writing—we despair and seek advice because no writing = no writer.

To commence, Anne Lamott (1995) suggests writing shitty first drafts. Richard Hugo (1979) urges us to write off the topic. To get and keep going long enough to have a draft worth working with, William Stafford (1987) predicts that we must first lower our standards. Natalie Goldberg (1986) advocates writing any place at all. Mihaly Csikszentmihalyi (1990) advises us to focus on process, writing for writing's sake, because this is an important aspect of flow states. Georgia Heard (1995) finds it useful to face inner critics and listen to good angels. Peter Elbow (1973) prescribes freewriting, and Donald Murray (1985) reminds us that pausing and percolating are productive—that sometimes, often times, not writing is the path toward writing again, and writing better. Great, Murray constantly reminds us, is the enemy of good.

But what do writers mean when they talk about experiencing these states, and what do those who study writers suggest is going on: how might we all move from stuck to (re)started? Every writer has stories of times when writing worked and didn't work, just as most have advice and prescriptions for getting into gear again. But writing block and procrastination are states of mind as well as physical states, and what writers believe clearly affects their production potential and actual activities. For every example of a famous blocked writer we can find one of a writer who goes on ad nauseam. For every truism we find a seemingly equally true opposite. It's worth seeing how beliefs circulate and gain currency and adherents.

BLOCKING IS NORMAL, ISN'T IT?

Studies of how writers learn suggest that William Stafford was correct in his estimation that many writers put an end to their own writing productivity by having overly high expectations. If you decide to compete with Shakespeare in the sonnet category, you may find it prudent to take endless walks around the block before undertaking your Herculean task. If, instead, you decide to investigate the sonnet form by reading and enjoying some sonnets, by writing strong imitations or approximations of your favorites (old and new), by getting as near as you can in a first try, you'll probably sooner rush to your nearest and dearest reader with your sonnet draft, your momentary success in the sonnet stakes. Of course, in order to do this, you must accept that a "good enough for now" sonnet may not be strictly metered. You do this because you realize you're not yet practiced enough and that it will take until your tenth or twentieth sonnet to achieve an enviable flow of iambs and rhyme. Without this sort of acceptance you're likely to walk away from the high wall surrounding your aspirations or to block. In that sense, blocking is a normal outcome of aspiration. Aspiration is necessary—not much ventured, not much gained—but overly high aspiration sets the creative stakes too high. Teacher Donald Graves explains it this way:

> Blocking is too often viewed as a negative experience. But blocking is a necessary by-product of any creative endeavor. If the child had neither voice nor strong intention, no desire to be precise with information and language, then there would be no problems to solve and therefore no thwarting in the creation. When children solve their blocking problems or emerge from a three-day or week-long slump, they have new energy and tools to apply to their writing. Teachers who know how writers change can help them through the normal pangs of composing and rejoice with them when they reach the other side of the impasse. (1985, 18)

Graves's observations suggest that we need challenges, but challenges of the right dimensions. Therefore, the aspiring sonneteer should not necessarily settle inflexibly for only a Shakespearean sonnet on the first attempt. A strong approximation, a poem that makes a lot of the turns of the sonnet form but is admittedly a draft, can let the writer move forward. To inhabit that complicated boxy fourteen lines with some initial success is necessary in order to want to write another, and another.

Pausing, blocking, and problem solving are not bad if we accept the corollary that practice makes more perfect. In fact, accepting reasonable drafting conditions and setting sensible challenges often dissolves the block that we wrongly erected in the first place.

Inspiration is a culprit in the blocking and procrastination game (see also "Author"). Writers would prefer to appear expert from the first day they write to the last. Often they feel that to admit to anything less than mastery, to reveal and examine composing processes, to evince a learning curve is to appear—or to be—uninspired and inexpert, a real novice. Equally, to have to toil, to work long and hard at craft is to admit another sort of deficiency. Surely the creative simply create, galvanized by a muse, unlike a lesser workaday mortal. And while we all want to be successful, it's sexier to appear effortlessly so. To work (the system) is tantamount to selling out. If it's popular, it can't be high art; if it was written without pain, it can't be inspired; and if it's done regularly, it can't be original and of high quality. These are the unexamined truisms that push writers to hide their narratives of productivity. Psychotherapist Robert Boice, who works with productive and unproductive writers in clinical settings, finds:

> Literary researchers tend to dismiss writers who produce a lot and who work hard. . . . Academics often suppose, erroneously, that those of us who write a lot necessarily suffer a loss in the quality and creativity of our work. . . . The facts say otherwise. . . . What these critics might better conclude is that being too obviously productive and nonprocrastinative can impair social approval of the less productive in academe. . . .
>
> Tradition holds special commendation for writers who claim they write without discipline, without really trying. (1996, 16)

Conversely (or perversely), if we can't claim to write without really trying, we can at least claim the pain of trying and not succeeding.

BLOCKING IS BAD, OR IS IT?

Afraid of success? Who wouldn't be? We can all name a first novelist who never wrote another. We hold our breath—half hoping for and fearing the fall from grace of our favorites. We trade examples of one-story wonders and published-only-after-death poets. We're reluctant to send out our story to the little journal we most admire because they might send it back. We're afraid to write the family story because we'll disappoint our parents. We assume we were made to write for the silver screen so we write poems and e-mails and somehow never buy that screenplay software that would make our task—now so hard with its required formatting—easier, doable.

In one line of thinking, blocking is always bad, an avoidance (no talent) or a confirmation of our mediocrity. Nothing hazarded, nothing lost. Better to sit in the café reading and critiquing. Better to make fun of the last reader at the open mike. Better to get drunk with the visiting writers and hit on the agent at the conference than to . . . find out the truth about ourselves. Drinking, of course, has long been associated with easing writer's block: "Many writers use alcohol to help themselves write—to calm their anxieties, lift their inhibitions." Yet heavy drinking can quickly lead to a vicious circle. Writing ultimately suffers because of drink, "the unhappy writer then drinks more; the writing then suffers more, and so on" (Acocella 2004, 116).

So, in the least admirable view: "Blocked writers are, in many respects, like phobics whose real fear is of public embarrassment; like overeaters who simply haven't learned to arrange their environment to ensure that they consume less; and like socially unskilled clients who need to learn to calm down, observe, and model the habits of others in threatening situations. The difference is that with, say, an agoraphobic (the person who fears leaving home for public places like supermarkets), we rarely attribute the cause of fear to some mystical force like lack of inspiration" (Boice 1985, 212).

But that's not really the whole picture. Certainly, many writers are blocked through fear. But many more work through that fear and enroll in classes, practice their craft diligently, seek advice and follow advice or interventions with useful results. Robert Boice himself has found success treating blocks with contingency management techniques, asking writers to refrain from a reward until the day's task is done—rewards as simple as a daily shower or a cup of coffee. Who hasn't worked to self-set rewards? In the case of this keyword, a walk to the local bookstore has been delayed until enough words have been logged on the screen.

But it's not simply that we need therapies or meds for the writing aversive, we need to understand that blocking can also be productive and is inevitably part of the journey. Every problem implies its solution: lack of information (research some more), lack of response (find a good reader to share a text or talk with), lack of maturity (try another project and come back to this one later). Donald Graves's studies of young writers showed him: "Writers of all ages and abilities have a common problem: They assume information is in their texts that is simply not there. Egocentricity is the lifelong problem of any writer. Writers need to be both the self and the other, both writer and reader, simultaneously. . . . A block can also arise because the child lacks adequate information. The child knows there is a discrepancy between his or her intention and the information on the page. . . . The writer has a gut feeling that the piece isn't right but lacks the objectivity or experience to summon the needed information (Graves 1985, 12–13).

We need to set up situations that help us make good matches between aspiration and ambition and ability. Writers need to pay attention to gut feelings and they also need training. Some get this training on their own, a lucky few find it in the company of others—in workshops, at conferences, under the guidance of dedicated editors. Most importantly, writers need to see that they have processes. When they do and learn to examine them, they learn how to optimize their opportunities. If writing at night isn't working, try writing in the morning. If the novel is going nowhere, outline again and break the chapters into scenes and finish just one scene and then another and then . . .

Equally, and perhaps more fundamentally, writers need success and positive reinforcement. All of them. However measured. This may be completing a certain number of pages, publication, or simply approbation from a supportive reader. Peter Elbow (1973) suggests that teachers can help students to like their writing by creating judgment-free zones and by encouraging them to write in low-risk environments, using journaling and freewriting. Writers have to get *somewhere* with language before they get somewhere better. After creating a form for assessing writing apprehension and researching that measure, John Daly observed: "A positive attitude about writing is associated with, and may even be a critical precursor of, the successful development and maintenance of writing skills" (1985, 44).

PROCRASTINATION (DOES) DOES NOT PAY

Readiness is not all, but it is something. You don't want to compete in a marathon with the flu or interview for a job without practice. Writers do need to prepare and sometimes pausing to do so pays off. "Each writer fears that writing will never come, yet the experienced writer knows it may take days, weeks, and months to produce a few hours of text production" (Murray 1985, 220). Murray argues that writers need information, insight, order, need, and voice as conditions for good forward progress. And Robert Boice sums up his extensive research by observing: "Said more simply, PB [procrastination and blocking] is a problem of not knowing how to work patiently, mindfully, and optimistically" (1996, 141). Reed Larson claims that "optimal [writing] conditions occur when a person feels challenged at a level appropriately matched to his or her talents" (1985, 40).

Robert Boice's work challenges the image of the writer waiting for a muse. The dailiness reported by William Stafford, who lowered his own standards every morning to rise in the dark and write a poem, or the doggedness that must propel Steven King to produce a novel year after year, or Elizabeth Bishop or Eudora Welty (and any number of other writers) who slowly craft work across a long life in letters, seem to support Boice's findings that "as writing becomes habitual it is both easier and more enjoyable" (1985, 205). And experience matters. Mike Rose (1990) found that inexpert writers use ineffective strategies and had a smaller set of rules of thumb with which to encounter challenging writing tasks. Those writers needed to learn options and how to work around a problem as it arose.

Writers' block and procrastination are psychosocial states as much as they are physical ones. The same is true of their obverse. Given the difficulties writers experience and the painful struggle that many report, why do writers write? For most of us, the state of being unblocked is a powerful one. When the writing is taking place, when we're in the zone, the groove, the flow, there is nothing . . . nothing . . . a writer would rather do. For an expert practitioner, there are rewards on a large scale, for the opposite of pain is pleasure:

> As our studies have suggested, the phenomenology of enjoyment has eight major components. When people reflect on how it feels when their experience is most positive, they mention at least one, and often all, of the following. First, the experience usually occurs when we confront tasks we have a chance of completing. Second, we must be able to concentrate on what we are doing. Third and fourth, the concentration is usually possible because the task undertaken has clear goals and provides immediate feedback. Fifth, one acts with a deep but effortless involvement that removes from awareness the worries and frustrations of everyday life. Sixth, enjoyable experiences allow people to exercise a sense of control over their actions. Seventh, concern for the self disappears, yet paradoxically the sense of self emerges stronger after the flow experience is over. Finally, the sense of the duration of time is altered; hours pass by in minutes, and minutes can stretch out to seem like hours. The combination of all these elements causes a sense of deep enjoyment that is so rewarding people

feel that expending a great deal of energy is worthwhile simply to be able to feel it. (Csikszentmihalyi 1990, 49)

The state of writing well, consistently, regularly, productively is the flow state most of us aspire to and one that can be achieved, one block, one delay overcome at a time—day by day, day after day.

CHAPBOOKS

Not quite a book. But almost. Collected. Circulated. Contests for. Used in classrooms. Fine press and electronic. Well and poorly produced. Counts for much and counts for little. Published by others. Self-published. Concrete object. Conceptual art space.

The creative writing chapbook is a chameleon form. We borrow the name from the eighteenth and nineteenth centuries and make it our own. According to the *Oxford English Dictionary*, the chapbook is "a modern name applied by book-collectors and others to specimens of the popular literature which was formerly circulated by itinerant dealers or chapmen, consisting chiefly of small pamphlets of popular tales, ballads, tracts, etc." A quick trip to the Web locates library collections like the one at the University of Pittsburgh, where the Elizabeth Nesbitt Room "houses approximately 250 chapbooks printed in both England and America between the years 1650 to 1850" (www.pitt.edu/~enroom/chapbooks). The genres of these older chapbooks are varied and include books on religion, ethics and morals, fables, tales, legends, prose, nursery rhymes, natural history, jests, riddles and satire, curiosities and wonders, history, travel, and so on. "In general, chapbooks were inexpensive publications designed for the poorer literate classes. They were typically printed on a single sheet of low-quality paper, folded to make eight, sixteen, or twenty-four pages, though some examples were longer still. Closely related to the chapbook were two other forms also hawked in the streets during the same period. Broadsides were texts printed on one side of an entire sheet of paper. Smaller slip-poems were printed on longer strips of paper cut from a larger sheet" (www.sc.e3du/library/spcoll/britlit/cbooks/cbook1.html).

Due to the small market for full-length collections of poetry—one assertion we've heard is that a first book of poems by a university press in the United States sells approximately three hundred copies—the contemporary poet often looks to the chapbook contests for first publication. If a poet wins a contest in a field of from three hundred to eight hundred entrants, his first-place chapbook is published, often with copies given out to other contestants, all having paid a fee to have their manuscript read. In this version of chapbook making, the chapbook manuscript is regularly described as "a 20–30 page collection of poems," though some contests specify shorter or longer manuscripts. Shorter manuscripts are usually required for handpress, limited, numbered, and signed editions, yet electronic chapbooks are now a regular feature of online journals, in which length is less of an issue. While most chapbook contests specify poetry, there are a few that focus on the short story and the novella, genres that typically require greater page lengths. Chapbooks are also not considered books due to their smaller press run, usually under five hundred copies. Not quite a book, or is it?

It makes sense that a book of two hundred or more published pages requires a greater investment from both writer and publisher. Paper and postage and printing costs are high, which is why many look to online publishing as the future hope and future home of creative writing. Therefore, the contemporary chapbook represents a smaller investment and in this sense remains closer to its historical predecessors and a more democratic form, since the chapbook allows a publisher, potentially, to publish more authors. A small press can more readily explore the fine arts book market by beginning a chapbook series or by devoting one issue of a multiissue journal each year to the chapbook. Unlike the case with early chapbooks, though, the contemporary chapbook publisher is not hawking wares to a mass market. Since the market is limited, publishers must charge fees to create a support base and a readership. Often the fee represents the price of subscription to a journal, or, as mentioned above, provides an immediate market for the winning chapbook if contestants are also given a copy.

However, the chapbook idea has often been more than just a pragmatic move by publishers to sample and circulate the work of a number of writers rather than investing all their publishing hopes on the single work of a single author. The chapbook has launched careers and journals. Elizabethan authors circulated their poems in court informally, the precursor to the chapbooks of the eighteenth and nineteenth centuries, mentioned above. Twentieth-century authors often published their own work and tried to sell it or were first published by patrons. A particularly famous example is that of Sylvia Beach, who ran Shakespeare and Company in Paris and brought

James Joyce to world notice. Among the works Beach published was "*Poems Penyeach* . . . a small twenty-page pamphlet in gray wrappers" (www.libweb. princeton.edu:2003/libraries/firestone/rbsc/aids/beach.html).

While self-publishing is a complicated issue, often viewed as self-aggrandizing by those in the field of creative writing today, there is certainly room for exceptions to the rule when we consider the fine arts book (see "Vanity Press"). Whether the fine arts book is a collaboration between artist and writer or completed solely by the writer, it reverses the original definition of chapbook: it is not democratic, for it is often quite expensive (unlike the "gray wrappers" of Joyce's *Poems Penyeach*). Instead, the artist and writer complete a limited edition press run, sometimes using rare and expensive papers and inks, original art, and unusual formatting. Sizes vary. Fine arts books may actually be boxes, filled with individually printed leaves, and so on. While attending the Santa Cruz Writers' Conference many years ago, we writers were given a tour of the special collections room at the campus library and shown a hand-printed collection of Robinson Jeffers poems, bound in the granite similar to that which Jeffers and his wife used to construct Tor House on the Monterrey peninsula where he wrote most of the poems we were being shown. Certainly a book like the one we admired that day seems to push the boundary of our definition of chapbook; it also suggests that there is room in this form for more thought and innovation.

Currently, most chapbook (and book!) contests refuse to consider collaborative writing (see "Collaboration"). One author is supposed to write a work that one editor wants to acquire and publish and circulate to a general reading public. Therefore, collaborative efforts, large scale to small scale, are rarely published. Yet due to its special positioning, the chapbook space seems promising for collaborative investigations.

Equally, many writing teachers have found the chapbook format to be an excellent teaching tool. Mirroring the movement in composition to ask students to collect and refine essays across the term and to present them for final evaluation in a course writing portfolio, creative writing teachers often ask their students to work toward a small chapbook as the final product of their writing workshop. Doing so asks students to write toward a theme, to revise and arrange material, and to consider how several poems or stories can work in concert. The chapbook is also a useful class text, allowing a teacher to assign and discuss works by several writers in the course of a semester without asking students to invest too heavily in the work of any single author.

Finally, the chapbook in the academy is equally a chameleon. In this arena a chapbook is often considered less than a book. Generally, university presses holding full-length first-book manuscript contests specifically label as a "first-book" author any writer who has not published a collection of more than thirty to sixty pages in an edition of more than five hundred copies. A first-book author is eligible to enter contests for first-book publication but ineligible for contests inviting second-book manuscripts. The writer who has published six chapbooks may have an advantage here over the writer who has published few or none, for she is still considered a first-book author. At the same time, the writer who has published six chapbooks may still find these chapbooks—though equal in page count or exceeding the page count of a regular-sized published book—do not translate as a "real book" in the academy. That is: six chapbooks by small-press publishers do not generally equal one book by a university or trade publisher according to academic scales. It is here that the chapbook's democratic roots—small books published by small-press editors who believe in the work—are poorly served. In the academic meritocracy, chapbooks do not make great headway with tenure and promotion committees.

Despite the vagaries of counting—how many chapbooks equal one book and under what circumstances and for what group of individuals?—writers for many good reasons continue to invest in and value the chapbook space. Visit a national creative writing conference like that held annually by the Associated Writing Programs and you'll find yourself in a book exhibit room full of tables where committed editors display their wares. In fact, they *are* hawking these wares like their more itinerant chapman predecessors. And the wares are lovely, lovingly produced, full of fine and exciting writing. Not the mass market many of us seek to avoid in our daily life but tables arranged on the communal village commons where good writing can flourish and be shared. Chapbooks exist because writers, editors, and readers want them to exist. And our guess is they will continue to evolve and flourish, in hard copy and on the Web, for the foreseeable future.

SOURCES FOR CHAPBOOK CONTESTS AND CHAPBOOK PUBLISHERS

Bentley, Chantelle. *Poet's Market*. Cincinnati, OH: Writer's Digest Books, annual.

Fulton, Len, ed. *International Directory of Little Magazines and Small Presses*. Paradise, CA: Dustbooks, annual.

Poets and Writers Magazine, published six times a year, 72 Spring Street, New York, NY 10012, www.pw.org.

Writer's Chronicle, published six times a year by Associated Writing Programs, Tallwood House, Mail Stop 1E3, George Mason University, Fairfax, VA, 22030, awpwriter.org.

COLLABORATION

For many, creative writing always has been, is, and always will be a solo art. For others, this assumption has not always—or doesn't at present—hold true. Consider, however, the entry requirements for the Associated Writing Programs' annual book manuscript contests: "Each manuscript must include . . . the following typed statement: 'This is an original work of which I am the sole author.'"

Traditionally, creative writers have focused on creating original texts for which they claim solitary authorship. They have done so despite cross-cultural, historical, and practical evidence that writing is often—some argue always—a collaborative act. Investigations of the history of authorship (definitions of which have demonstrably changed over time) and philosophies of postmodernism challenge this unitary assumption, suggesting that our thinking and our writing are socially constructed and that our inventions and ideas are influenced by all that we encounter in the world. Definitions of collaborative work and practices, while complicated, may help us productively reconceptualize the creative composing process, encouraging writers to continue to challenge genres, create hybrid forms, and participate in constructionist and cooperative practices, including bricolage, collage, and alternate discourses.

For example, one of our most often taught verse forms, the haiku, derives from an ancient collaborative composing activity. In the *Haikai no Renga* tradition. Japanese poets, circa 1200, would gather to create linked verse together, each striving to produce the "hokku"—the stanza that begins a renga series, in which "each poem in a series was linked to the immediately preceding one either by witty association or verbal play" (Yuasa 1975, 12). In this competitive collaboration—a sequential composing act that produced a multiauthored product—poets often found themselves with many leftover hokku, which became haiku.

However, U.S. poets and writers rarely, if ever, gather with the intention of composing together in a similar manner, for there are a number of artistic and economic pressures on them to focus on the singular.

Obstacles to such collaborative work include the difficulty of finding editors willing to publish coauthored work and the fact that coauthored work is regularly excluded from the thesis and dissertation processes as well as from contests and grant applications like that of the AWP awards contests mentioned above. Indeed, coauthored creative writing is almost an oxymoron and is generally treated with suspicion by other authors. That this should continue to be so may prove problematic in a century that is already grappling anew with definitions of intellectual property and academic arguments over what constitutes plagiarism, as those definitions are being continually challenged by advances in writing technologies.

Instances of coauthorship in creative writing are so rare as to be memorable to those who have encountered them. Early in his career, Mark Doty published with his then wife Ruth as M. R. Doty, and Louise Erdrich and her husband, Michael Dorris, successfully pushed a coauthoring agenda during a number of the years preceding his death, regularly sharing insights into their collaborative composing during interviews. One of the few novelists to investigate collaborative coauthoring—prior to the advent of electronic publishing—was the late Ken Kesey, whose fiction-writing class wrote a novel together. The next best thing to published coauthoring of a literary product in the fine arts is the artistic correspondence. While Rilke's *Letters to a Young Poet* represents one side of a conversation, epistolary correspondents like Leslie Silko and James Wright shared insights and ideas about their writing in letters edited and introduced by Anne Wright (1986). Rare but notable is William Stafford and Marvin Bell's *Segues* (1983), a lyric exchange between two already widely published solo artists.

If coauthoring seems to diminish the uniqueness of the creative act and raise questions about the division of labor that goes into producing a coauthored text (and the awarding of merit for that product), it also challenges our assumptions concerning originality and influence. Intentionally, advocates of collaborative learning and teaching practices raise these and other related issues. Though now widely accepted as a meaningful pedagogical tool, as evidenced in creative writers' workshops (see "Workshop"), the writing and reading response groups advocated in composition pedagogies today are based on assumptions that learners benefit from supportive response to their work (including peer tutorials in writing centers). Influential in bringing the workshop concept to composition was Peter Elbow, in *Writing without Teachers* (1973, 1998), and the many MFA-holding writing teachers who staffed required composition courses within traditional English literature departments during the

1970s, when open-admissions students increased the need for time-intensive writing instruction, particularly at the first-year level.

To deal with the complicated needs of first-generation college writing students, these writing teachers drew on the work of creative writers and the work of diverse thinkers and theorists like Richard Rorty (1979), a philosopher who argued that knowledge is a social construction; Kenneth Bruffee (1984), who argued that collaboration was a useful and necessary part of a democratic process; and Carl Rogers (1961), a psychologist who was investigating group response dynamics in the early 1960s—to name just a few whose thinking influenced the growing field of composition studies. Compositionists developed new classroom practices based on several premises: that collaboration could increase writing students' audience awareness; allow learners to pool and increase knowledge; create supportive environments for taking risks in learning and writing; offer a more accurate reflection of the way meaning is made (in discussion and negotiation among and between communities of learners); and challenge hierarchies and encourage investigations of power relationships—to name a few.

Of course, it did not take long for critics of these new practices and pedagogies to raise useful critiques, particularly that of the possibility of forced acquiescence and community norming. While group consensus about what would help improve a writer's text can be profoundly useful to a writer who is seeking reader response, consensus may also prove stifling to those writers who are eager and ready to push against conventions and conventional thinking. Think of the collaborators in Vichy France and the nobility of the Resistance served up in our favorite movie, *Casablanca.* Historically, to collaborate is to buy in to the assumptions of the power structure, and to resist is to remain free and original.

Writers who give in to editorial or community demands, to the temptations of genre writing and its problematic economic rewards, are often viewed on the professional level as sellouts or worse. One need only note a common belief among writers that to suffer and remain in poverty—to live the bohemian life—is more meritorious than to succeed and have one's artistic struggles tainted by the seductions of success and luxury—or, as Jane Tompkins explains, "The first requirement of a work of art in the twentieth century is that it should do nothing" (1980, 210). In this vision, the paid literary collaborator hides her artistic light, her real talent, under a bushel basket in order to boost the prestige of someone who couldn't produce real work. This writer is a hack, a drudge, factotum, plodder, scribbler; such coauthoring is to be abhorred and avoided if at all possible or undertaken only to return the writer to her art. Equally, the ghostwriter succumbs to the temptations of earning a living by prostituting his talents, taking dictation for the stars (or other nonliterary but successful figures), or overseeing the continuation of a successful series by a now-deceased genre author in order to assure the success of, say, a blockbuster mystery or romance series. Hacks and ghosts include the once famous, now fallen, like F. Scott Fitzgerald writing screenplays in Hollywood instead of completing his last novel.

But concepts of collaboration are more complicated than a concern over "false or forced consensus" or the worry over "who wrote which words?" or "words for money are less valuable than words for art's sake" might suggest.

Collaboration takes place when we talk through ideas or derive an idea from a life experience. It occurs when we interact with another artist's work. Collaboration takes place when we coauthor as well as when we share our writing and ask for response that we feel free to use or not use. These are only a few of the many instances of fruitful collaborative and, potentially, knowledge- and art-making activities that have long been part of the writing life. While some argue that all writing is inherently collaborative (Thralls 1992), others restrict the term to discussions of coauthoring. Therefore, a few more definitions and explorations are in order.

WHERE COLLABORATION HIDES

It is fairly easy to illustrate that writers do not write alone. Even if we were able to ignore theories of influence, we would still encounter the practicalities of production. Most writers find other authors' acknowledgment pages a transparent primer of influence, collaboration, and community. Here we find the traditional and expected tropes of thanking the publisher, editor, research assistant, the writers' reading group, the writer's university that offered sabbatical support or a state arts council that provided grants, the writer's retreat where good conversation and well-prepared food greased the inspirational wheels, the nanny (oh, lucky writer), and the helpmeet, spouse, or significant other. Even, at times, the muse is acknowledged.

One does not have to go far to find traditions of collaborative authorship, though most instances are found in non-European-influenced cultures or, in the United States, imbedded within traditions of vernacular and oral literatures. If authorship is a social construct, stemming from nineteenth-century romanticism, which valued the concept of autonomous, original (often male) composition as a reflection of an individual character and mind at work on a page—a page that could then be owned via copyright legislation—then collaboration is the act that undermines that construct. We'll never know if some unsung editor of Shakespeare's work suggested that he add an extra "Never" (or advised taking away one we now value) from Lear's memorable lament on the death of his daughter Cordelia. We could as usefully speculate on what version of the *Wasteland* might we be reading (or not reading?) without Ezra Pound. Ditto, Pound without Chinese and other world literatures to mine. Editors and authors collaborate. Readers and writers collaborate. Writing teachers and writing students collaborate.

Collaboration can be seen as a way to compound knowledge: surely two good minds can often remember more than one, two can sometimes work more quickly to see and make connections between disparate facts or analyze options (we know this holds true in the hard sciences, where research teams are the dedicated norm). It's also easy to imagine that our tools are singular (the paintbrush, the keyboard), although that's rarely true. The painter tends to lay down "versions" as often as does the writer (*pentimento* is the term for an earlier layer of painting that shows through the next layers). There are times when some of those layers and drafts are set down by different hands in a collaborative effort, potentially enhancing the product but certainly complicating current notions of ownership. In fact, collaboration has often been the way of apprenticeship. Renaissance painters had workshops, guilds had articled apprentices, and writers' workshops have students who are seeking to learn from professional writers via imitation, workshop response, and editorial direction and correction.

Collaborative theory suggests that such relationships are more complicated *and* more important than is commonly admitted. For some, the publishing senior writer is *the expert*, perhaps a gatekeeper, someone to emulate and eventually to dethrone. For others, the senior writer is a mentor, introducing able novices into a guild, society, school, or community. Not either/or, but both/and. Even if few of us coauthor, clearly none of us writes alone. Writing is not entirely a social activity, nor is it a provably solitary one. It is at once an act of individual cognition but also always an act of intellectual and social negotiation with other thinkers. We think and write in the presence of and as a result of our influences, and we can choose to make what is tacit more explicit and interactive. Such a choice is often made by writing teachers, by feminist authors, or by writers interested in connecting writing with social activism and reform and identity politics. It is also the normal experience of workplace writers and writers in other academic genres.

COLLABORATION IN ACTION

In the sciences, coauthored research is the given. Research labs work on a variety of funded group projects. Senior scientists direct and compile the work of assistants, training younger researchers and reaping the benefits of that training in contributions to coproduced reports. Credit and authorship are acknowledged in ways different from those composing in the arts and humanities: sometimes seniority and hierarchy are indicated and sometimes funding agencies are given great credit. At other times, coauthorship or joint authorship is evenly spread across a team of senior researchers. That is, credit may be hierarchical *or* dialogic; in certain group writing projects, workers contribute data and brainstorming to a product that is orchestrated by the dominant member. In other projects, colleagues work in tandem, in dialogue, each cocontributing to the final product.

The same is true in workplace writing environments, where a document may be produced on an assembly-line model in which the constituent parts arrive separately on the desk of a coordinator who assembles the whole, smoothes out the text, and produces an introduction or executive summary. More interactively, a team may produce "versions," one member sending a draft to another to revise before sending it to another member of the team (or the document recirculates and accretes through multiple iterations), although the composite document may still eventually move through an editorial or proofreading hierarchy. Composition researchers have identified and detailed these sorts of models, including the influence of computer systems on our understandings of coauthoring as we produce hypertext or linked texts that are loosely but usefully associated (Ede and Lunsford 1990; Landow 1992, Smith 1994).

Technology challenges our ideas of authorship and increases our options for creative composing (see "Electronic Literature") in the workplace *and* in academic environments. Technology challenges Jane Tompkins's (1980) definition of twentieth-century art. In the twenty-first century, art does many things and is sure to circulate in new ways across evolving platforms. Indeed, through the use of classroom Web boards and e-mail exchanges, student writing already is doing so. Sharing work online can allow students informal and formal writing opportunities, increase engagement and dialogue, and encourage revision in a writing space

(Conroy 2001), which may feel "alternative" for students' instructors, yet is likely to feel comfortable and productive for writing students, many of whom have never actually seen or touched the museum object called "the manual typewriter."

For creative writers, then, a promising first step (though market forces still appear to hinder the publication and circulation of the same) would be to explore the values of coproduction, as detailed here by Lisa Ede and Andrea Lunsford. They explain how dialogic writing and "versioning" *both* were elements of their coauthoring processes (at least during their pre-e-mail days of collaborative composing when this was written):

> When we are working, whether in Vancouver, Corvallis, or Seattle's University Inn, our halfway meeting place, we usually stake out different rooms to write in. But we move constantly back and forth, talking, trading texts (one of our favorite collaborative strategies is to revise one another's writing), asking questions. Often when one or both of us is stuck, we'll work together on the same text, passing a single pad of paper back and forth, one of us completing the sentence or paragraph that the other began. By the time that most essays are finished, we simply couldn't say that "Lisa wrote this section, while Andrea wrote that." Our joint essays are truly collaborative efforts. (1990, 126)

Creative writers might consider the potentials of collaboration, because doing so could lead to balance. Received images of solitary writers at the word processor might be balanced with equally real images of writers talking about aesthetics together and founding schools of poetry, of editorial board meetings for literary journals with their convivial and contentious discussions that help shape the future of U.S. letters, of the public reading where writer shares ideas with writer, with the popularity of writers' lists and online salons, with the continued growth of academic degree programs, university workshop classes, and community-based writing programs and all the writerly discussion that takes place in those locations. Teachers and writers in school, prisons, shelters, and retirement homes continue to compose within intensely collaborative settings and often testify to those environments' important cocontributions to their creative work. It's worth asking, then, how coauthoring and copublishing might usefully enliven a rapidly changing publishing landscape on and off the Web. How can reconceptualizing the creative composing process open new avenues for writing, for writers, for the teaching of writing? How might collaborative practices support social and institutional change?

Last, but not the least important, we might consider the fact that collaboration and coauthoring often prove both productive *and fun* for writers and can change their attitudes vis-à-vis a highly competitive and often discouraging publishing environment.

"I want my ideas to generate talk, to make sense, to provoke. I want a good story. And the only way to get there for me is through the challenges of tough readers," says Lil Branon. "That's why I write a lot with other people. That and it's never quite as lonely. That and it's just plain more fun. You get to talk a lot. You get to hear yourself think . . . The essay or chapter was just the by-product of the talk. The talk was the important part. The talk was important because it would generate hundreds of ideas which didn't fit the paper but which could become papers later on. The talk created a future for ideas. The writing never seemed hard either—time consuming but not hard" (1988, 26).

Not only have creative writing communities supported a bias against art that "does something," but many also hold to tacit associated assumptions that art-making should entail relentless hard work and suffering, perhaps a poor inheritance from a long Puritan tradition (see "Author"). Consider the lilies of the field. Consider the Japanese Hokku writers, who are reported to have enjoyed their group poetry sessions, working hard to prepare, traveling long distances to participate, balancing the insights of the solitary observer with the joys of gift giving, of poetic observation shared in community—and along the way producing haiku that we read with respect and enjoyment some eight hundred years later. Consider creative writing as—at times—a pleasurable collaborative practice. There's a lot to be said for it.

COMPOSITION

Composition is an activity (what we do when we write), an institutional practice (a type of assigned first-year writing within a required undergraduate college course), and, nowadays, it's also a course of graduate study that represents a field of specialists who call themselves compositionists (and sometimes rhetoricians). *Composition* is a term that has been in regular use since the late 1970s, and it describes a still-developing and multidisciplinary field (see North 1987). Those in composition studies draw on research in composing practices, theories of reading and writing, linguistics and literature, and the history of rhetoric. Patricia Bizzell and Bruce Herzberg's *The Bedford Bibliography* (2003) provides both a useful overview to the field as well as an extensive annotated bibliography of readings that together represent the variety of texts found on degree reading lists in contemporary graduate composition programs.

Most creative writers become teachers of college composition as part of their MA, MFA, or PhD degree work. The first-year writing course (formerly freshman composition, with its developmental or basic writing pre-freshman equivalent) became a core one- or two-term sequence in most American colleges and universities by the mid-twentieth century and remains the course that is most often taught by graduate teaching assistants within English departments today. These literature, creative writing, or composition graduate students are given some-to-minimal preparation for such teaching (via a summer pedagogy course, a one-week in-service orientation, and/or a one-day introduction to the assigned textbook and department syllabus). Historically, at schools where two terms of writing are offered, tenured literature faculty, who are also sometimes required to teach composition, often have opted to teach the second-term course because they could organize this class as a reading course. In this incarnation, the second-term writing course turned into an introduction to literary genres, a way of teaching both more familiar to and more valued by these faculty members. In a composition program with a composition-trained director, however, these courses are more often organized as writing courses that include a mixture of reading theory, introduction to critical or cultural theory, and/or research or argumentation. (See also "Reading.")

During the 1950s and 1960s, the first-year writing course—then freshman composition—was modally organized; that is, students were asked to compose a sequence of essays in prescribed forms: description, narration, exposition, and persuasion. In these courses the focus was on the text, the written product, and not on the processes of composing those texts. During the 1960s and 1970s, research into composing practices of basic and professional writers (as well as an examination of narrative accounts offered by creative writers) led to the deeper understanding of writing as a recursive activity and to the development of process pedagogies. These included teaching practices that encouraged students to develop writing fluency and metacognitive awareness of their writing processes. Students were taught to develop topics, share initial drafts in small-group and collaborative settings, and to revise and complete writing portfolios.

In many of these courses, the focus shifted from the production of texts to the development of *students as writers*. At this time, composition classrooms came to more closely resemble the graduate creative writing workshop course, while the graduate creative writing workshop became a model for undergraduate creative writing courses, which, in turn, began to be informed, in some cases, by composition theory, research, and practice (see Bishop 1998).

Writing in 1986, Lester Faigley outlined three broad categories of composition research: expressive, cognitive, and social. Expressive theories were complicated by cognitive research and cognitive research, in turn, was amplified by social theories of instruction. At the end of the century, social theories of composing were dominant, though process practices were still challenging modal (current-traditional) curriculums around the country. Process theory and practice, however, face challenges from both cultural and postprocess theorists who are in tune with movements in critical theory that are prominent in English literature departments. Such movement—the rise and fall of models and groups aligned to those models and the evolving theories of writing based on developing research into composing practices—speaks to the growing disciplinarity of the field of composition. This evolution asks compositionists to look at why their particular discipline has developed as it has, just as it should prompt creative writers to inquire where they might fit into those discussions.

In the early 1970s, an abundance of graduating literature PhDs encountered a lack of positions, and many of these graduates either left the academy or took on untenured adjunct teaching, sometimes moving from one institution to another. Frequently, these gypsy scholars found work teaching large numbers of first-year writing students, whose enrollment fueled English departments by providing teaching assistantships for graduate students as well as a limited number of term positions for adjuncts. Traditionally and still, adjuncts perform highly specialized and professional work but often at very low salaries, and they are rarely offered benefits or job security. (See also "Adjunct and Temporary Faculty.")

In departments that do not recognize the MFA as a terminal degree, creative writers who have not yet published a book often form a large part of this adjunct composition teaching pool. Unfortunately, because MFA programs have not generally offered an introduction to composition teaching—much less pedagogy courses in creative writing—and because English literature departments generally hold the teaching of teaching writing in low esteem, creative writers typically align themselves with their colleagues in literature. (See Starkey 1994 and Scholes 1986 for a discussion of English department hierarchies.)

The many negative attitudes toward freshman composition have been challenged only in the last thirty years as degree programs in composition and rhetoric began to develop a profile on the national English department scene, in part because of the increase of jobs for all English degree holders in this very area. By the early 1980s, many institutions were offering the MA and PhD degree in composition, notable among these are the programs at Indiana University of Pennsylvania, the University of New Hampshire, Carnegie Mellon, Ohio State, Texas Christian, Rutgers, Syracuse, Miami Ohio, Penn State, the University of South Florida, and the University of Nebraska. At the largest universities around the country, large-scale writing programs (with first-year writing programs of over three thousand students and up to one hundred graduate teaching assistants and adjuncts) have undertaken the more systematic pedagogical training of teachers and graduate students, and many now offer exciting and diverse graduate course offerings, including courses in the history of rhetoric, composition theory and practice, psycholinguistics, sociolinguistics, ESL, cyberliteracy and computer-assisted instruction, basic writing, literary and composition theory, and reading theory. Every several years, the journal *Rhetoric Review* surveys and reports on these programs and their course offerings.

Large-scale writing programs are often run by trained Writing Program Administrators (WPAs), who hold degrees in composition studies and are supported by and support in turn campus writing centers and computer-assisted classrooms. Since 1949, college composition instructors have been organized via the Conference of College Composition and Communication (CCCC), a conference within the parent organization, the National Council of Teachers of English (NCTE). Currently, CCCC has over eight thousand college-level members and NCTE over ninety thousand kindergarten- through college-level members. Information on both organizations—their annual conventions and their activities to promote the interests and working conditions of teachers of writing—can be found at the NCTE Web site: www.ncte.org. (See "Associated Writing Programs" for a discussion of the equivalent organization for teachers of creative writing.)

These days, composition and rhetoric are engaging fields of study that offer graduates in this area regular opportunities for university-level employment. Many who run those programs note that an increasing number of MA- and MFA-holding creative writing graduates are now continuing on for a PhD in composition because that field is offering interesting avenues for enhancing a creative writer's understanding of his or her own writing practices and supporting his or her work as a writing teacher. In tandem with the rise of degree programs, composition presses now provide a growing body of publications for the field; prominent among these are the National Council of Teachers of English, Boynton/Cook, Oxford University Press, Southern Illinois University Press, and Utah State University Press. Journals such as *Writing on the Edge* publish articles of interest to both creative writers and compositionists, and major journals in composition—*College English, College Composition and Communication, Journal of Advanced Composition, Composition Studies, Rhetoric Review*—also publish an occasional creative writing oriented essay or article.

In addition to referring to the *Bedford Bibliography*, those interested in recent developments would do well to consult the last several years of the above journals as well as the ERIC database through a local university library. Those who wish to join the many vibrant ongoing electronic conversations about writing can access a number of online lists. Among the most popular listeservs are the WPA-L (www.wpacouncil.org/wpa-l), H-Rhetor (www.h-net.org/~rhetor/), and TechRhet (www.interversity.org/lists/techrhet/). Interested teachers should also refer to online journals such as *Kairos* (english.ttu.edu/kairos/) and *English Matters* (chnm.gmu.edu/ematters/) and online resources such as Paul Matsuda's links page (pubpages.unh.edu/~pmatsuda/resources.html) and rhetcomp.com.

A good history of rhetorical theory can be found in Bizzell and Herzberg's *The Rhetorical Tradition* (1990) and useful introductions to classroom issues and management are Thomas Newkirk's collection *Nuts and Bolts* (1993) and Lad Tobin's *Writing Relationships: What Really Happens in the Composition Class* (1993). Victor Villanueva's *Cross-Talk in Comp Theory* (1997) collects key texts of the field in one volume. Paul Heilker and Peter Vandenberg's *Keywords in Composition Studies* (1996) introduces readers to the most compelling discussions in composition, those that have dominated the journals, classrooms, and conferences, and Joseph Harris also approaches the field through keywords and discussions in *A Teaching Subject* (1997).

Narrative histories of composition are available in Duane Roen, Stuart Brown, and Theresa Enos's *Living Composition and Rhetoric* (1999) and Joseph Trimmer's collection *Narration as Knowledge* (1997). Three other engaging edited collections include Susan Hunter and Ray Wallace's *The*

Place of Grammar in Writing Instruction (1995) (new teachers of writing are always pressed to address the "grammar question"); Art Young and Toby Fulwiler's *When Writing Teachers Teach Literature* (1995), which represents an intersection of interests between writing and literature teachers; and David Starkey's *Teaching Writing Creatively* (1998), which does the same for the intersection of creative writing and composition. Many creative writers may already be familiar with Peter Elbow's vastly influential *Writing without Teachers* (1973, 1998), which arguably marks the beginning of the writing process movement and still yields pleasure and insight to the student of creative writing about to enter or begin teaching her or his first writing workshop.

CONFERENCES, COLONIES, AND RESIDENCIES

Because the larger world is generally indifferent to creative writing, places and times where writers can concentrate on their writing lives are infrequent. Always, obligation beckons. Most creative writers must work in jobs outside their field. Many have families to shepherd through the day. The phone rings, the trash must be taken out, a friend e-mails to request a luncheon date. One after another the daily duties mount so that a writer may feel she is *never* going to get her work accomplished. This entry discusses opportunities for writers to escape their normal responsibilities, to grow and develop as writers in a space specifically designed for that purpose.

CONFERENCES

One of the easiest and most productive ways for beginning writers to meet and engage with others who are practicing the same craft is to attend a writers' conference. Conferences are held around the country (and around the world), and may last for anywhere from part of a single day to several weeks. Perhaps the most famous is also the oldest (established in 1926), the Bread Loaf Writers' Conference at Middlebury College in Vermont. The idea for the conference is attributed to Robert Frost, who hoped to bring young writers together in an inspiring setting, and this goal remains central to most contemporary conferences.

Attending a conference is not possible for all writers, as it requires time and money, but financial assistance is sometimes available. At Bread

Loaf, for example, this takes the form of reduced rates on tuition fees or scholarships that require students to serve as waitstaff during meal times. However, because there is such a wide range of offerings, most people can find one to satisfy their needs and financial circumstances. Writers' Conferences & Centers Online has the most comprehensive site on the Web; it can be found at www.awpwriter.org/wcc/index.htm.

For attendees, conferences serve a number of different purposes. New writers benefit from the guidance of established writers via workshops, craft lectures, or one-on-one conferences. They can mingle informally with these writers at parties and hear them read from their work. As literary agent Michael Seidman notes, at a conference "there is a large and varied support group waiting not only to ensure that you are not lonely, but to provide the kind of help and lessons the writer needs to grow" (1993, 102). New writers can meet influential agents, like Seidman, and editors who may become interested in their work. Prestigious conferences like Bread Loaf or the Sewanee Writers' Conference serve as a kind of fraternity or sorority for writers. Participants meet other writers who act as a support network, offer encouragement, and give advice about publication opportunities. Ideally, new writers are both nurtured and challenged, and leave the conference eager to do more work.

For writers teaching at the conference, there are also a number of benefits. It is prestigious to be asked to teach at a conference, and one conference may lead to another. If new writers hope to benefit from contacts with editors and agents, established writers have even more hope of turning their contacts into publications. Conferences provide a paid semivacation, usually in an attractive locale such as a resort or a college campus. Even well-known writers, unlike pop singers or movie stars, are generally not recognized by the general public, so the close attention of adoring fans is another stimulus.

Ultimately, some writers are put off by the occasionally circuslike atmosphere of a writing conference. At times, the art of schmoozing (q.v.) seems to be practiced more than the art of writing. Nevertheless, for new writers hoping to step into "the business," there are few comparable opportunities for such a full-throttle experience.

COLONIES

If a conference offers the chance to immerse oneself in the world of writing for a short time, a writers' colony makes that immersion long term. One of the most famous writers' colonies is the Fine Arts Work Center in

Provincetown, Massachusetts. The Work Center "provides seven-month fellowships to twenty fellows each year in the form of living/work space and a modest monthly stipend." Writers are expected to live and work in the space provided by the sponsor. Typically, days are spent working, while nights are free for socializing with other artists.

All the benefits of the conference are increased in the residency. There is more than ample time to write. Creative energy abounds. The support from one's fellow "colonists" is broader and deeper, and friendships made with writers in the colony tend to be long lasting. Opportunities to schmooze with visiting writers are more frequent, and the resulting encounters may be more intense. Those living in an artist rather than a writers' colony can exchange ideas with people working in mediums other than their own.

On the other hand, colonies are impractical for most writers with work and family responsibilities. For these people, the luxury of taking seven months, or even a month, off to work solely on their writing is unthinkable. Consequently, however diverse their aesthetic points of reference may be, there is a certain group resemblance to the members of a writers' colony. They tend to be young, highly educated, and largely unencumbered.

RESIDENCIES

While the term "residency" is sometimes applied to a stint in a writers' colony, here we mean time spent alone, rather than with fellow artists. The residency at the University of Arizona Poetry Center, for instance, promises to provide "an individual writer with a place to create in a quiet neighborhood." The Philip Roth Residence in Creative Writing at the Stadler Center for Poetry at Bucknell University offers "a studio in the Stadler Center, a furnished two-bedroom apartment in Bucknell's Poet's Cottage, meals in the University Dining Service," and a small stipend, with all "campus academic, cultural, and recreational facilities available for the Resident's use." (www.bucknell.edu) Like a writers' colony, a residency provides writers with an opportunity to write; occasionally, some part-time teaching may also be required.

One of the most interesting, and geographically wide-ranging, artist-in-residence programs is offered by the National Park Service (NPS; www.nps.gov/volunteer/air.htm). While the residency is unpaid, artists and writers chosen to participate in the program live for free in NPS-supplied housing while they work on projects inspired by their spectacular surroundings. The residencies are offered at parks ranging from Voyageurs in Minnesota, on the shores of Lake Superior, to the Everglades in Florida, from Acadia in Maine to Joshua Tree National Monument in the California desert.

Again, the standards for acceptance at most residencies are fairly high—a writer must have some record of success and must demonstrate even more potential. Once those standards are met, however, the decision about whether or not to join a writers' colony or take an individual residency depends on the writer's own needs and personality. Writers who live far from large cities may welcome the opportunity to discuss their work with other artists. On the other hand, a parent who has somehow managed briefly to disengage herself from her family would likely cherish her every free moment to work and would prefer the solitude of a residency.

CONTESTS

Publication of most literary novels occurs through a process that has become established over the last half century. Aspiring authors send their completed manuscripts around until they find an interested agent. The agent, working through a network of connections, shows the manuscript to editors he believes will find the novel exciting. Eventually, if the author is lucky, a publishing house accepts the novel and—assuming the writer has no celebrity connections—prints anywhere from two thousand to ten thousand copies. The novel is then marketed through traditional means. Copies are sent to reviewers. Advertisements are placed in trade journals like *Publishers Weekly* and large-circulation magazines like the *New Yorker* and the *Atlantic*. Publishers may also arrange readings and book-signing tours. Unfortunately, the author and her novel will most likely soon be forgotten, though that is not always the case.

Despite decades of decreasing sales, literary novels retain some profitability. Granted, literary authors do not post the same numbers as blockbuster authors like Tom Clancy, John Grisham, Mary Higgins Clark, and Sue Grafton. However, proven names such as John Updike, Anne Tyler, Alice Hoffman, Wally Lamb, and Joyce Carol Oates manage to win the praises of highbrow reviewers while also selling respectable numbers of books. Moreover, literary novels can create a buzz and increase sales by winning prizes like the Pulitzer and the National Book Award. If they are made into movies—even if the movies themselves are not spectacular successes—these novels can find themselves in the front windows of bookstores next to much less accomplished work. Even though Jonathan Demme's movie was a commercial disaster, its prerelease hype greatly increased sales of Toni Morrison's *Beloved*. And Michael Cunningham's *The Hours* would not have entered the national conversation the way it briefly did if not for the film staring Nicole Kidman, Meryl Streep, and Julianne Moore.

Therefore, while there are risks in publishing a literary novel, there are also potentially large rewards. The same cannot be said for collections of short stories, even books of related short stories, which have the texture of a novel. Volumes of poetry—with the rare exception of collections by celebrities like Jimmy Stewart, Jimmy Carter, and Jewel—do not make so much as a blip on the radar screens of most major publishers. As Pulitzer Prize winning poet Henry Taylor once said when asked about his relationship with his agent: "Poets don't have agents. There's not enough money in poetry."

So what are poets and short story writers—and literary-minded publishers—to do? In the last twenty years, the answer has been to hold contests. Ideally, a contest to publish, say, a collection of short stories works as follows. First, an announcement is made in magazines that writers read. Normally, a prestigious writer is named as judge of the contest. If the advertising is effective, at minimum several hundred authors enter their manuscripts at $20 to $25 per entry. The contest fees of $4,000 or (sometimes considerably) more allow publishers to finance publication of the book. If there is an especially large surfeit of contest fees, publishers might use the money to publish a second book, conduct an aggressive marketing campaign, or simply pay themselves a stipend for the hard work they have done.

Contests also offer advantages from an author's perspective. Because writers have paid a fee to the publisher, they can expect to receive a closer reading than they would from an editorial assistant in a large publishing house who has little incentive to spend time with the work of an unproven author. Writers know, at the very least, that their work *will* be read, rather than sit unnoticed in a "slush pile." And if a writer is lucky and talented enough to overcome the long odds and win the contest (after all, winning a short story contest is easier than winning the lottery), she can be assured of some renown. Everyone who has entered the contest will know her

name; some of those contestants will want to read the winning book. The
publisher is likely to announce the winner in trade publications and to
mention the contest in all advertising. The final judge will write a flatter-
ing foreword and may be able to introduce the winner to other influential
people.

With so much going for them, no wonder contests are so popular. And
yet their reality is sometimes quite different from their outward appearance. A contest, as its etymology implies, promotes competition. Writers
who submit frequently to contests may come to see other writers as rivals
rather than as friends. In a contest, the perception exists (despite publishers' "Dear Contestant" letters) that there are not many excellent writers,
but one winner in a sea of losers. Furthermore, judges in large contests
normally read only the finalists; all other manuscripts are screened by
editorial assistants, whose tastes and training will necessarily be different
from the judge's. And though contests are supposed to be judged "blind-
ly," judges may well be tipped off that a friend or student has entered the
contest. In fact, according to editor George Bradley, in its early years, the
judges of the Yale Series of Younger Poets—one of the most prestigious—
sometimes openly asked their protégés to send in manuscripts.

While the back-scratching and logrolling that go on in poetry book
contests was an open secret, many writers refused to discuss the issue publicly, fearing that their own chances of winning—however slim—would
be destroyed if they became whistleblowers. However, in April 2004 the
prestige and legitimacy of these contests received a serious blow with
the creation of foetry.com. The Web site was created by Alan Cordle, a
Portland, Oregon, librarian whose wife, he believed, had repeatedly and
unfairly lost book contests to people who were unconscionably close to
the judges. Cordle charges that the "celebrity poets" who generally have
the final say on which manuscript wins a contest "routinely award prizes
to their students, friends and lovers." He argues that this is "cheating.
It's criminal. If this was anything other than poetry, the Department of
Justice would be involved" (Tizon 2005, A1). To support his contentions,
foetry.com lists the winners and their ties to the judges and sponsors of
what are generally considered the most prestigious contests. Though not
all winners have close connections to their contests, it clearly doesn't hurt
to know the judge or to have attended a university that publishes books
through competitions.

While foetry.com had been generating a great deal of controversy in literary circles, it reached the wider world when the *Los Angeles Times* made

it a front-page story in June of 2005. Reporter Alex Tizon remarked, "In today's literary climate, winning a major contest is one of the only sure tickets to continuing life as a poet" (A1). Thought Tizon is obviously exaggerating—many fine creative writers continue their careers without ever winning a major literary prize—it is certainly true that without a prize it is difficult to land a tenure-track job in a college or university (see "Teaching Jobs"). And the controversy flared so brightly in large measure because foetry is so aggressive in its condemnation of book competitions. Its mission statement calls for "Exposing the fraudulent 'contests.' Tracking the sycophants. Naming the names." At the bottom of a list of contest winners is the inflammatory rhetorical question: "Is your professor's poetry career built on academic integrity?" Indeed, Cordle encourages those who have entered contests and lost to those who have suspiciously close ties to the publisher to take every remedy from asking for a refund to filing a fraud complaint with the state's attorney general.

Not surprisingly, many of those on the winning and judging side of the contests took issue with Cordle's claims. Probably the most persuasive argument against Cordle is that the poetry world is so small—the number of truly accomplished poets is probably in the hundreds or thousands, rather than the hundreds of thousands—it is inevitable that judges will know, or know of, the winning contestants. Yet for every defender of poetry publishing's status quo, there are likely many more who would agree with Neal Bowers: "This confirms what anyone involved in poetry over the past 30 years has known for a long, long time. . . . The world of poetry is all about hustle and connection" (Tizon 2005, A33).

Whatever the morality of contests, every issue of *Poets and Writers Magazine* and the *Writer's Chronicle* is chock full of them. Poetry chapbooks (volumes of less than thirty-two pages) are the clear favorite of publishers (see "Chapbooks"); however, contests also tend to target authors who have not yet published a full-length book. Some contests, like Converse College's Julia Peterkin Award, offer writers of a winning manuscript cash prizes and the opportunity for a public reading.

Perhaps the most profitable variation on this theme is the contest to select a prize story or poem for a literary journal. While these contests normally charge only half the fee of a book contest, they offer far less than half the exposure for a winner. Advantages for the editors are much more obvious. Even if the top two stories or three to five poems are all published in the magazine, the editors need to devote only a small percentage of the total pages of their journal to the winners. Yet contest fees may provide enough money to finance publication of the entire issue. As a consolation prize, contestants typically receive a year's subscription to the journal, another clever editorial tactic that boosts exposure of the magazine.

If the authors of this book sound skeptical of contests, it's not because we haven't been on the winning end. Both of us have won contests and been pleased when friends and strangers have recognized our accomplishment. We simply yearn, unrealistically perhaps, for a publication climate that is more communal than individualistic, that acknowledges shared achievement as fully as personal triumph. However, as long as writers continue to hunger for fame, and as long as editors and publishers (q.v.) at cash-strapped university presses, nonprofit presses, and small presses desperately require funds to produce their work, contests are likely to remain a staple of the literary landscape.

Contributor's Copy

The contributor's copy is the coin of the realm in the kingdom of the small and literary press. In exchange for the right to publish an author's work, the editors of a vast majority of literary magazines "pay" the author with one or more complimentary copies of the magazine. While the standard payment is one to three copies, some publishers give their contributors up to ten or twenty copies and also provide offprints of the author's piece. (Those journals that aren't even willing to ante up a single contributor's copy—even if they have legitimate financial reasons for not doing so—are generally shunned by writers with established reputations.) To many new writers, this situation is a source of grave wonder. They had assumed that when they were finally published the financial reward would be commensurate with their happiness at seeing their name in print. Alas, that is not the case, and the disappointment they feel is likely to be compounded by friends' and relatives' astonishment at the paltry compensation literature receives.

Yet, in a sense, this arrangement is beneficial to all parties. Writers have the pleasure of seeing their names in print, and they may attract the notice of more influential editors and publishers (q.v). Moreover, the contributor's copy provides a writer with a window on the literary scene, helping him to assess the current market for his work. The minimal payment may even seem ironically appropriate. After all, to an author who has invested a great deal of time, energy, and imagination in a piece of writing, almost any financial recompense is likely to seem inadequate. The contributor's copy is, therefore, merely a fitting symbol of the meager value the larger world places on serious art.

For publishers, the contributor's copy is a godsend. It allows them to indulge in the pleasure and prestige of running a magazine without having to worry about paying to fill their pages. The major investments for editors and publishers of print magazines are printing and mailing; for editors of e-zines, the only expenditure is time (see "Electronic Literature"). Still, one might ask why someone would go to *any* trouble at all to produce a magazine when there is no monetary reward. One answer may be that many editors are also writers themselves, and their journals allow them to engage in the mutual (if often unspoken) back-scratching—you publish mine and I'll publish yours—that has become such a prominent feature of contemporary literary publishing.

Though contributor's copies quickly come to seem inevitable to most literary writers, an important question does arise: How much is literature of this sort actually worth? While both authors and publishers might argue that, in a spiritual sense, the answer is "a great deal," viewed from a financial perspective one's response has to be "obviously not much." Granted, magazines whose sole payment is in contributor's copies can usually claim to be more serious than their commercial brethren. Because their modest outlays are often covered in part or in full by universities or government funding agencies, they can focus on publishing work that will be well received by the literary cognoscenti rather than by the general public. Nevertheless, authors who are not affiliated with institutions of higher learning and must earn their living through writing clearly cannot afford to subsist on a diet of contributor's copies, and charges that literary magazines have become effete, out of touch, and self-important are not without merit.

COPYRIGHT AND INTELLECTUAL PROPERTY

According to the World Intellectual Property Organization, which was founded in 1970 to promote worldwide protection of industrial property and copyrighted materials:

Intellectual property refers to creations of the mind: inventions, literary and artistic works, and symbols, names, images, and designs used in commerce. Intellectual property is divided into two categories: Industrial property, which includes inventions (patents), trademarks, industrial designs, and geographic indications of source; and Copyright, which includes literary and artistic works such as novels, poems and plays, films, musical works, artistic works such as drawings, paintings, photographs and sculptures, and architectural designs. Rights related to copyright include those of performing artists in their performances, producers of phonograms in their recordings, and those of broadcasters in their radio and television programs. ("About Intellectual Property" n.d.)

Recent advances in technology, particularly the widespread use of the Internet, have made copyright and intellectual property hot issues for everyone involved in the creative arts. There is even a World Intellectual Property Day, April 26, designed "to promote, inform and teach the importance of intellectual property as a tool for economic, social and cultural development" (World Intellectual Property Organization 2004). Of course, events such as this occur because it is so simple to violate copyright law and steal intellectual property, especially works of literature. Step one: scan or cut and paste a block of text. Step two: upload it to a Web site. Voila: anyone in the world with a computer can access the poem, story, or essay for free. While the owner of the copyrighted material may eventually force the transgressor to take the material off his Web site—or even shut down the site altogether—another malefactor can come along at anytime. Unless the work of literature has a large profit potential, the cost of the legal fees to enforce the copyright will quickly outweigh the potential income from the work. Even then, it may be impossible to halt the violation. Robert Frost's "Stopping By Woods on a Snowy Evening," for instance, is copyrighted by Henry Holt and Company, which jealously guards the print rights. Yet a recent Google search found more than twenty-four thousand occurrences of the poem's full text on the World Wide Web.

Because the Web has made it incredibly easy to copy and distribute print, today's creative writers may feel particularly vulnerable to theft of their literary works—and particularly in need of legal defense—yet Paul Goldstein traces "the moral impulse to protect authors" all the way back to the Roman poet Martial. The famous epigrammatist was partly responsible for coining our word "plagiarism" when he complained that others were kidnapping (*plagium*) his works by reciting them aloud. However, "until the printing press, few occasions arose to assert these moral claims. A pirate who copies an author's manuscript by hand had to invest the same physical labor as the author or scribe who penned the original; the cost advantage of the pirated copy was virtually nil" (Goldstein 2003, 31).

After Gutenberg, all that changed. Initially, it was the legal rights of the publishers to control and market their books that was at stake. Authors— even Shakespeare, as we know—freely stole phrases, sentences, and even entire passages from other authors. Gradually, however, as legal scholar Mark Rose explains, "the abstraction of the concept of literary property from the physical book and then the presentation of this new, immaterial property [came to be seen] as no less fixed and certain than any other kind of property" (Best 2004, 60). Thus, copyright came to protect not only the book itself but the *expression* of the ideas in it—although the ideas themselves could not be copyrighted. Screenwriter Max Adams puts it bluntly: "You cannot copyright an idea. You can copyright the execution of an idea. As in a script. But not the idea itself. Which means anything you want to stamp yours, legally, you have to write. On paper. Then you own, if not the concept, at least the script. Which is as close as you're going to get" (2001, 103).

At the beginning of the twentieth century, the definition of what an artist could copyright expanded even further. Stephen Best cites a case centered on the reproduction of circus posters as one of the most important instances in America of "the extension of intellectual property doctrine to include new forms of mechanical reproduction." In the majority decision on that case, Justice Oliver Wendall Holmes wrote: "*Personality always contains something unique.* It expresses its singularity even in handwriting, and a very modest grade of art has in it *something irreducible*, which is one man's alone. That something he may copyright" (2004, 61). If second-rate circus posters were protected by copyright law, it didn't take long for equally inferior works of literature (and painting, music, and so on) to deserve equal protection.

Today, the standards for creating something that can be copyrighted are low indeed. In order to qualify for copyrighting, a work "must be fixed in a tangible medium of expression," which can be anything from a book to code stored on a computer's hard drive, and "the fixed expression must be original and creative" (Lutzfer 2003, 9–10). According to Arnold Lutzker: "*Originality* means the work is not copied; *creativity* means that it evidences at least a modicum of thought. If the expression is extremely short, a word or a phrase, then trademark law takes over. However, string together 15–20 words (much like a poem) and you have sufficient creativity for copyright" (2003, 10).

Lutzker's *Content Rights for Creative Professionals* may be the most complete and current work on copyright law that pertains to creative writers. The book covers everything from advertising jingles to educational materials, but writers will find it most useful for the facts it provides about their basic rights and obligations. Lutzker himself finds copyright law "fascinating from a legal perspective" because it sets at odds two core principles of the Constitution: "Article I, Section 8 entrusts Congress to pass laws granting to *authors exclusive rights to their writings for limited times,* while the First Amendment prohibits Congress from passing laws that inhibit free speech" (2003, 3). The attempt to reconcile these tensions can be found in the Copyright Act of 1976 and the Digital Millennium Copyright Act of 1998. The statute developed in these two laws:

- Defines a copyrighted work and what is meant by *exclusive rights* in that work.
- Sets forth a term of years during which the author can commercially exploit the copyrighted work.
- Governs the ways in which copyrighted works are owned and can be transferred.
- Provides penalties for those who would take an author's copyrighted work without permission.
- Establishes limited exceptions so that important public policies can be advanced. (4)

Once a copyright is established, the owner does not necessarily have carte blanche to do whatever he or she wants. However, the copyright holder *does* have six exclusive legal privileges:

The right to

- reproduce the work;
- prepare derivative works based on the original;
- distribute copies to the public;
- perform the work publicly;
- display the work publicly;
- copy, publicly distribute, and prepare derivate works that are digital audio sound recordings. (Lutzker 2003, 21)

No copyright lasts forever, though: at a certain point, literary works pass into the public domain, where they are considered public property and can be freely reproduced and transmitted by anyone. Works copyrighted prior to 1923 passed into the public domain after seventy-five years. Works published between 1923 and 1977 retain copyright for ninety-five years. And literature created in 1978 or later will pass into the public domain seventy years after the death of the author ("Public Domain" 2002).

The need for copyright is in direct proportion to the market for the product. Financially speaking, screenwriters normally have the most to lose if their intellectual property is stolen, so they tend to be sticklers about their contracts and about registering their screenplays with the Writers Guild of America (www. wga.org) even before they are sold. Registration, which essentially "date stamps" a script, can be done online with a credit card for $20. Members of the Writers Guild who sell their scripts can also rely on the organization's Minimum Basic Agreement, "which stipulates a foundation of creative protections and financial incentives for . . . intellectual property" (Lent 2004, 80). When "an original script is sold, the [screen]writer usually transfers the copyright as part of the sale" (79). Screenwriters are atypical creative writers in that when they sell their work, they often give up all control over how the final product will look. Unfortunately, they are at the bottom of the creative food chain in Hollywood, so even if their films become hits, screenwriters normally see less of a return than the director and featured actors.

Novelists, too—especially if they are successful—fiercely safeguard their work. In addition to copyrighting their books, their agents negotiate aggressively for subsidiary rights. Among these rights are first serial, second serial, book club, foreign, reprint, performance, audio book, electronic and merchandise. Like film studios, trade book publishers "wield their economic control with the deftness of a surgeon's scalpel": "A publisher charges more for the initial hardcover edition of a novel than for the softcover edition that follows months or years later, not so much because the hardcover costs more to produce—though it does—as because the publisher knows that some readers will pay a premium to read a new book as soon as it is published, while other readers will trade immediate gratification for the lower price of a cheaper edition issued later. By adjusting its prices to these differing tastes, the publisher can earn profit from each for both itself and the author" (Goldstein 2003, 5).

The average new play *loses* money, and the most common reward for a published short story is a contributor's copy (q.v.) of the magazine in which the story appears. Yet playwrights and short story writers can create a piece of intellectual property worth protecting if a film studio options their work. Moreover, playwrights whose work finds favor on Broadway, and subsequently appears on the stages of America's regional theaters, can earn their living as writers. Neil Simon, Edward Albee, A. R. Gurney, Tony Kushner, and August Wilson all make handsome incomes from their plays alone. For playwrights without agents, copyrighting a play is similar to copyrighting a screenplay. Members of the Dramatists Guild of America can register their work with the organization, and anyone who pays the annual fee may become a member.

A screenplay or blockbuster novel that has the potential to generate millions of dollars will find itself the subject of much legal scrutiny. In contrast, a new poem or short story by a neophyte writer is not likely to be stolen by anyone. Indeed, one of the quickest ways novice poets and fiction writers betray themselves is by the © symbol they insert after the names on their manuscripts. (Magazine editors looking for an easy way to separate good from bad will often toss these submissions into the reject pile without a second look.) Taking for granted the fact that the work they publish has negligible commercial value, many small-press publishers don't take the trouble to copyright it—although that doesn't mean an occasional poem or story isn't filched. The authors of this book have both come across poems we've written pasted onto someone's Web page without our permission, but the poems were credited to us, and ultimately we felt gratified rather than bamboozled.

A fascinating exception to the general rule that poetry has too little value to bother being systematically stolen is detailed by Neal Bowers in his book *Words for the Taking: The Hunt for a Plagiarist* (1997). In the early 1990s, Bowers realized that someone calling himself David Sumner was taking poems Bowers had already published in literary magazines and republishing them himself (usually with different titles) as his own work. Bowers hired a lawyer and a private detective to find the man, who turned out to be more pathetic than sinister. Ironically, Bowers is now probably more famous for the story of his quest to find the plagiarizing poet than he is for his own poetry.

For those writers who wish to claim title to their work yet also make it available to the general public without making a profit, there is creative-commons.org. "Creative Commons helps you publish your work online while letting others know exactly what they can and can't do with your work." Among the free licenses the organization offers are those that put the work in the public domain and those that "invite a wide range of royalty-free uses . . . in developing nations" while allowing the author to "retain full copyright in the developed world." Sampling licenses "invite other people to use a part of your work and make it new." The entire catalog of Creative Commons' licensed content—including creative writing, music, film, and visual arts—is listed at creativecontent.org.

CREATIVE DISSERTATION

Scene: A Starbucks coffee shop in a university town. Two friends, Amy and Andy, sit at a table drinking latte.

AMY: I'm going on for my PhD in creative writing.

ANDY: *(astonished)* Why? You hated going to workshop all during our last year.

AMY: Yeah. But I went to a writers' conference and listened to the options the panelists on "Living the Writing Life" gave me. And I decided that—unlike you, Andy—I don't want to flip burgers and write. And sex, drugs, and Hollywood isn't me either. Anyway, I hated the workshop because I was young and unsure. Because I didn't want to read *Mao II* that year. I mean, I was trying to write poetry. It was a bad mix of classes. And one bad professor, too, but let's not go there. Besides. Now I'm ready. I want to be Dr. Narrative. I'm back. I'm a fiction writer now. I want to teach. I need to get going. Hey, you know I love Don DeLillo.

ANDY: *(dubious)* Okay. But maybe you'd better see what it's all really about. Sounds pretty unlike you to me.

(Exeunt.)

In American universities, graduate students can complete one of three English department degrees that allow for a focus on creative work: the master of arts degree (MA), the master of fine arts degree (MFA), and the doctor of philosophy degree in English (PhD), each with a creative writing emphasis. The master of arts degree usually consists of coursework in English literature, craft and workshop courses, and the completion of a master's thesis, a collection of original writing. While this could also roughly describe the MFA degree, the MA degree requires fewer hours than the MFA, sometimes a shorter thesis, and is considered a preparatory degree for the PhD. The MFA degree, on the other hand, requires more units of work, which in turn requires a longer residency in a graduate program, and a substantial thesis—often described as a book-length work in the genre studied (generally poetry, fiction, nonfiction, or screenwriting/drama).

As the professional association representing college-level creative writing teachers, the Associated Writing Programs has long supported the MFA as the terminal degree in creative writing, but many programs now offer a PhD in English with an emphasis in creative writing and a creative dissertation (see "MFA" for an alternate view of the situation described in this entry). Students in these programs take the same number of courses as English students who emphasize literature or composition and rhetoric, but they focus on writing-related courses and workshops. They generally complete comprehensive exams on reading lists in specified areas: some choose to focus on major writers, major time periods in literature, or special topics such as folklore and linguistics and/or to minor in rhetoric and composition. (Note: some programs require qualifying exams—reading exams taken before a student is admitted to a PhD program—with comprehensive exams to follow at the end of PhD coursework.) A PhD student generally is trained to teach first-year writing as part of her degree work (and to study and master one or two foreign languages as well).

In many senses, until it is time to complete the creative dissertation, there is no difference between the course of study for completing a PhD in literature, composition, or creative writing in many programs (though in our experience creative writers certainly attend and participate in more readings series, while composition students gravitate toward pedagogical events). In literature, the dissertation is often an extended scholarly work of five to eight chapters that will eventually, for many of these degree candidates, be submitted to university presses for publication. For the candidate in rhetoric and composition, a dissertation is an in-depth scholarly or research project that combines primary and secondary research and often helps theorize issues in teaching, explores current knowledge about and theories of composing, and/or investigates literacy history. For the candidate in creative writing, however, the creative dissertation is generally a book-length manuscript of original creative writing.

While some programs have restrictions about how much of the dissertation may be work that originated in courses the candidate took prior to sitting for qualifying (reading) exams, most creative dissertations begin in the degree-program workshop. The writer shares work in her genre, meets professors, finds one who is interested in her work, and proposes a collection of poems, short stories or novellas, a collection of nonfiction, a novel, a screenplay, or a play. To date, programs resist coauthored work and genre writing (mysteries, science fiction, and so on). The focus is on the candidate proving himself in a literary genre like those he has been studying in his coursework in the English department.

Although a PhD program, including the writing of a creative dissertation, can be completed in three or four years—on paper—studies show that most candidates take from five to ten years; the dissertation is a not inconsiderable part of that work. After completing coursework, reading for and taking and defending comprehensive reading exams, the candidate forms a dissertation committee, beginning with a dissertation chair. First a prospectus is drafted—often describing the candidate's interest in the project, history with similar work in that genre, readings of similar works; then a detailed analysis—in some cases, a detailed outline—of the proposed dissertation is presented. A working time line is set up and the candidate begins drafting, sharing chapters with the dissertation chair who has agreed to work with her and continuing to read widely while revising chapters, until a complete first draft is shared with other members of the committee.

Usually dissertation committees consist of three department members, including the committee chair, and a fourth member from somewhere else on the campus whose job is to make sure the university's standards are met by the English department and the candidate. A chair must have doctoral directive status (as must the outside committee member), which has been conferred upon him, usually when he achieves tenure, by his department and college.

At the end of the drafting cycle, the candidate prepares a final creative dissertation manuscript and defends the project before being awarded the doctor of philosophy degree. It is assumed that the candidate will then seek to publish her book by submitting it to editors and agents; in some cases portions of the manuscript will already have appeared in print in literary journals, and in even rarer cases a candidate will end a degree program with both a dissertation and a publishing contract in hand.

To further illustrate the diversity of requirements as well as their commonalties—and to highlight the tensions that those in English departments appear to feel about these requirements, particularly the "special case" of the creative dissertation—let's look at five different program descriptions posted on the Web.

It should be noted, though, that some scholars of English literature find the "creative" dissertation suspect because they don't believe it is generally submitted to the same type of scholarly scrutiny or rigor as is the research-oriented dissertation. While it is true that it would be possible for a committee to pass on a novel or book of poems that did not require extensive commitment, learning, or development from a PhD candidate, such an event would not be due to the "creative" quotient of the manuscript. Clearly, creative texts can be assessed if a committee discusses its standards with a candidate and applies those standards in a systematic way. Equally, standards for assessing the merit of a scholarly dissertation are not universal nor are they, in our experience, applied equally within programs. Both types of dissertation present the same challenges (and opportunities) to candidates and committees; the literary dissertation is simply more often the more familiar genre to all concerned.

Now let's look at how such tensions play out in published descriptions:

> Florida State University—After filing a prospectus, the candidate will write the dissertation in close consultation with the major professor and the committee. The dissertation may be an extended essay, three or more essays related by subject, or an extended original work in fiction, poetry, or drama. The candidate will defend a draft of the dissertation in a 1-to 2-hour oral examination by the supervisory committee. (English.fsu.edu/graduate/brochure.htm)

Here is the first inkling of the quality issue. We see that the dissertation is of some length, original, and defendable.

In the next description, notice that students are encouraged to be active as creative writers by taking at least one workshop a year. Many writers feel that attending graduate school in creative writing poses a special challenge. While completing the other scholarly and pedagogical requirements of such programs (reading and teaching), a writer may feel that it is difficult to simultaneously find the extended periods of writing time she first aimed for by entering a graduate program. Not a surprising reaction when we look at the many requirements of such programs:

> University of Georgia—Doctoral-level students complete a degree that consists of coursework in English and American literature and related fields. Doctoral-level students generally take at least one workshop per year. Doctoral students

also take the comprehensive examination and fulfill foreign language requirements. In general, Ph.D. candidates in creative writing complete all degree requirements, except for the creative dissertation, which is a book-length work of fiction, poetry, creative-non-fiction, or a combination of genres, in four years. (www.english.uga.edu/grad/applinfo.html)

In the next entry, you'll see some further tensions between the literature and creative writing dissertation camps: this program requires that only one dissertation committee member be a creative writing faculty member. They wish the creative thesis to be read and discussed by literature scholars (perhaps including those in linguistics, folklore, composition, and other areas). Writing quality is desired—clear and graceful—and the work is defended not only before a committee but also as part of a public discussion:

> Western Michigan University—The dissertation will be a book length manuscript of scholarship, criticism, research, or creative writing comprised of either a single piece of work or a coherent collection of shorter pieces that are methodologically, structurally, or thematically related. The dissertation must be approved by a committee of at least three members of the graduate faculty, one from outside the department. In the case of creative work, no more than one faculty member may be from the creative writing faculty. The dissertation should be so designed as to take no more than one year to complete. Clarity and grace of writing will be important criteria of acceptability. When the dissertation is complete, the candidate will present it in a public discussion chaired by the members of the dissertation committee.
>
> Our dissertation requirement further defines the special qualities of our Ph.D. program. We do not want the dissertation to devour years of the student's life. We are not, as a primary aim, training research specialists but rather preparing future teachers with a thorough grounding in reading and an ability to write. Thus, for the Ph.D. in literature, English language, or pedagogy, we encourage not only the more traditional kind of dissertation, exploring a single focussed theme or author, but as an alternative, a coherent group of thematically or methodologically related critical essays. The creative dissertation option ensures that the student leave the program with a manuscript of publishable quality—a novel, a book-length collection of poems or short stories, a full-length play or a collection of shorter plays. (www.wmich. edu/english/phd/diss.html)

This final paragraph addresses the issue of how long it takes to complete a degree, mentioned above. In an effort to reduce the degree process from seven to ten-years to a more reasonable period of three to five years (about the time spent by most students earning their MFAs), the literature dissertation has been modified to include a group or collection of essays. The creative dissertation remains one that should be "publishable." (Note: the common term for having passed comprehensive exams but not yet finished with the dissertation is ABD, All but Dissertation. Some candidates remain ABD for life: they have completed a lengthy course of study and taken exams on those studies but not filed a completed and defended dissertation.)

The next school requires a creative dissertation of publishable quality but also asks for a critical preface. This program also goes into some detail describing the process a candidate should follow. Note the critical preface requirement is echoed in the defense, where the candidate should be able to talk about the implications of her work. Note also that "publishable quality" is a flexible and vexed term: publishable by whom, under what conditions, on what terms, for what audience?

> University of Denver—A dissertation of publishable quality that is a significant contribution to its field. This will take the form of an extended scholarly and critical work (usually between 150 and 250 pages) *or* a creative work (fiction or poetry). The creative dissertation must include a critical preface which situates the dissertation in its literary context. . . .
>
> When the dissertation is completed, it must be defended by the candidate. The Defense must take place no later than three weeks before graduation. . . . The student will defend the dissertation before a Committee of five readers of the work, including the dissertation advisor, three members of the English Department, and a Committee Chairperson from outside the English Department. The Department Chair, in consultation with the Director of Graduate Studies, will assign the English department members and the Committee Chairperson. The Defense takes the form of a discussion concerning the content, context, and implications of the work. The Defense may result in a pass, a pass with minor revisions, or a pass with major revisions. . . . Once the Defense is passed, the candidate will prepare the dissertation in final form, incorporating, with the advice of the dissertation director, any revisions required by the full examining committee. (www.du.edu/english/phdregs.html)

In this program a great deal of committee oversight is in place, including having the entire committee reading revisions.

Finally, the creative dissertation at some schools is viewed as a possible but potentially more rigorous option.

University of Iowa—Ph.D. *with creative dissertation*—The Program in Creative Writing confers only the M.F.A. degree. However, it is possible for unusually well qualified students in the Department of English Ph.D. program to obtain permission to submit a creative dissertation for that degree. In such a case, all application and course work deadlines and requirements are those of the English department's Ph.D. program, and the Program in Creative Writing assumes responsibility only for granting permission to do the creative dissertation and approving it once it is completed. . . . While the standards for admission to the M.F.A. program are formidable, those for approval of the creative dissertation are more so. Denial of a manuscript for the creative dissertation does not jeopardize that person's candidacy for the Ph.D. with scholarly dissertation. (www.uiowa.edu/~iww/admissions/degrees.htm)

In this description, we hear the echo of an earlier description suggesting that only one committee member be a creative writer.

To reprise (and this, now, is what we would tell Amy, the character in the opening dialogue), commonly, in English departments, there is a suspicion that the creative writing dissertation could be viewed as an easy option, an escape from the rigors of literary scholarship. This also explains why the degree requirements for the PhD in English with a creative writing emphasis and creative dissertation in most English departments are the same as those for literature students, right up to the moment of the drafting of the creative dissertation. We'd like to think that programs reviewing their procedures would look toward making their program "tracks" equivalent but would also strive to become more innovative and useful; that is, that the paths of literature, creative writing, and composition students might not need to remain identical until the dissertation (see North 2000 for a discussion of one such experiment).

Most writers soon realize that creative work is just as rigorous and demanding as scholarly work. Often it includes primary and secondary research, and certainly it is as critically challenging as much of the work done by writers of literary scholarship. In some programs, creative dissertation writers are writing metafiction, preferring to include critical prefaces, enjoying their work in literary theory and bringing it back in productive and innovative ways to the creative genres they are qualifying in. Creative writers are often in the vanguard, reenvisioning dissertations as they craft them.

Certainly, there are a number of similarities between the MFA thesis (potentially a book of publishable quality) and the PhD creative dissertation (also potentially publishable). Supporters of the latter would point to the difference in duration (longer courses of critical study capped by exams), the types of work done (literary, critical, creative, study of foreign language—though some MFAs do this work as well), and the way this text provides an entrance into a particular academic community—the university English department—the members of whom prefer to replicate themselves whenever possible. These supporters would further argue that a writer hoping eventually to work in a PhD degree-granting institution will find working through one of these programs on his own is the best preparation for the "culture" of that type of English department. In other words, aiming for a PhD in English with the creative dissertation is not just a matter of liking to write, liking to teach, and hoping to be Dr. Narrative. At the same time, extended study of and attention to writing within these department environments may be the best hope creative writers have of surmounting the overwhelming odds of ever being hired to a tenure-track position.

CREATIVE NONFICTION

THE RISE OF CREATIVE NONFICTION

The genre du jour in writing programs, creative nonfiction (or cnf, as initiates refer to it) in reality is as old as the hills, or at least the Romans. In *The Art of the Personal Essay*, Phillip Lopate traces the genre's background from Seneca and Plutarch to Japanese and Chinese writers such as Kenko and Ou-Yang Hsiu through Michel de Montaigne—"the giant, the mountain of the form" (1994, xlvii)—to eighteenth- and nineteenth-century British writers like Joseph Addison, Richard Steele, Charles Lamb, and William Hazlitt. Among his model essayists in the twentieth century are Virginia Woolf, George Orwell, Natalia Ginzburg, H. L. Mencken, James Thurber, James Baldwin, Joan Didion, Annie Dillard, Scott Russell Sanders, and Richard Rodriguez. According to Lopate, what this diverse collection of writers has in common is the ability to succeed in a genre that can be overwhelming for lesser writers because its boundaries appear so limitless: "The essay is a notoriously flexible and adaptable form. It possesses the freedom to move anywhere, in all directions. It acts as if all objects were equally near the center and as if 'all subjects are linked to each other' (Montaigne) by free association. This freedom can be daunting, not only for the novice essayist confronting such latitude but for the critic attempting to pin down its formal properties" (xxxvii).

Lopate calls Montaigne the "fountainhead" of the genre because the sixteenth-century French writer was able to move so dexterously from one idea to another, to quote from a Latin authority in one sentence and in the next to reflect on what happened to him the previous night at dinner. This elasticity of form and thought, frightening though it may be at times, is a central component of the personal essay, one particularly valued by contemporary writers. Nevertheless, in his introduction to the anthology, Lopate manages to isolate a number of qualities that most personal essays have in common:

- The personal essay is conversational—often ironic, humorous, even "cheeky"—in tone.
- It values honesty and confession—self-disclosure is a necessary component of the genre.
- It has "a taste for littleness," dwelling on the often-ignored minutiae of daily life, while at the same time it expands the importance of the writer's self.
- It goes against the grain of popular opinion.
- It wrestles with the "stench of ego," trying to reveal the writer's true self without seeming narcissistic and proud.
- It demonstrates the learning of its author while distancing itself from the scholarly treatise.
- Perhaps most importantly, it is a mode of thinking and being, an attempt "to test, to make a run at something without knowing whether you are going to succeed."

However, for all its appeal, the personal essay does have its detractors. According to Harriet Malinowitz, "the personal essayist disclaims authority; she is not teaching a lesson so much as candidly revealing the process by which she has learned one. . . . Traditional argument musters and deploys the author's strengths, breaking down the defense of the skeptical or hostile reader; the personal essay disarms the reader by laying bare the author's defects, demonstrating that the writer poses no threat and subtly winning the reader's sympathy" (2003, 319).

Written during the same period as Montaigne's informal pieces, the work of Francis Bacon represents this second strand of essay writing:

"the traditional argument." Bacon prizes clarity, order, conciseness: the qualities that, until very recently, have dominated our thinking about what a good college essay should be. From a postmodern (q.v.) point of view, Bacon looks hopelessly naive—he wants to condense the world into crystal-hard sentences, to say everything there is about a topic in a few pages—but he remains an ideal of succinct, argumentative writing.

These two essayists are often held up as conflicting models for creative nonfiction, with Montaigne recently having become the clear favorite among those making the comparison. Bacon is authoritative and final in his pronouncements, while Montaigne is open to changing his mind. Bacon has a clear thesis statement and follows it ruthlessly to its obvious conclusion; Montaigne meanders from thought to thought, like a child chasing a butterfly, who stops to examine the flowers each time the butterfly alights. Bacon dictates; Montaigne suggests. Bacon instructs; Montaigne delights.

A great deal can be said for this contrast, but even Lopate agrees that Montaigne and Bacon "should not be viewed as opposites; the distinction between formal and informal essay can be overdone, and most great essayists have crossed the line frequently" (1994, xlvii). Nevertheless, the two strands have persisted. For every Hazlitt and Lamb, there has been a Macaulay and Carlyle, essayists who work in a belletristic tradition yet see their primary purpose as informational and rhetorical, who are far more concerned with persuading their readers to *do* something differently than they are in revealing the charming, idiosyncratic details of their own lives.

Clearly, then, writers have been assaying some version of "creative nonfiction" for a very long time, but when did the term itself gain general currency? According to Caroline Abels, "in the 1970s the National Endowment for the Arts helped bring [the term 'creative nonfiction'] into academic parlance. The agency needed a word to categorize grant submissions of nonfiction that appropriated fictional elements such as dramatic tension, dialogue, shifting points of view and attention to detail and rhythm" (1999). Lee Gutkind gave the name a permanent home when he founded the journal *Creative Nonfiction* in 1993, just as the term was gaining widespread currency.

WHAT IS IT?

What exactly *is* creative nonfiction? Because it covers such a broad swathe of writing, some scholars have felt "creative nonfiction" has become hopelessly confusing as a descriptor. Robert Root laments "[h]ow useless the existing definitions of nonfiction are, particularly in light of the current popularity and prominence of certain of its forms. Given the breadth of achievement a term like 'non-fiction' (meaning really 'non-everything-other-than-whatever-it-is') is assumed to cover, we will either have to write a new definition that names what nonfiction is now or find an appropriate modifier to add to 'non-fiction' (unhyphenated), such as 'literary' or 'creative,' to distinguish it from 'non-literary' or 'non-creative' forms, whatever they might be" (2003, 243).

As this passage indicates, a number of different subgenres are often stuffed into a single bag with one name on it. However, since Gutkind has been given the moniker "the godfather of creative nonfiction," we will let him have the first crack at defining it. In issue no. 6 of his journal he describes "the five Rs" of creative nonfiction (1995):

- Real Life: "the foundation of good writing emerges from personal experience"
- Reflection: "a writer's feelings and responses about a subject"
- Research: "I want to make myself knowledgeable enough to ask intelligent questions. If I can't display at least a minimal understanding of the subject about which I am writing, I will lose the confidence and the support of the people who must provide access to the experience"
- Reading: "almost all writers have read the best writers in their field and are able to converse in great detail about the stylistic approach and intellectual content"
- "Riting": "This is what art of any form is all about—the passion of the moment and the magic of the muse."

Most essayists would have trouble arguing with *most* of these characterizations, but the inclusion of research clearly places Gutkind's definition closer to journalism than to memoir. Indeed, in the first issue of *Creative Nonfiction*, Gutkind claims that reportage is "the anchor and foundation of the highest quality of journalism and of creative nonfiction" (1993). In this respect, many of the essays published in *Creative Nonfiction* are in the camp of literary journalism, or New Journalism, which came of age in the 1960s and 1970s. Books like Truman Capote's *In Cold Blood*, about a gruesome murder in Kansas, and Tom Wolfe's *The Electric Kool-Aid Acid Test*, which followed the exploits of Ken Kesey's Merry Pranksters, found the authors imaginatively re-creating scenes they didn't witness (Capote) and participating directly in the lives of their subjects—Wolfe was "on the bus," and even experimented with LSD to understand the lives of the Pranksters. While traditional reporting insists on the fiction of the invisible reporter "objectively" collecting facts and passing them on, without comment, to the reader, literary journalism acknowledges the reality that *which* facts reporters choose to write about and *how* they convey those facts makes an enormous difference in what particular version of the truth is being told. Consequently, literary journalists employ many of the tools of fiction. Descriptions of places and people are far more lavish than in conventional reporting. Dialogue is used extensively. The writer's own point of view, her opinions about what she is witnessing, become part of the story. Style is foregrounded, a recognition that the piece is being written by an individual writer with personal tastes. Finally, though, journalists trade in facts, and readers must believe that what is on the page actually happened. Getting the story *and* writing it artfully can be, Norman Sims admits, "a difficult and tedious method of reporting": "Tracy Kidder spent a year in a nursing home, day after day, taking notes, listening to conversations. 'I just wanted to be there when something was happening,' Kidder said. 'I've done this enough to be patient. I can spend five hundred hours taking notes and use none of them, and then in ten minutes everything happens'" (1995, 18).

A less time-consuming but centuries-old version of creative nonfiction is cultural criticism, which includes writing about other writers and their work. This type of nonfiction can be found everywhere from first-year English classes to *Harpers* and the *New Yorker*. While an essayist working this territory may wander far and wide in his commentary, ultimately he must return to his subject. Cynthia Ozick explains: "With an essay you have your goal in your pocket: you know where you're going. At least you know what it's about. For instance, I'm in the process now of reading *The Awkward Age* by Henry James, which I've never read before, and I intend to write an essay on it. Well, I know what the essay is about. It's about *The Awkward Age*. I don't know yet what I'm going to say, what I'm going to discover, and I will surely make discoveries. Nevertheless, there's a premise, there's something to work with, there's something already pre-existent. But in fiction the challenge is an abyss" (Watchel 1992, 15).

Nature and travel writing represent a similar bridge between reporting accurately on the world outside the writer while focusing on the writer's own responses to that world. The nonfiction of John McPhee, Loren Eisley, Rachel Carson, Barry Lopez, and Annie Dillard is carefully researched and factually accurate, yet the writer's impressions of the natural world ultimately matter as much as what is being observed. Likewise, in the travel narratives of Pico Ayer, Paul Theroux, and V. S. Naipaul, style shapes the reading experience in an especially prominent way—how something is said is at least as important as what is said. In recognition of the quality of the nonfiction being written in these fields, there are now annual anthologies of both *The Best American Science and Nature Writing* and *The Best American Travel Writing.*

Another link between writing about the world and writing about the self is the autobiographical craft book. Annie Dillard's *The Writing Life,* Natalie Goldberg's *Wild Mind,* and Anne Lamott's *Bird by Bird* all purport to be volumes on how to write fiction, yet they are just as compelling (if not more so) as examples of autobiography. As Lamott, for instance, writes about plot, character, dialogue, writer's block, writing groups, and "shitty first drafts," she uses her own life experience to illustrate each point. The ultimate result is highly readable as memoir, and it's not surprising that the nonfiction books by Lamott and Goldberg have in fact sold better than any of their works of fiction.

Of course writers of "straight" autobiography and memoir need no subject other than their own lives, and undergraduate creative writing students—who may not feel they know much about anything *except* their own lives—are drawn to memoir. Indeed, "life writing" is popular among beginning creative writers from seventeen to seventy. Our lives are portable—we bring them with us wherever we go—so there is never a sense of being removed from the subject matter in the way a fiction writer may find herself separated from a character she wants to write about. Moreover, since our lives are infinitely fragmentable, we find occasions for autobiographical essays wherever we look. Perhaps the "purest" form of memoir is the journal or diary, with which many students will have extensive experience. Glorious examples of the form exist—from Sei Shonagon to Samuel Pepys to Gail Godwin—but the private nature of this type of writing makes it problematic as a subject for classroom teaching.

Those writing autobiographically for a reading *public* quickly face one of the central ethical questions of creative nonfiction: how much truth can you tell about your own life? "What can you decently write about other people?" Mary Clearman Blew wonders. "Whose permission do you have to ask? What can you decently reveal about yourself?" Her answer: "I own my past and present. Only I can decide whether or how to write about it" (1993, 62). This decision can be a vexing one, though, and ethical (and artistic) issues abound. What liberties can one take with the past? Can you invent dialogue for a conversation that took place years ago? If the dialogue approximates what was actually said, is that close enough to the truth? Can you change the location of an event? Someone's hair color? Gender? Name? At what point does a story about one's life become "just" a story and no longer a factual recounting of what happened? What *did* happen anyway? How trustworthy is a writer's memory? What's to be gained by shading the truth? And on and on.

At the end of "Never Let the Truth Stand in the Way of a Good Story," Bronwyn Williams reveals that he never actually heard his father use the title phrase, although throughout his essay he has claimed that it was something his father often repeated. The truth is he simply thought the line did a neat job of summing up his father's character. Williams goes on to disclose that his father "suffered from devastating bouts of depression and unemployment" (2003, 303), then ruminates on whether he should have revealed this information—his mother is still alive and may be wounded by the public disclosure of her late husband's faults: "I think that in composition when we discuss teaching creative nonfiction, we spend too little time on the effects of our work on those we write about, on the ethics of reportage and observation and representation. It is easy to wrap ourselves in the comforting blankets of the social construction of truth and postmodern theories of subject and subjectivities and not feel the chilly breezes of pain and hurt that may come from those we write about" (304). Ironically, as Williams's own essay makes plain, revealing the awful secrets of others may be the best way to serve the narrative and rhetorical strategies of our writing.

Whatever the subgenre, the distinguishing feature of "the fourth genre" appears to be the "non" preceding "fiction." Creative nonfiction purports—in a way that poems and stories and plays do not—to be the "truth." "To be credible," Lynn Bloom maintains, "the writer of creative nonfiction has to play fair. This is a statement of both ethics and aesthetics. The presentation of the truth the writer tells, however partisan, cannot seem vindictive or polemical" (2003, 284). Bloom emphasizes the writer's responsibility to her audience, the need to be honest, to present oneself as someone the reader can trust.

WHO OWNS IT, WHO TEACHES IT?

Perhaps because it is both profitable and less clearly defined than other genres, creative nonfiction is currently the subject of a power struggle in

English departments. One reason for this conflict is the corporatization of American universities and the increasing rewards given to high-profile work: "Write a successful memoir like Susanna Kaysen's *Girl, Interrupted* as an English department member in the 1980s and this seemingly 'minor' accomplishment would have been mentioned patronizingly, if at all, during tenure discussions. Do the same and be optioned for a film in the 2000s, and you'll accrue praise, cash, envy, and a promotion" (Bishop 2003, 264).

So, does creative nonfiction belong in the creative writing camp, where it has exploded as a subject of practice and study? After all, this faction of the English department has long been the home of the most visible, the most media-friendly faculty members. Or should cnf be the responsibility of compositionists, who can make a much stronger claim to being experts in nonfiction prose, having taught that subject exclusively for many decades?

On the one hand, the swelling numbers of faculty teaching and students taking courses in creative nonfiction would argue for cataloging creative nonfiction courses next to fiction, poetry, and drama. Many graduate and undergraduate creative writing programs now offer emphases in creative nonfiction, and graduate students, especially, are required to write in a range of essayistic modes. At the University of Pittsburgh, for instance, the MFA with a concentration in creative nonfiction asks students to explore "autobiography, biography, history, speculative or personal essays, new journalism, investigative reporting/analysis, and quality feature writing" (University of Pittsburgh Department of English, 2005). Surely, students working in such a wide variety of styles could expect to receive a comprehensive education in the subject.

Yet creative nonfiction has, in the last century, taken a long excursion through the first-year writing curriculum in the form of the composition essay, and creative nonfiction as composition was (re)claimed by this wing of English studies in the January 2003 issue of *College English*. At first glance, it seems obvious that compositionists would welcome the opportunity to teach the essay in its expanded form. Too many teachers, and their students, share Douglas Atkins's experience in the Baconian tradition of formal essay writing: "We wrote 'essays' as if they were 'compositions,' entities that smack of the artificial and the mechanical, whose parts might be simply *assembled*, like those of a small engine" (1994, 630). And most English teachers, whatever their current specialty, originally went into the field because they loved literature. Granted, many freshman English instructors *have* embraced creative nonfiction like a long-lost wealthy uncle.

There is a buzz in the air in faculty lounges across the country, and sessions on creative nonfiction at the Conference on College Composition and Communication are nearly always packed with enthusiastic audiences.

However, as Doug Hesse notes, until recently, "in light of compelling rhetorical and cultural theory produced during the 1980s and 1990s, to assert the literariness of the essay struck many in composition studies as quaint, or worse, complicitously conservative" (2003, 239). If being labeled "conservative" is one reason some compositionists have been wary to fully accept creative nonfiction, another is their lack of confidence in their students' ability to write it well. "I see essayistic power and style all the time in the writing of students," Chris Anderson says (1990, 88), but many more instructors will have shared the experience of Gordon Harvey, who claims student writers "haven't defined (for themselves or for the reader) what they found interesting enough to pursue and why it should interest a real person (besides their instructor) . . . why an essay needs writing" (1994, 650). Moreover, as Robert Root points out, some compositionists worry about being placed in the dubious company of poets and fiction writers: "Tacking the adjective 'creative' in front of the noun 'nonfiction' may help link it to other forms of 'creative writing' as a literary genre but it also helps to marginalize it in the same way that creative writing is marginalized in most English departments—as something chiefly of interest to an artsy contingent of student and faculty writers rather than to the student and faculty littérateurs, scholars and critics, and readers who make up the majority of the department" (2003, 246).

These fears aside, creative nonfiction does seem to have injected composition with a new glow of enthusiasm, with teachers who haven't themselves written for years suddenly joining their students in essay making. Ultimately, as Root says, "Maybe the question regarding nonfiction and composition isn't how to infuse nonfiction into the comp course. Maybe the question is whether, when we name composition, we aren't simultaneously naming nonfiction" (2003, 255).

CREATIVITY

We use the term "creative writing" throughout this book, but while we examine various writing processes in some detail, we spend less time discussing creativity itself. Yet the adjective modifying the noun is thought by many of our academic colleagues to make us a discipline apart. (Some of them suspect we are practicing a form of black magic in our classrooms.) Even other English teachers claim they're not capable of responding to an original student poem or story—although those same teachers may have spent their entire careers writing and talking about canonical poems and stories. What makes *creative* writing so different from the expository writing done in other classes across the curriculum? And what exactly is creativity?

Readers of the authors' earlier articles and books will know that our response to the first question is that, in many ways, creative writing isn't so different from any other kind of writing. We believe all writing—even the one-minute, uncorrected e-mail—involves some creativity, some thinking, some *imagination*. In this belief, we have not always been in accord with some of our academic colleagues. Most significantly, a sharp distinction is often drawn between creative and critical thinking. Definitions of "critical thinking" vary, but they generally point to a complex, advanced, and organized cognitive activity that includes the willingness to question one's own beliefs and to tolerate ambiguity and uncertainty. Teaching students to think critically is a focus of many educators in the more "serious" disciplines, but for creative writers such as Katherine Haake, this focus on metacognitive reflection (thinking about thinking) is an essential part of the creative writing process as well. Indeed, book-length studies such as Haake's *What Our Speech Disrupts* (2000) insist that intense and persistent self-assessment are crucial to a writer's development.

Granted, beliefs about the origin of creativity have changed over time. Dean Simonton notes that "creativity was originally viewed as something mysterious. According to the ancient Greeks, creativity was literally the gift of the Muses, the goddesses who presided over all major forms of human creativity. This basic idea persisted in various forms well into the Italian Renaissance." Gradually, however, those studying creativity came to acknowledge that it involved a strong element of conscious thought, that creativity was at least as much a rational as a natural phenomenon: "the creative person was someone who applied a logic, method, or set of techniques to a given domain of expertise" (Simonton 2004, 83). And this application of logic and method does not occur in a vacuum. Without education and socialization, "sophisticated inborn capabilities simply cannot exist. Outside mythology, nobody begins life having proclivities that can guarantee the emergence of high abilities" (Howe 1999, 188).

In other words, highly creative people are *made* at least as much as they are *born*. Shakespeare could never have displayed his creative genius if he hadn't learned how to write and been given at least a modicum of schooling; Mozart could never have composed his music if his father hadn't taught him how to read the notes on the staff and play the pianoforte.

Consequently, most current explanations of creativity see it resulting from both nature and nurturing. Creativity studies is now an active and interdisciplinary field, drawing on biology, psychology, medicine, literature, sociology, and, indeed, any area of inquiry that attempts to explain why and how humans do what they do. Nearly all theorists differentiate between creativity and simple novelty: "A merely novel idea is one which can be described and/or produced by the same set of generative rules as are other, familiar, ideas. A radically original, or creative, idea is one which cannot" (Boden 2004, 51). (The disparity between creativity and novelty is not dissimilar to the distinction Coleridge draws between imagination and fancy in his *Biographia Literaria*.) To demonstrate true creativity, "the task as presented [to the creator] must have been somehow open-ended, with no clear and straightforward path to a single solution." Moreover, the expression of creativity must be valued by people other than its creator: "the [creative] product or response cannot merely be different for the sake of difference; it must also be appropriate, correct, useful, valuable or expressive of meaning" (Amabile and Tighe 1993, 9). In other words, "Creativity is the interplay between ability and process by which an individual or group produces an outcome or product that is both novel *and* useful as defined within some social context" (Plucker and Beghetto 2004, 156).

Indeed, the social reception of a work determines whether its creator is classified as a genius or a crackpot. The following comment about visual artists can be applied—with slight modifications—to creative writers: "One does not become an artist simply by making art. To earn a living and develop a self-concept as a bona fide artist distinct from a dilettante, one must be legitimated by the appropriate art institutions. Only when the artist's work has been recognized by the *field* of art—the critics, historians, dealers, collectors, curators, and fellow artists—can the artist continue to focus his or her energies on creating art. . . . If an artist creates artwork that does not fulfill the needs of the field, that artist will be dismissed or ignored" (Abuhamdeh and Csikszentmihalyi 2004, 37).

Admittedly, many creative writers make a living from their teaching salaries rather than from selling their writing, but even if their publications don't earn sufficient money to pay for rent and food, those publications are nevertheless essential: without them, creative writing professors at colleges and universities lose their jobs. And someone who claims to be a creative writer but has no validation from recognized professionals in the field will very likely be "dismissed or ignored."

Ironically, while creativity must ultimately be endorsed by the larger world, highly creative people are often snubbed or scorned for their eccentricity. And since creativity involves disruptions of routine ways of thinking, it's not surprising it has long been associated with mental illness (see also "Therapy and Therapeutic"). In the *Ion*, Plato has Socrates chastise the title character because he passes on the madness that inspires poets to the listeners of their poems. In *A Midsummer Night's Dream*, Theseus says: "The lunatic, the lover, and the poet / Are of imagination all compact." Shakespeare goes on to show how "strong imagination" leads to a kind of hallucinatory power:

> The poet's eye, in a fine frenzy rolling,
> Doth glance from heaven to earth, from earth to heaven;
> And as imagination bodies forth
> The form of things unknown, the poet's pen
> Turns them to shapes, and gives to airy nothing
> A local habitation and a name. (V.i)

Any student of literature will quickly be able to bring to mind another half-dozen literary examples equating madness with creativity, but creativity theorists tend to be skeptical of received ideas about their subject and insist on compiling documentary evidence to support conventional wisdom. In *Strong Imagination*, his book-length examination of creativity and mental illness, Daniel Nettle does just that. Among the studies he cites is one by Kay Jamison analyzing the lives of all the major British and Irish poets born between 1705 and 1805. Jamison learned "that to be a poet in Britain in the eighteenth century was to run a risk of bipolar disorder 10–30 times the national average, suicide 5 times the national average, and incarceration in the madhouse at least 20 times the national average" (2001, 142). In a more recent study Nettle cites, Arnold Ludwig scrutinized the biographies of more than a 1,000 people who achieved eminence in their fields from 1960 to 1990. Ludwig found a strikingly high 59 percent incidence of psychiatric disorder among the people he studied, although this percentage "pale[s] into insignificance when compared with those observed in creative pursuits: 87 percent for poets, 77 percent for fiction writers, 74 percent in the theatre" (144). In standardized diagnostic interviews with students enrolled in the Iowa Writers Workshop, Nancy Andreason "found a staggering 80 percent of the writers qualified for a diagnosis of affective disorder" (143). Yet another study, published in *Science* magazine, found "[a]bout twice as many writers as nonwriters had some form of mental disorder" (Holden 1994, 1483). For Nettle, at least, the results are "very clear": "There is an increased risk of psychosis and related disorder among those who become eminent in the creative arts" (147).

Not everyone, however, is entirely persuaded that there is a definitive correlation between mental illness and creativity. Holden commented on another study—this one focusing on women writers—"[T]he variety of problems in the writers . . . studied suggests that a state of general 'unease' and 'tension' is conducive to creative activity. But being weird doesn't make you creative . . . it only acts as a spur in those with a creative bent" (1994, 1483).

If madness has traditionally been considered one avenue to inspiration, drinking and drugs are another time-honored way to spark creativity, especially among novices. Yet the majority of serious writers find they cannot write as well when they are impaired as when they are sober. And, of course, sustained abuse of any stimulant may lead to addiction and debilitation—the opposite of creativity. A number of writers have moved from intoxicants to spiritual pursuits in order to achieve their creative moments. They pray, meditate, go on retreats, sit zazen. Jane Hirshfield finds "the willing embrace of pain" in the search for creativity and enlightenment a "mystical paradox": "Fasting, sleeplessness, and exposure to the elements are part of many rites of passage. Just as Whitman allied himself with the most difficult human circumstances, Dickinson too acknowledges the necessity of pain in the enduring transformation of the threshold" (1997, 219). (Of course the latter poet famously reminds us, "Much Madness is divinest Sense.")

Whether it is following a regimen of mindfulness or drinking oneself to the point of oblivion, writers engaged in these pursuits clearly believe they can achieve creativity through conscious effort. However, even if we no longer quite believe in the Muses, creativity is still often thought to come unbidden, when the writer is least expecting it. Some writers believe that true creativity is largely spontaneous and ruined by later attempts to gussy it up. "First thought, best thought," Allen Ginsberg often said, echoing Zen artists and poets from the past. The romantic poets, too, "promoted spontaneity with varying fervor . . . for Wordsworth, poetry is *emotion recollected in tranquility*—so a first draft's passionate outpourings could presumably be revised. But a Shelley would likely leave them untouched, since the moment of frenzied inspiration for him provided truthful revelation supreme" (Abra 1988, 428). While most experienced contemporary writers would side with Wordsworth, believing that revision is an essential and creative part of the writing process, many beginning writers sympathize with Shelley, holding fast to the belief that the first thing that comes from their pens or keyboards should be cherished—— immaculate and uncorrected.

Creativity appears to be an intrinsically human trait, though some researchers have tried to transfer this quality to sophisticated computer programs. Super computers may be able to defeat chess champions, but so far there have been no budding writers in the bunch. Story writing programs are unable to overcome several apparently insurmountable obstacles. Most importantly, it is currently impossible to program the complex psychological processes of human beings—the heart and bone of creative writing—into a machine. Computers that can predict hurricanes and economic trends cannot arrange the vast and idiosyncratic background knowledge of human experience, which every writer brings when she sits down to her desk, into anything with much aesthetic value. Moreover, when research is necessary to aid a plotline, computer programs are unable to discern what information is valuable to the story and what should be discarded. Granted, random word generators have managed to produce some interesting Language poetry, but for the time being, "Emily Bronte . . . is not in the picture. Occasionally, however, today's computers can *seem* to do almost as well as Aesop" (Boden 2004, 177).

Ultimately, literary creation is an act of human will. It signifies the creator's belief that something does not exist that should exist, that the world needs redefinition or redirection or reconstruction. "A creative contribution represents an attempt to propel a field from wherever it is . . . to wherever the creator believes it should go" (Sternberg, Kaufman, and Pretz 2002, 10). Even if a writer's goals are more modest, he is likely to agree with Jean Baker Miller that "[p]ersonal creativity is a continuous process of bringing forth a changing vision of oneself, and of oneself in relation to the world" (1976, 24).

EDITORS AND PUBLISHERS

Marc Aronson locates the emergence of the modern American editor in a single publishing event at the very end of the nineteenth century. Editor Ripley Hitchcock made significant revisions to Edward Noyes Westcott's manuscript *David Harum*, which had previously been rejected by a number of publishers. The novel subsequently became "the number one best-seller for 1899," with almost three-quarters of a million copies sold by 1904. According to Aronson, "The work Hitchcock actually did on the manuscript was not unusual—other editors had also made suggestions for radical cuts and had turned rejected manuscripts into hot sellers—but there were two crucial differences this time: the book sold at a record-breaking pace, and people found out what the editor had done" (Gross 1993, 11). The idea that an editor could be just as, if not *more* important than the author was a new one, and Hitchcock's achievement gave editing a cachet it lacked at a time when most book editors when were seen as little more than glorified proofreaders.

Aronson further traces the evolution of the editor as virtual coauthor to Max Perkins, who turned the massive, unwieldy manuscripts of Thomas Wolfe into the now-classic novels *Of Time and the River* and *You Can't Go Home Again*. Perkins, modest to a fault, ennobled the editor's role by refusing to take credit for his work, although it was clear to those on the inside that his editing was crucial to the books' commercial and artistic success. From the 1940s through the 1970s, editing became a haven for smart, driven people who faced discrimination elsewhere in the white-collar world. Young Jewish men established a number of now-prominent publishing houses, including Alfred A. Knopf, Simon & Schuster, Viking, Random House, and Farrar, Strauss & Giroux. These houses, in turn, opened their doors to women and people of color. This is not to say that, for much of America's literary history, there has not been, as Zora Neale Hurston wrote in 1947, a dismal "lack of curiosity [by Anglo-Saxons] about the internal lives and emotions" of African Americans. "The fact that there is no demand for incisive and full-dress stories around Negroes above the servant class is indicative of something of vast importance to this nation" (54). Yet the situation has gradually become less egregious, as authors have become editors and editors became authors. One of the great novelists of the century, Toni

Morrison, had her entrée into the world of New York publishing as an editor at Random House in the 1960s, when the field was full of excitement and intellectual activity.

Unfortunately, in the 1980s, "as many publishing houses were subsumed into a new group of international conglomerates, the individual editor became less and less familiar to the public" (Aronson 1993, 19). That trend has continued to this day so that, outside the industry itself, editors at large houses are now, once again, generally anonymous. Indeed, Aronson only half-jokingly foresees a time in which "[f]ully computerized editing programs could take quantified focus-group studies, mix them with marketing figures, and generate genre paperbacks from text through bound books untouched by human hands" (20).

For the time being, however, editorial positions continue to be occupied by real people. Despite earning "average salaries even though they have above-average educations and responsibilities" (Editors Association of Canada, 1991), some editors appear to have satisfying and varied careers. Elizabeth Demers, the history acquisitions editor for the University of Nebraska Press, describes her life as a book editor this way:

> My job takes me from the lofty halls of academe to schmoozy fund-raising events and cocktail parties; from discussions of intellectual ideas to the very serious contemplation of the economics and market for potential books, often within a very short span of time. A typical day for me might include reading manuscripts; meeting with authors and donors, or potential ones; flying to a conference, both to acquire new titles and to give a talk; meeting with our marketing department, managing editor, or designers; finding reviewers for manuscripts; and, of course, doing the core work of editing, accepting, and rejecting projects. (2004b)

Alan Williams—an editor at both Viking and Grove Weidenfeld—maintains that book editors have three constant and specific duties: "First they must find and select the books the house is to publish. Second, they edit (yes, Virginia, they still do edit, no matter what cries you hear about bottom lines, heartless conglomerates, and the defeat of taste by commerce). And third, they perform the Janus-like function of representing the house to the author and the author to the house" (Gross 1993, 4).

As selectors, and rejecters, of manuscripts, editors exercise a great deal of influence over who and what will be read. At this point in the process, editors are gatekeepers, potential queen- and king- (and taste-) makers. Authors and/or their agents are friendly, accommodating, and on their best behavior. A certain amount of seduction is involved, with the author/ agent wheedling and persuading, promising a financially successful book, and consenting to editorial conditions that the author may later find onerous. "[H]ow well you can write your book, indeed how good a writer you are, doesn't initially come into play. First, an editor must determine if your project is, in concept and focus, commercially viable" (Rabiner and Fortunato 2002, 39). (Of course, if an author is already a proven commercial entity, the editor and publisher will be "doing the wooing.")

It is in Williams's second category that the relationship may sour: "Some writers . . . would rather see their dentist than their editor" (Editors Association of Canada, 1991). In fact, if getting and signing a book contract is in some respects like courtship, the actual editing phase may more closely resemble the student-teacher bond. Unless the author is a proven moneymaker, the editor normally continues to occupy the position of power. She tells the author what he must do to bring his work up to the level she expects. Like a teacher dealing with a recalcitrant student, she may cajole, harangue, plead with, and threaten the author to elicit a product she finds satisfactory. Though the author may—like a disgruntled student—sometimes grouse about an editor's suggestions and demands, he knows he must please her to achieve his ultimate goal of publication.

Williams claims that the "third function—editor as Janus, or two-face— occupies most of the working editor's office hours. . . . Unceasing reports, correspondence, phoning, meetings, business breakfasts, lunches, dinners, in- and out-of-office appointments leave active editors feeling like rapidly revolving doors as they attempt to explicate author and house to one another" (1991, 7). This constant juggling of duties is common to both trade and university press editors. Both are businesspeople engaged in hard work, much of it tedious, designed to make money for the companies that employ them.

Yet when it comes to profitability, there is a significant difference between the New York publishers and the smaller presses. While there may be more imprints than ever, the established publishing houses are now under the control of just a handful of corporations. Trade publishing is a multinational industry, mergers and acquisitions are rampant, and it takes a scorecard (and an eraser) to keep up with who owns what:

> Rupert Murdoch's Australia-based News Corporation acquired HarperCollins
> (formerly Harper & Row), William Morrow, and Avon, plus many other

American, Australian, and British publications as well as television and radio stations. Doubleday, along with its houses Delacorte and Dell, was bought by the German firm Bertelsmann and merged with Bantam; when Bertelsmann later (1998) acquired Random House, it became the largest U.S. trade publisher. Robert Maxwell of England bought Macmillan, the New York *Daily News,* and many other publishing enterprises. Maxwell's empire collapsed in the early 1990s, and Macmillan was eventually acquired by Viacom, which already owned Simon & Schuster. Viacom (which also owned Prentice Hall, Scribner, and other companies) later (1998) sold many of these publishing operations to the Pearson Group of England. Pearson's holdings now include Allyn & Bacon, Appleton & Lange, Macmillan, Penguin Putnam, Prentice Hall, Silver Burdett Ginn, and Simon & Schuster. ("Book Publishing" 2000)

As in the music and film industries, this concentration of power in just a few hands has resulted in a pronounced aversion to risk. Editors who once might have taken a chance on an unproven author—hoping that, over time, she would develop an audience and grow as an artist—now increasingly look only for books with best-seller potential. "[E]ditors . . . now spend more time marketing books than editing them, which results in the production of longer, sloppier . . . books" (Foer, 1997). Whether or not one would include fan favorites such as the *Harry Potter* series in this group, there is no doubt that publishers rely on blockbusters to generate a significant share of their revenue each year.

In 2002, the big five publishing houses—Random House, Penguin, HarperCollins, Simon & Schuster, and AOL Time Warner Group—"had estimated domestic revenue of $4.10 billion," accounting for "approximately 45% of all sales generated in the adult, children and mass market segments." By far the largest among these in North America was Random House, with total sales of $1.45 billion (Milliot 2003). In December 2004, that publisher's home page featured six books: three works of nonfiction (two memoirs and a cookbook) and three works of fiction, all by proven genre specialists: John Grisham (law and crime), Dean Koontz (horror), and Jonathan Kellerman (crime). While it makes sense that a publisher will want to put its prized possessions on show, it is equally obvious that the bottom line dictates what is and is not published. Look at any recent edition of *Publishers Weekly,* the industry's newsmagazine, and one notices that most news and feature articles focus far more on profitability than they do on art. Editors at the commercial houses must keep at least one— if not both—eyes on the market, on forecasts and media synergy and growth strategies. Certainly, an editor who develops a productive working relationship with a superstar—a Stephen King or John Grisham or Sue Grafton—will be rewarded with some job stability, but most editors at large houses find themselves constantly scrambling to find the next big thing.

In contrast, editors at university presses more closely resemble the "old school" editors from the thirties and forties. With their presses funded by institutional budget lines, the commodity they trade in is prestige rather than profit. These editors can concentrate on developing authors whose work they admire and on tackling intellectual and social issues they think are important. On the downside, university presses editors will probably be paid even less than their New York colleagues. They also typically receive lower starting salaries than beginning teaching faculty, although they "don't have the same kind of flexibility as faculty members in their schedules," working a full day, five days a week, with only a few weeks of vacation each year—rather than three or four months (Demers 2004b).

Editors for nonprofit literary publishers have even more control than university press editors over what they do and don't publish. Scott Walker, founder and editorial director of Graywolf Press, writes: "Most small-press editors not only acquire books but serve as line editor, managing editor (coordinating scheduling and the work of copy editors and proofreaders), legal department, receptionist, and administrative assistant—i.e., as the entire editor half of the old-fashioned author-editor relationship. The small-press editor's acquisition won't get shot down in an editorial or marketing committee meeting" (1993, 264).

Although Walker refers to himself as a "small-press" editor, publishers like Graywolf, Coffee House, Copper Canyon, Milkweed, Sarabande, and Story Line should more properly be called nonprofit presses. Milkweed, the second-largest nonprofit literary press (after Graywolf), is fairly typical in its goals: "Regardless of the genre, our books and programs are driven by a single-minded mission: to present the public with literary works that have the power to illuminate, challenge, and change" (n.d.). Nonprofits take advantage of—and are confined by—tax codes. While they may earn more money than they spend, they are prevented from "distributing their net earnings to individuals who control the organizations" (Tenenbaum 2002). Nevertheless, nonprofits do still need to make money in order to survive.

To this end, Thomas Woll contends that all publishers who eventually want to make a profit must be committed to the following goals:

- funding the enterprise yourself or through loans
- developing your editorial concept and niche
- producing quality products your target audience wants at a price it can afford
- marketing your product and getting the word out about it (2002, 3–4)

For university and nonprofit press editors and publishers of creative writing, this clearly means lots of hard work. Poetry, especially, is a notorious money loser, so publishers must rely on grants and wealthy contributors to keep the money flowing. And while most university and nonprofit presses know what sort of literature they want to publish, the trick is finding a niche that is not already occupied by a dozen other publishers. Granted, desktop publishing has made a huge difference in small publishers' ability to produce quality products; however, with chain bookstores closing down the independents, distribution is a major problem. Add to this the fact that "nonbookstores (department stores, grocery stores, discount outlets, etc.) sell 53 percent" of all books (Foer, 1997), and it is easy to see why an adventurous first novel is unlikely to receive much exposure. Moreover, because contemporary literature continues to be published in quantity (even while relatively little of it is actually sold), "getting the word out" requires plenty of research, strategic advertising, a significant amount of trial and error, and a very large dollop of luck.

On the very bottom rung of the commercial publishing ladder are small-press editors and publishers (often they are the same person). These generous and idealistic people know they aren't going to sell enough books to fund their operations, so they typically bankroll their presses out of their own pockets. True small presses—or "micropresses," as they are sometimes called—operate simply because the person in charge loves literature. Editor/publishers of small presses may engage in self-publishing or publication of the editor's friends, but their ultimate goal—getting work they love in the hands of people who will appreciate it—differs markedly from the profit-driven objectives of vanity presses (q.v.). Using desktop publishing (anyone with a computer and a printer can make a chapbook), micropresses print editions as small as fifty copies, and they often only "print on demand," that is, when there are sufficient customers to justify a print run. While this can be a tedious process, print-on-demand books don't take up warehouse space and they are never remaindered since they exist chiefly as code on the editor/publisher's computer.

Like nonprofit and small-press editors, editors of literary journals normally come to their work through a love of literature rather than a desire to make money. In fact, literary magazines tend to be money pits, and most long-standing journals have a university sponsor (the *Kenyon Review, Ploughshares,* the *Southern Review*) or some other source of outside funding (*Grand Street,* the *Partisan Review, Poetry*). Without this funding, the vast majority of literary magazines simply fold up after a few issues—the editor/publisher's initial enthusiasm nearly always meeting with deafening apathy from the magazine-buying public. Not surprisingly, because of the forbidding cost of printing a high-quality, flat-spined color magazine, many new editors have begun turning to e-zine publishing instead (see "Electronic Literature").

Whatever the drawbacks, editing a journal can still be a joy. Whether the magazine is online or in print, when editors are in the thick of putting together what they know will be an inspiring collection of stories and essays and poems, they, like their small-press counterparts, may well feel that the lack of financial remuneration is counterbalanced by the excitement of being part of—and helping to create—a literary scene. Joyce Carol Oates, longtime editor of the *Ontario Review,* describes the buzz this way: "[O]ne picks up a magazine, weighs it in the hand, it appears to be a *thing,* but in fact it isn't a *thing* at all. It's a symposium. A gathering. A party" (1980, 145). This festive atmosphere energizes editors—the sense that when readers "step into" a literary journal they never know whom they'll meet or what the guests will have to say. David St. John, former poetry editor for the *Antioch Review,* writes: "Certainly it takes no great courage to publish a poet who's already been well-received and acknowledged. The real delight is in discovering the work of a new or relatively unknown writer, and in being able to bring this work to the attention of a larger audience" (1990, 3). Robert Stewart, an editor at *New Letters,* echoes this notion that moving beyond the bounds of the ordinary is one of the great pleasures of editing a literary magazine: "In choosing poetry for publication, an editor needs both discipline and freedom. A little craziness, in fact, keeps him from bottoming out on poems that fit a predisposition, whatever kind" (1990, 58).

Before the boom in creative writing teaching jobs in the 1960s and 1970s, many writers made their living as editors. With the current dearth of teaching jobs, writers are once again turning to editing as a career. While hardly anyone will be able to make a living editing a literary magazine or small-press publication, earning a living wage editing for a trade house or university press is feasible. Writers who wish to pursue this path must be persistent and willing to gain experience however they can, even it that means working for a while as an unpaid intern. While recent graduates of creative writing programs may have to work extra hard, as they will likely be perceived as less studious and diligent than their peers who have studied literary theory or rhetoric and composition, "many of the skills acquired in graduate school are useful in publishing" (Demers 2004a). Moreover, "Editors are encouraged to read voraciously and think critically, whether they edit in the humanities or in more technical fields. They never stop learning" (Editors Association of Canada, 1991). Dedicated creative writers *are* voracious readers and learners; consequently, they have the potential to thrive outside their area of specialization. And of course university-trained creative writers will inevitably have an especially clear sense of how and why a novel or a collection of stories or poems does or doesn't work well.

The authors of this book have been on both sides of the editor-author relationship, in both scholarly and creative projects. We've learned that there are several guidelines editors and authors should follow if they are to have a congenial and fruitful working association. Good communication is essential: the more clearly all expectations are initially articulated, the less frustration there will be later on in a project. Authors need to feel free to ask potentially dumb questions, and editors need to know that it's all right not to be able to answer every query immediately. Editors and authors should be respectful of one another; they should be diligent and follow through in a timely way on the promises they make. Most importantly, though, both sides must be patient. Authors need to realize that editors are almost certainly juggling a number of projects. Likewise, editors should understand that authors have lives outside their manuscripts that can interfere with its completion. In an "open letter" to prospective editors, M. Lincoln Schuster advises: "Learn patience—sympathetic patience—so that you will not be dismayed when you ask an author how his new book is coming along, and he tells you: 'It's finished—all I have to do now is write it'" (1962, 24).

Fortunately, many editors are, or have been, writers, so they are familiar with the problems authors face. In an ideal relationship, the editor acts as the author's conscience. He forces her to buckle down and do the work when she would rather be at the beach; he pushes her to double-check that arcane fact she's not quite sure of (and he does it himself when she forgets to do so); he elicits better work from her than she ever thought she was capable of producing. And, when the process is over, and the editor and the author hold the new book or magazine in their hands, they can take great pride in knowing their collaboration was a successful one.

ELECTRONIC LITERATURE

The arrival of the computer age has affected creative writers profoundly, and no doubt will continue to do so in ways most of us can't yet imagine. Indeed, if any entry in this book has the potential to become obsolete overnight, it is this one. "Early" writing about Internet culture, which often focused on MUDs and MOOs, a few years later seems as quaint and outdated as discussions of the telegraph or the Pony Express. And "electronic literature" might well include everything from imaginative writing that was never intended to appear on a computer screen but has somehow found its way there to work that cannot be viewed in any other format. As such, most creative writing produced in the future will ultimately fall into this category. However, our focus in the short space we have here will be on a few of the ways that e-creative writing differs from its print equivalent. Even our notion of who we are as writers has shifted. As Sherry Turkle says, "We come to see ourselves differently as we catch sight of our images in the mirror of the machine" (1995, 9).

Before looking at any specific manifestation of electronic literature, we should first consider how significantly the computer has affected the creation and distribution of writing itself. We now take for granted the ease and speed of word processing, but, particularly for those working in book-length forms, the ability to cut, paste, and edit huge blocks of text has radically altered the composition process. Writers no longer hesitate to make small changes deep in a manuscript that might result in re-pagination, and editorial suggestions that once might have taken hours to implement can now be accommodated with the click of a few keystrokes.

In the computer age, writers begin their hunt for information—the name of a city street, the year an event took place, facts about a disease that will make a character seem more believable—via search engines. Research that previously might have taken days at the library can now be accomplished in a few seconds with a Google query. Many contemporary novelists have remarked on how much more realistic their writing now is, with fact-checking so much easier than it once was. And there is no excuse any longer for a misremembered quotation or an inaccurate date when it is so easy—for both writer *and* reader—to search for the correct version.

Once a piece of writing is finished, the writer's quest for publication now usually begins online, with electronic information about publishers likely to be far more current than anything in print. A typical literary journal listing in *Writers' Market* or *The International Directory of Little Magazines and Small Presses* can take up to eighteen months from the time it is filed with the press to the day it actually appears on paper—plenty of time for an editor's preferences to change or a magazine to go out of business. By contrast, journal editors with online listings can update their publishing needs and contact information immediately. The classifieds page in *Poets and Writers Magazine* (www.pw.org/mag/classifieds.htm), the searchable members directory at the Council of Literary Magazines and Presses (www.clmp.org/directory/), and the links page of LitLine (www.litline.org/links/index.html) all contain full, and free, listings of literary publishers. (See also "Contests," "Submissions," and "Writers' Resources.")

One the earliest types of literature specifically designed for computers is hypertext, which provides authors with ways to challenge the traditional notion of storytelling. In a typical hypertext, the reader is presented with a short narrative passage called a "lexia," which is often no larger than a computer screen; several key words or phrases in the lexia are highlighted as hyperlinks. Depending upon which link the reader clicks, the narrative may move in any number of directions. The multilinear story may take sudden turns or repeat previous lexia, which, now that the reader has new information, will be seen in a different light; however, it is unlikely that someone will view every lexia on any given read-through. Normally there are one or more "end" lexia, which signal that the story has finished.

Roland Barthes's ruminations on the nature of text in "The Death of the Author" are frequently cited by critics as suggestive of the hypertext experience: "a multidimensional space in which are married and contested several writings . . . a fabric of quotations, resulting from a thousand sources of culture" (1968, 149). Less sophisticated readers tend to compare the form to the "Create Your Own Adventure" series of children's books. In either case, hypertext has clear pleasures and obvious faults. The interactive nature of the genre means readers play a far more

significant role in the construction of the story than they would in traditional fiction. Because of its open-endedness, its ceding of a large measure
of authorial control, its resistance to making conventional narrative sense,
the hypertext has been touted as the postmodern fiction par excellence.
Indeed, the indeterminate nature of the text ensures that no "correct"
reading is ever possible, and a well-written hypertext novel like Michael
Joyce's *Afternoon* presents readers with an astonishing range of pleasures.

Unfortunately, hypertext writers are limited to a certain pattern of storytelling. Because of the randomness built into the form, hypertext novels
move in fits and starts. Authors who prize the ability to closely influence their readers' reactions are especially frustrated by the medium.
Digression is the norm. It is easy for a reader to give up on a long piece
of hypertext, since the end is rarely in sight (even it is really only one click
away). Moreover, as hypertext can exist only on-screen, the pleasures of
sustained reading are limited: even the most sophisticated "electronic
books" have yet to rival the simple felicities of their paper counterparts.
While trade editors and publishers (q.v.) have worked diligently to acquire
copyrights (q.v.) for electronic distribution of previously published work,
they, too, have found e-books to be unwieldy. "Even Ann Godoff, presi-
dent and publisher of Random House Trade Group and creator of the
digital imprint, admitted that she had not yet managed to enjoy reading
a book off a screen, or read a whole electronic book. Neither has almost
anyone else in the industry" (Kirkpatrick, 2000). Granted, literary software publishers such as Eastgate Systems—which also publishes the most
popular program, Storyspace—have sought to commodify longer hypertext works; yet electronic novels have proven to be no more lucrative than
any other form of avant-garde literature. In the words of Eastgate's Web
site: "Important writing is not necessarily popular."

If hypertext has been difficult to market, easier (and free) access to
shorter works of electronic literature is offered through Web-based literary magazines, often called e-zines. Early e-zines were usually nothing
more than offshoots of their creator's vanity home pages. On these pages,
writers of dubious ability and no reputation would chiefly post their
own work and occasionally the work of other writers. Then, during the
high-tech boom of the mid- and late-nineties, many academically trained
creative writers found themselves working computer jobs. As they gained
experience in Web design, suddenly the *look* of some e-zines was far superior to anything their print equivalents could offer. In addition to a sleek
appearance, e-zines offered other advantages. Though literary magazines

remain as unprofitable as ever, the cost of an e-zine is modest enough to make nearly anyone with time, energy, and a small amount of Web savvy a potential literary editor. Compared to the thousands of dollars it takes to produce a thousand copies of a glossy 100-page paper journal, e-zines cost only as much as the annual fee for a server, or, on a server sponsored by an academic institution, nothing at all. Access is unlimited, and the number of "pages" possible per issue is far greater, potentially almost limitless. An editor could conceivably print an epic poem or a full-length novel in every issue—and still have plenty of room left for other material.

Ironically, though, the very technology that makes this vast space available for storing literature also creates a prejudice against extended reading. Web surfers are acclimated to quick viewing. They don't stay long with a single page; therefore, editors have discovered that the shorter the work, the more likely it will be read. The more successful e-zines have a variety of short offerings and take full advantage of the electronic medium. Short Quicktime films or Shockwave graphics may accompany works of literature. Writers can be heard and seen reading their work aloud through audio/video devices like RealPlayer. E-zines are also a natural medium for hypertext, although this resource is surprisingly underutilized in most magazines.

Among the advantages of online publication is the close relationship it fosters between writers and readers. The author's e-mail address is generally available at the end of her piece, so readers can immediately weigh in with their opinions. Literary discussions that in the past would have been conducted in cafés, bars, or through the post can now take place online. On a more mundane level, e-mail manuscript submissions to e-zines have made electronic submission of material to some print journals more acceptable, too, providing creative writers with a faster and more convenient way of submitting material than through the postal service.

Publication in the best e-zines still does not carry the same prestige as publication in the best print journals. However, there are signs that this is changing. E-zines like the *Blue Moon Review* have been included in *Writer's Digest*'s "50 Best Poetry Markets." E-zines such as *BeeHive* regularly feature fine writing *and* spectacular visual effects. One of the first places writers and readers looking to explore e-zines should begin is webdelsol. com. A long-standing locus for all things literary and electronic, Web Del Sol (WDS) includes everything from links to the Web sites of print and electronic journals to newsletters and columns about e-publishing to its own e-zine and online chapbooks by WDS authors. The evolution of the site mirrors the evolution of e-zines in general. Web Del Sol began with a few links to magazines, a lovably cantankerous editorial perspective, and an annoying MIDI (Musical Instrument Digital Interface) theme jingle. These days, WDS has a slick design, links to *USA Today*, and advertisements for workshops, magazines, and movies—proving yet again that e-commerce follows on the heels of *any* online endeavor.

Though traditional literary magazines were initially hesitant to move to the Internet, most print journals of any standing now also have a Web site. Typically, this site consists of the table of contents for current and past issues, submission information, selected works from the magazine, and links to other literary journals. Of course, some journals have been more ambitious, and generous, with their e-offerings. For a time, the *Kenyon Review* made each new issue, in its entirety, available as a pdf download, and *Ploughshares* has put most of its back issues online at www.pshares.org.

Because Internet users are accustomed to getting their online literature for free, they have proven to be bad customers for electronic books. Granted, a few optimistic and persistent e-book publishers, such as Boson Books (www.cmonline.com/boson/), continue to sell books designed to be read on computers or handheld personal digital assistants. However, most electronic publishers of creative writing offer their product gratis and hope to cash in on advertising. The results can be mixed. A site like Bartleby.com, which unites economics with art, offers a peculiarly incongruous reading experience. Milton's "On the Death of a Fair Infant Dying of a Cough" is accompanied by a flashing promise that the reader can make $125–$175 per hour working from home. Edmund Burke's *Reflections on the French Revolution* is festooned with ads for AT&T wireless service. Nevertheless, despite these commercial intrusions, free admission to many of the world's classics books ought to be a boon for aspiring lower-income writers, provided they can circumvent the obvious impediment of Internet access.

Of course, even when the reading experience isn't interrupted by pop-up ads, a notable difference exists between the process of following text on-screen and on the page. One of the most vocal critics of electronic literature has been Sven Birkerts. In "'The Fate of the Book,'" he argues for the advantages of the hierarchical and closed systems of that "artifact." Without books, Birkerts maintains, the style of individual authors will gradually become more and more alike. Moreover, the words they write will be in some ways less important: "When we read from a screen, or write directly onto a screen (without printing out), we in fact never cross the border from atom to bit, or bit to atom. There is a slight, but somehow consequential, loss of gravity; the word is denied its landing place in the order of material things, and its impact on the reader is subtly lessened" (1996, 198).

Whether or not Birkerts's gloomy predictions come true, the poetics of digital code is still clearly evolving, and the consensus to date is that electronic literature has not yet lived up to its potential. (See "The Electronic Labyrinth" at www.iath.virginia.edu/elab/elab.html for a concise, readable analysis of the subject.) Granted, increasing numbers of young writers are turning to the Web for publication: they are exploring the impact of technology on the ancient acts of writing and reading. And Richard Lanham is more optimistic than Birkerts: "We will learn to use volatile electronic text to do the work of the world, just as we have learned to use fixed text" (2003, 232). Yet electronic literature is currently an unstable medium. Links go dead: a page that is accessible today may disappear tomorrow. And to date, no genius has yet emerged to fully exploit the possibilities of word and screen. Until there exists a serious literature that can only be accessed via computer, what Charles Bernstein slyly calls B-O-O-K technology will likely remain the industry standard.

FICTION

The rise of creative nonfiction—which began in the late 1960s with the New Journalism and became a seemingly unstoppable force in the 1990s—threatens to preempt fiction as the sexiest—that is, the most marketable—literary genre. Yet fiction remains the backbone of the creative writing industry. While the popularity of other genres waxes and wanes, fiction is the economic engine that keeps the business running, and for that reason in this entry we will look at the financial aspect of creative writing, which receives scant attention elsewhere in this volume. Of all the creative writers, fiction writers appear to have the most legitimate chance of achieving fame and fortune. No publisher believes that a book of poetry will become a best-seller, but even the most erudite publisher of small-press fiction secretly hopes that one of the novels on this year's list will manage to break through to a large audience. And those lucky books that are translated into films will garner rewards most creative writers only dream of.

As all creative writing program administrators know, fiction continues to draw the highest percentage of students, young women and men who envision themselves hobnobbing with celebrities and pitching their latest novels on talk shows. Every semester they come in droves, the Great American Novel just out of reach of their fingertips. And it isn't just the hope of material rewards that brings these students in. If undergraduates typically consider poetry abstruse and difficult, and scriptwriting for television and film is a largely invisible and undertaught art, every budding writer has a favorite novel that has nursed him through hard times as an adolescent. Fiction offers students an opportunity not just to tell their (life) stories, but to embellish them as well.

The first disjunction for many new fiction writers begins the moment they enter the classroom. More often than not, undergraduates arrive in introductory courses enamored of genre fiction. In their apprentice stories, robot vampires battle for supreme control of Mars. Plucky ingénues woo tongue-tied but good-hearted hunks. Drug-dealing cops exchange gunfire with wisecracking CIA agents. Clever gnomes outsmart lusty witches in a land that time forgot. But if genre fiction draws students into class, their teachers are usually unsympathetic readers of this work. New creative writing teachers are particularly appalled. Veteran teachers like Jerome Stern get over it by writing books like *Making Shapely Fiction*, which takes a perverse joy in making fun of bad undergraduate fiction. Stephen Minot's admonishment in his widely used textbook *Three Genres* is typical of the hardened instructor's attitude toward "popular" fiction: "Like fast food, formula writing serves a wide market and often earns top dollars, but it usually sacrifices subtlety and insight" (2003, 155).

Clearly, the struggle to define "fiction" is always at the center of the fiction writing course. What constitutes a "legitimate" story or novel in class? Outside the classroom? And obviously, any attempt to definitively identify fiction per se (as opposed to what?) will necessarily exclude other definitions. So: a couple of pertinent questions and a few provisional answers. What is fiction and who decides what receives that name? Who, and what, is fiction for?

WHAT IS FICTION AND WHO DECIDES?

At the beginning of *The Art of Fiction*, his classic meditation on the subject for aspiring writers, John Gardner warns against constructing too rigid a set of principles for telling stories: "What the beginning writer ordinarily wants is a set of rules on what to and not to do in fiction. . . . but on the whole the search for aesthetic absolutes is a misapplication of the writer's energy. When one begins to be persuaded that certain things must never be done in fiction, and certain other things must always be done, one has entered the first stage of aesthetic arthritis, the disease that ends up in pedantic rigidity and the atrophy of intuition" (1984, 3).

George Garrett similarly hesitates to make ultimate pronouncements about what fiction is. He writes, "Say anything you want about 'the creative process,' but what is clear and certain is that we don't really understand it. It breaks all the rules as fast as we can make them. Every generalization turns out to be at best incomplete or inadequate" (1999, 2).

All relativism about what constitutes a work of fiction aside, we have already seen how flippant writing teachers can be about nonliterary fiction. (Both Gardner and Garrett would likely agree with Minot's dismissal of it as a subject for serious study.) In part this snobbery may stem from a realistic assessment of the place of literary fiction in the economic order of things. Saul Bellow believed that "[t]he literary masterpieces of the 20th-century were for the most part the work of novelists who had no large public in mind. The novels of Proust and Joyce were not intended to be read under the blaze and dazzle of popularity" ("Writers on Writing" 2004, 7). Out of necessity, most creative writing teachers would endorse this view that serious fiction ought not to be read *too* widely. Barry Gifford says, "It's clear that the general public in the United States doesn't read literary fiction. There may be more books being sold now than ever, but what are the books? They're mysteries, romances, cookbooks, how-to books. There's very little commerce when it comes to literary fiction, and this is just a fact. The evisceration of the independent bookstores has guaranteed this kind of awful future, and I can't help but feel any other way" (Petracca 1999, 492).

Like Gifford, the majority of fiction writing teachers have made their reputations—and therefore earned their place in the academy—as novelists. Therefore, for them the novel is the ne plus ultra of fictional writing. However, because of the time constraints of the quarter or semester, in most creative writing classes fiction comes to mean the short story. This makes for yet another unexpected twist in students' educations. They've come to class wanting to write the next *Lord of the Rings*, yet their instructors want them to write "The Lady with the Dog" instead. And they soon learn that most instructors are unwilling to spend the many additional— and *unpaid*—hours required to read and comment upon a student-written novel. As a result, conscientious students eventually begin writing literary short fiction. Regrettably, as beginning writers learn when they visit the fiction sections of libraries and bookstores, there are always plenty of novels for sale or on loan, but far fewer collections of short stories. Consequently, students find themselves writing the least profitable form of fiction: their transformation from Stephen King to Stephen Dixon is complete.

Indeed, despite, or—to follow the illogic of the creative writing industry—*because* of their lack of marketability, shorter fictional forms have become increasingly popular in creative writing classes over the last fifteen years. Of course short tales have been around for millennia; and throughout the twentieth century—Borges's *Ficciones* is just one example—master writers have produced expert work in the very short form. Recently, however, there has been an explosion of short-short stories, works of fiction one to five pages in length. Grace Paley writes, "A short story is closer to the poem than to the novel . . . and when it's very short . . . should be read like a poem" (Shapard and Thomas 1986, 253). This close attention to the words on the page is a boon for writers, but, alas, microfiction is currently about as marketable as poetry among book buyers.

With the popularity of computer-generated media, one might reasonably assume that computer-based fiction would thrive also. And if the narratives constructed by computer gamers count as stories—voyages through outer space, shoot-'em-ups, popular movies reconstituted as games—that has, in fact, turned out to be the case. However, if one's definition of fiction continues to be text-based, the future of fiction doesn't look as bright. Granted, hypertext—a story or novel written and read on a computer that proceeds via links from screen to screen—had a brief period of popularity in the 1990s, and publishers invested some time and money into promoting downloadable e-books, but the pleasures of reading an actual book appear to have triumphed over the chore of reading text on a computer screen (see "Electronic Literature").

WHAT IS IT FOR?

Peter Rabinowitz points out in "Canons and Close Readings" that *how* we read a text determines the sort of fiction we value. Rabinowitz notes, "Once you give priority to close reading, you implicitly favor figurative writing over realistic writing, indirect expression over direct expression, deep meaning over surface meaning, form over content, and the elite over the popular." Rabinowitz compares Harriet Wilson's *Our Nig* with Henry James's *What Maisie Knew* and demonstrates that while James's focus on psychology and symbolism makes his novel more palatable to contemporary critical tastes, "the racist brutality endured by Ms. Wilson's heroine is arguably more important for our culture—and thus more deserving for our consideration—than the affluent sexual merry-go-round that dizzies Maisie" (1988, 219) (see "Reading").

Alberto Rios says, "Fiction's cruel burden is that it must be more believable than real life" (1999, 261), and in many quarters this belief that literary fiction should strive for mimesis continues unabated. Tobias Wolff makes a similar claim in his introduction to *The Vintage Book of Contemporary American Short Stories*: "It is this quality, above all, that puts . . . writers on common ground—the ability to breathe into their work distinct living presences beyond their own: imagined others fashioned from words, who somehow take on flesh and blood and moral nature" (1994, xvi).

We saw earlier that escape from reality is a common goal of student writers, but many writers of serious fiction also have escapist tendencies. Ursula K. Le Guin's science fiction, for example, often leaves this world and time to deal with issues of the day. And Marcela Christine Lucero-Trujillo locates an escapist vein in Latino literature that returns obsessively to the past: "Some Chicanas' literature has been a vehicle whereby they could escape into another temporal scene of our folklore, our legends and modus vivendi; of that particular past which seemed a safer and saner word, the world as it ought to be, albeit a very traditional romantic view" (1980, 621).

Of course, modernist novelists like Woolf, Proust, Joyce, and Faulkner, and postmodernist novelists like Barthleme, Barth, and Pynchon have, for almost a century, been working actively *against* the traditions of mimetic and escapist fiction. If Pynchon's *The Crying of Lot 49* is in some ways a Bildungsroman about Oedipas Maas, it is even more a complex literary game in which the real subject is the shifting and usually invisible structures that undergird our society. This type of fiction responds to the uncertainty of postwar American life as described by Ruland and Bradbury: "Mathematics examined the fiction of numbers, linguists described the slippage of words, architects learned the vast simultaneity of all styles and the certainty of none, as codes gave way to decodes" (1991, 371) (see "Postmodernism").

Mimetic and escapist fiction tends to have a clear moral center, while, as the editors of *Postmodern American Fiction* note, "If any one common thread unites the diverse artistic and intellectual movements that constitute postmodernism, it is the questioning of any belief system that claims universality or transcendence" (Geyh, Leebron, and Levy, 1998, xx).

Indeed, African American critics such as Valerie Smith have pointed out that "feminists and Afro-Americanists alike have considered the extent to which they may betray the origins of their respective modes of inquiry when they seek to employ the discourse of contemporary theory" (1989, 675). And yet despite the anti-Foundationalist gestures made by postmodernists, fiction writers keep returning to the idea that fiction has a moral purpose. Wayne Booth writes in *The Rhetoric of Fiction*: "When human actions are formed to make an art work, the form that is made can never be divorced from the human meanings, including the moral judgments, that are implicit whenever human beings act. And nothing the writer does can be finally understood in isolation from his effort to make it all accessible to someone else—his peers, himself as imagined reader, his audience. The novel comes into existence *as* something communicable, and the means of communication are not shameful intrusions unless they are made with shameful ineptitude" (1961, 397).

Booth is writing in 1961, but Charles Baxter has something similar to say in 1997. He uses the adjective "dysfunctional" "to describe a structural unit (like the banking system, or the family, or narrative) whose outward appearance is intact but whose structural integrity has been compromised or collapsed." "No one is answerable from within it," Baxter claims. "Every event, every calamity is unanswerable, from the S&L collapse to the Exxon Valdez oil spill" (11–12). Baxter goes on to remark: "In the absence of any clear moral vision, we get moralizing instead" (18). Even writers like Joyce Carol Oates, who believe the purpose of fiction is to test (and sometimes violate) established moral codes, nevertheless implicitly acknowledge the importance of those codes: "To write is to invade another's space, if only to memorialize it. . . . Art is by its nature a transgressive act, and artists must accept being punished for it. The more original and unsettling their art, the more devastating the punishment" ("Writers on Writing" 2004, 19).

Oates hints here at the political nature of fiction writing, its ability to persuade readers to change their minds about an issue, to work effectively for social justice (see "Identity Politics"). In America, the politicizing of fiction is often looked at suspiciously, especially by those on the right, who argue that one must inevitably sacrifice art for partisan ardor. Yet Richard Powers sees this either/or stipulation as false: "Aestheticize politics or politicize art: the old, iron-clad dichotomy bewilders me. I don't mean I'm bewildered by having to make the choice. I'm bewildered by those who think we can. We've reified these two terms of creative engagement and made them out to be incommensurable. Should fiction be concerned with beauty or morality? It's a little like asking whether humans ought rather to eat or to breathe, or whether sentences ought really to consist of nouns or verbs" (Powers and Morrow 2000, 177).

Ultimately, then, even the greatest and most experienced writers return to the recurring question of purpose and audience, which so vexes beginning creative writing students. We write stories for ourselves, certainly, but once we take the step to show our fiction to other readers we can be sure that it will be met with a complex and conflicting set of responses, many of which are out of the writer's control.

GENRE

"Genre" comes from the French word meaning both "kind" and "gender." While in English we use genre mostly to refer to categories of literary, musical, and artistic compositions, in the past there has also been a sense that some of these types of work are more "masculine" or "feminine"—more or less privileged—than others. According to M. H. Abrams, since the time of Plato and Aristotle, works of literature have generally been placed in three main classes: "poetic or lyric (uttered throughout in the first person); epic or narrative (in which the narrator speaks in the first person, then lets his characters speak for themselves); and drama (in which the characters do all the talking)" (1981, 70). A poet or dramatist's success or failure in any one of these genres was judged by how well he (nearly always the writer was a man) adhered to the standards articulated by classical theorists like Plato, Aristotle, Horace, Longinus, Plotinus, and others.

> From the Renaissance through much of the eighteenth century, the recognized genres—or poetic "kinds," as they were then called—were widely thought to be fixed literary types, somewhat like species in the biological order of nature; many neoclassic critics insisted that each kind must remain "pure" (there must, for example, be no "mixing" of tragedy and comedy), and also proposed *rules* which specified the subject matter, structure, style, and emotional effect proper to each kind. At that time, the genres were also commonly ranked in a hierarchy (closely related to the ranking of social classes, from royalty and the nobility to peasants), ranging from epic and tragedy at the top to the short lyric, epigram, and other minor types at the bottom. (Abrams 1981, 70–71)

Of course, even when ideas of genre were supposedly most rigid, a brief glance at world literature shows us that minor rather than major writers worried more about sticking strictly to narrow ideas of what one could or couldn't do in a work of literature. Shakespeare, for one, was an egregious offender in the crime of genre-mixing. From act to act, scene to scene, even from line to line, he ranges from the tragic to the comic, from high diction to low. In Polonius's speech introducing the traveling players in act II, scene 2 of *Hamlet*, Shakespeare famously satirizes the subdividing of literature into absurdly particular varieties. These are "[t]he best actors in the world," Polonius boasts of the troop, "either for tragedy, comedy, history, pastoral, pastoral-comical, historical-pastoral, tragical-historical, tragical-comical-historical-pastoral, scene individable, or poem unlimited."

Genre features may no longer be as stable as critics once wanted them to be, but bookstores still classify their wares by nonfiction and fiction, and within these categories are many subcategories. Indeed, "genre fiction" refers to novels found in sections labeled Romance, Horror, Crime, Spy, Science Fiction, and so on. Genre fiction gets its name from the fact that books written in the genre adhere to a specific set of conventions that readers of the genre expect, if not demand. Because these conventions may be so specific and unrelenting, the writing itself may become formulaic, so reliant upon a set of rigid conventions that there is little room for creativity.

Yet if mainstream creative writers once derided genre fiction as unimaginative and mechanical, many literary novelists of the past thirty years have enjoyed playing with, and against, those same conventions. Erica Jong believes that "genres themselves matter less and less. The most enduring books of the modern era are, like *Ulysses*, full of exposition, narrative, dramatic writing and even poetry" (Arana 2003, 69). Postmodern writers have been especially engaged in "the repudiation of narrative and generic boundaries" (Geyh, Leebron, and Levy 1998, 1). In novels that were *almost* recognizable as science fiction, William Burroughs, for instance, employed "nonlinear techniques of narrative composition works together with . . . thematic explorations of domination and resistance, sexuality and drug use, to challenge the structures and taboos of contemporary society." Among the many novelists who have followed Burroughs's example and expanded and challenged the definitions of genre in their work are Kurt Vonnegut, John Barth, Samuel Delany, Ursula K. Le Guin, Octavia Butler, Paul Auster, Maxine Hong Kingston, and Gloria Anzaldúa

The influence of postmodernism, which "jams things together, and, in so doing, calls attention not just to their convergences but also to the artificial construct by which they are produced" (Haake 2000, 272), has clearly had an effect on writing in composition (q.v.) courses as well, making them more open to genre-mixing and resulting in the validation of expository essays that may look quite creative indeed. The very site where most writing now occurs—at our computers—is as much a world of imagery (icons on our toolbars and desktops, illustrations and photographs on Web pages) as it is a world of text, and writing any document—creative or scholarly—for an intelligent, attentive audience (*Keywords in Creative Writing*, for example) is likely to involve dipping into and drawing from a number of "genres." As writers toggle between e-mail and the Internet, online databases and print books and journal articles, "it becomes pretty clear that we *already* inhabit a model of communication practices incorporating multiple genres related to each other, those multiple genres, remediated across contexts of time and space, linked one to the next, circulating across and around rhetorical situations both inside and outside of school" (Yancey 2004, 308).

Tom Romano, one of the first scholars to catalog productive ways of crossing genre boundaries in school essays, traces his interest in the multigenre paper to a reading of Michael Ondaatje's *The Collected Works of Billy the Kid* (1970), which consists of "songs, thumbnail character sketches, poems, a comic book excerpt, narrative, stream-of-consciousness passages, newspaper interviews, even photographs and drawings" (2000, 3): "Out of his inquiry into Billy the Kid, Ondaatje created a complex, multilayered, multivoiced blend of genres, each revealing information about his topic, each self-contained, making a point of its own, unconnected to other genres by conventional transitional devices. I cannot emphasize enough this idea of separateness. Each genre is a color slide, complete in itself, possessing its own satisfying composition, but also working in concert with the others to create a single literary experience" (4). Interestingly, as Romano implies here, even when authors are madly mixing genres, the frisson we feel as one type of writing is juxtaposed against another can only occur when we can identify the different genres.

If we can now speak of the multigenre composition essay as a genre in itself, contemporary rhetoricians have taken the study of genre even further and applied it to areas far outside traditional literature. For these theorists, "genres and the activity systems they are part of provide the forms of life within which we make our lives. This is as true of our systems of work, creativity, community, leisure, and intimacy, as it is of our system of tax obligation—each mediated through language forms along with whatever other embodied and material aspects there are to the interactions" (Bazerman 2002, 15). From this perspective, any type of written or oral communication can constitute a genre. In *The Rhetoric and Ideology of Genre*, a recent book on the subject, genre theory is used to explain everything from political party Web sites to doctor-patient interviews to school geography classes to architecture students' sketchbooks (Coe, Lingard, and Teslenko 2002). If we can indeed recognize each of these texts as a separate genre, that is because our socialization "has trained us to immediately perceive the purpose and intended effects, i.e., the social function, of most texts we are confronted with. . . . The majority of these texts have some practical function . . . which can be related to the real world around us" (Verdonk 2002, 12).

Clearly, genre is shaped by social forces and by the expectations of different readers during different historical periods, and "a given type persists only so long as it remains a functional response to exigencies" (Campbell and Jamieson 1990, 104). The rise of the novel in eighteenth-century England, for instance, is often linked to the increased education and leisure time of middle-class women. The novel has remained a popular form because literacy and leisure time have continued to expand. However, the relative *un*popularity of the novel compared to television shows and movies can be explained by the fact that, for many people in postindustrial societies, leisure time is now limited; these people would rather seek brief release in a visual medium rather than invest days or weeks in reading a novel.

Because the definitions of genre change over time, it is naive to suppose that those definitions will not be contested in the process of their shifting. As Daniel Chandler (2000) points out: "The classification and hierarchical taxonomy of genres is not a neutral and 'objective' procedure. There are no undisputed 'maps' of the system of genres within any medium (though literature may perhaps lay some claim to a loose consensus). Furthermore, there is often considerable theoretical disagreement about the definition of specific genres. . . . One theorist's *genre* may be another's *sub-genre* or even *super-genre* (and indeed what is *technique, style, mode, formula* or *thematic grouping* to one may be treated as a *genre* by another)." In short, there can be no universally agreed upon characterization of genre.

Despite all the work currently being done in genre theory, many American creative writers would be surprised to learn that anyone is particularly concerned with more than just the four "main genres": poetry, fiction, drama, and creative nonfiction. From a pragmatic point of view, when submitting work to editors and publishers, writers just need to know which genre editor to send their work to. Those editors, in turn, will expect the writer to have a fairly clear idea of the conventions of their genre.

Moreover, genre remains important for graduate students in creative writing since most programs require students seeking an MFA (q.v.) or writing a creative dissertation (q.v.) to declare a "major genre" in which they will write their book-length thesis. In the work that will ultimately determine whether or not they receive their degrees, graduate student writers may feel hesitant to cross lines that confuse or frustrate their thesis or dissertation committees. (And committee members may feel unqualified to assess work outside their own area of specialization.) Once they have their degrees in hand and begin looking for jobs, creative writers will again find that genre plays a significant role in their professional lives. College and university hiring committees typically specify a particular genre they want candidates to teach; not surprisingly, applicants without extensive experience in that genre are unlikely to be asked to teach it.

Consequently, while genre-mixing may be on the rise among established writers and those outside the academy, there are practical reasons for emerging writers to select a major genre to specialize in and to adhere to the expectations for that genre. Though some writers may find these external forces restrictive, others will be comforted by the fact that once a writer chooses a particular genre, she "has chosen in some respects a template, a standard . . . an interaction of contexts and an appropriate reflection of those contexts in sets of expectation." And even within the boundaries of the genre, there remains "a range of possible variations, room within the standard to meet the demands of the individual situation and the individual's creative choices" (Devitt 2004, 217).

GRANTS

As Christine Cassidy notes, "grants come in many forms—cash, time, publication, or a combination of all three" (1996, 17). This entry focuses on the first form: money. Interested readers should also consult the entry on "Conferences, Colonies, and Residencies" for grants that focus on organizations primarily offering time and/or a quiet place to write.

"Contests" discusses venues offering award money in conjunction with publication.

"Free money" is every writer's dream, and, once in a very great while, some of it may fall directly into a talented writer's lap. A few grants don't even have to be applied for; they are simply given to writers an organization deems worthy. Most famous, perhaps, is the MacArthur Foundation Fellows Program, the so-called genius grant, which currently pays recipients $500,000 over five years. Beneficiaries of this grant are selected based on "their expertise, accomplishments, and breadth of experience," and they may do whatever they wish with the money (MacArthur Fellows Program 2004). Awards from the Lannan Foundation and the PEN American Center may not be nearly as lavish, but most of their grants are similar to the MacArthur fellowships in that there is no application process.

The majority of grants, however, require that the candidate actually send in an application. Luckily, the grant application process is often easier for creative writers than for others. The applicant fills out the required forms and may have to show some evidence of past accomplishments (writers applying for grants from the National Endowment for the Arts must have a certain number of recent publications to their credit); he then attaches multiple, usually anonymous copies of his work and waits for the results. Ideally, the strongest writers get the grants, although different judges will obviously have different notions of what "strong writing" is. In any case, a careful appraisal of the application form is crucial: "The whole package should be read carefully again and again. And again. And *again*. Each reading will reveal something that was missed during an earlier reading" (Karsh and Fox 2003, 38). Among the easy mistakes grant applicants can avoid are submitting a rejected grant application without making major changes to the new version, assuming that the funding source has no changes in its budget situation from year to year, and spending insufficient time and money in making the grant proposal look as professional as possible (Browning 2001, 245–47).

Most grants come with some restrictions: there are strict deadlines, and only authors living in certain places or writing in certain genres may apply. Especially if it is funded from public coffers, the grant may stipulate how the prize money is used. Yet for all the strings attached to them, grants from national and state governments have become increasingly scarce in the past two decades. The U.S. Congress, which funds the National Endowment for the Arts (NEA), has been controlled by a conservative Republican Congress with a demonstrated suspicion of, if not outright hostility toward, the arts, in particular arts that challenge the status quo. As a result, lawmakers have been increasingly keen to have a say about what will or won't be funded. The NEA has managed to keep afloat in the face of threats to eliminate it altogether in some measure through the agency of conservative poet Dana Gioia, appointed chair of the NEA during the first term of George W. Bush. While Gioia, a former advertising executive, has been criticized by many writers on the left, he has been successful at his job because he is able to speak the language of his budgetary masters.

Overall, though, difficult fiscal times have caused many state and local governments to decrease arts funding dramatically. As of this writing, the statewide budget for the California Arts Council is practically nonexistent. Ironically, though, the Marin Arts Council, representing a wealthy county north of San Francisco, was at the same time offering creative writers grants of $4,000 to $10,000. Because funding for state and local arts organizations is so uncertain, some private foundations have emerged to pick up the slack. The Artist Trust in Seattle (www.artisttrust.org), for instance, only awards grants to writers and artists living in Washington State, but it is not associated with the state government itself. In fine, searching for grants is a hit-and-miss process, but a thorough investigation is likely to turn up some surprising opportunities.

So where do creative writers go to look for grants? The Foundation Center in New York (www.fdncenter.org) is a good place to start. The center has an "Opportunities" page and publishes an inexpensive annual, *Foundation Grants to Individuals*, with more than six thousand listings, many of them relevant to writers. PEN American Center publishes the biannual *Grants and Awards Available to American Writers*, but at a list price of more than $150, most writers will have to use this book in the reference room of their libraries. *The International Directory of Little Magazines and Presses* (Dustbooks), along with *The Writers Market* (Writers Digest Press) and its associated specialty guides—*Poet's Market* and *Novel and Short Story Writers Market*—also contain a section of grant listings. Unfortunately, with up to eighteen months' lag between when the grant information is submitted to the publisher and when it actually appears in print, these listings may be out of date by the time writers read them. And many books with promising titles such as *Funds for Writers* or *Money for Writers* are not updated annually, and so are virtually worthless. Probably the most reliable and up-to-date Web link is the *Poets & Writers*

Grants & Awards page (www.pw.org/mag/grantsawards.htm), which is accessible whether or not a writer subscribes to the magazine. The page lists the deadlines for and briefly describes upcoming grants, contests, and residencies; normally, there is also an e-mail address and link to the grantor's home page.

IDENTITY POLITICS

"Not *politics* again," sighs the white guy in a gray shapeless sweatshirt on the far side of the table. "I'm here to learn to write a novel."

"*Woman* poet?" she whispers audibly to her neighbor during the reading. "Not a *black* poet. Not a *black woman* poet. A *poet.*"

WHO CARES . . . AND WHAT ABOUT?

On tour, at readings, during workshops, the visiting writer fields any number of predictable questions: "How did you arrive at the idea for your poem (novel, play)?" or "How can I get an agent?" or "What time of the day do you write?" or "What contemporary writers have influenced your writing?" In published interviews, questions range over process, product, poetics, the profession, and personal politics, but politics are, for some, the shark under the surface. It is far easier to discuss the first four Ps—including technique and talent and "the business" of writing—than to articulate the way the fifth P—politics, or ideology—affects a text or reflects the way a writer's identity has been formed in response to intersecting communities. The *Writer's Chronicle,* as the publication representing "professional" creative writers, focuses on the first four Ps—particularly the fourth and the situation of writers within English department hierarchies—while *Poets and Writers,* which features regular themed issues focused on groups of writers, more regularly focuses on the fifth P: identity politics.

A perennial conference panel question: "As a self-labeled lesbian feminist, why did you choose a male speaker for your historical persona poem?" The possible subtext here? "Shouldn't you have written and celebrated a woman's life since these have been so often overlooked; as a woman shouldn't you write about women?" Try another version of the question: "Can a white, middle-class, male liberal like you truly present the Vietnamese experience as you attempt to do in these short stories?" The possible subtext here? "Aren't you unfairly appropriating the voice of the 'other'?"

Depending on their understanding of writing as based in aestheticism—which is championed within institutions of higher learning—or on writing as a social process—a focus that reflects the daily realities of many freelance writers—the answer to these questions will vary from author to author: The poem needed to be constructed, with a male speaker, no matter the gender politics of the writer, because *women* during that period *couldn't* take the initiative in a love affair; the story's Vietnamese character *demanded* that the author follow him from the old country to the new. For these writers, art and verisimilitude shape inventiveness. For another poet, representing her own gender's experience, even in historically based poems, might be paramount, and for another novelist, the narrator's character is crucial but can only be developed in the context of what the writer has experienced, researched, and decided he is ethically able to claim; that is, character development may at times be a matter of following but is always a matter, as well, of shaping and deciding. In fact, these and all writers are guided by innumerable other constraints as well: genre (mystery), audience (young adult), assignment (fewer than three thousand words) . . . to say nothing of the ability to put an idea into action.

Put another way:

- The Aestheticists say "Yes"; the artist (and the art) requires a writer to use his or her unique imagination to create new textual realities of the highest order.
- The Political Activists say "Maybe," particularly if one's heart and motives are honorable (often this means green, liberal, socialist, or Marxist).
- The Foundationalists say "No," because *only* someone of Vietnamese heritage may credibly share these events, having earned that right via untransferable experiences.
- The Postmodernists say "Which Vietnamese? American born? Biracial? Still living in country? Fishermen in Louisiana bayous? Old, young, gay, Catholic, of the professional class now fallen on hard times? There is no unitary 'Vietnamese experience but 'many Vietnamese experiences.' And by the way, who is the audience? How will the text be received and read?"

Here, we can recast Mikhail Bakhtin's claim that "[t]he word in language is half someone else's. It becomes 'one's own' only when the speaker populates it with his own intention, his own accent, when he appropriates the word, adapting it to his own semantic and expressive intention" (1975, 294). So too, most theorists and many writers this century acknowledge that identity in culture is always mediated. Writers, if they focus exclusively on constructing creative worlds, risk overlooking their own construction, the myriad experiences and influences that combine to make up the ever-evolving identity each individual recognizes as "self."

RACE, CLASS, GENDER, AND OTHER "OTHERS"

For the theory aversive writer, the term "identity politics" may be less familiar than the critical mantra: raceclassandgender. It doesn't take long as a professional to understand that it was not only during the McCarthy era that the relationship of a writer's politics and activism influenced an agent's willingness to read a script or an editor's decision to recommend a book. Some years certain narrators are bankable, sometimes they are box office poison. Financial gain (particularly for the publishers) can focus the flame of attention down to certain groups or genders or political positions. Because of this, an author's choice of a narrator may be influenced by community relationships and an investment in that community (developing a work to highlight the loss of an ecology or a group of individuals); on a writer's willingness, desire, and ability to be seen as a spokesperson for this (or other) communities (writing out of and to illustrate the black experiences in America); and on a writer's ability to understand and successfully negotiate the power relationships inherent in "the writing business" at the local, national, and global levels.

Equally, and sometimes without fanfare, identity politics may determine creative writers' choices of genres and techniques (feminists refusing traditional genre constraints), shape their literary taste (subscribing to Gay Lesbian Bisexual Transgendered [GLBT] literary journals), impact their values and beliefs (resisting being labeled as a woman poet, editing a book that highlights the writings of authors whose work has been banned in their home countries) support their efforts to form or leave writing communities (starting a new theater to highlight working-class dramatists and drama), and influence their writing theories and teaching practices (teaching poetry in homeless shelters).

Which is to say that a writing life is built upon, grounded in, and shot through with cultural influences and beliefs that we place under this umbrella term. Consider this brief compilation, a litany of "politics r us":

On the Environment

I do not believe we can bypass our relationship to the land if we hope also to improve this culture's relationship to women, to children, to people of color, to the poor, the illiterate, the homeless. . . . We can't be good to each other if we can't even be good to a tree, to a forest.—Rick Bass

On Race

Although I am quite Americanized, my book focuses on many of my feelings and identity and my "Cubanness." I intended for my book to commemorate at least a few aspects of the Cuban psyche (as I know it).—Oscar Hijeulos

Writing becomes a way to be exacting about images in a world where generalizations lead to stereotypes; it is a way of showing how varied and complicated the black experiences (yes, plural) are in this country, on this continent, on this planet.—Colleen McElroy

On Class

I saw that the people I was working with . . .were voiceless in a way. In terms of the literature of the United States they were not being heard. Nobody was speaking for them. And as young people will, you know, I took this foolish vow that I would speak for them and that's what my life would be. And sure enough I've gone and done it.—Phillip Levine

I see my work emerging from some kind of imaginative collectivity, not from solitary genesis. That approach has been nurtured by my working in writers' groups. As a writer, I still strongly identify as a worker . . . partially as a result of my class background.—Valerie Miner

On Gender

"Coming out" is partially a process of revealing something kept hidden, but it is more than that. It is a process of fashioning a self—a lesbian or gay self—that did not exist before coming out began.—Shane Phelan

Did you come out while you were at Penn State?
I don't want to go too much into that. . . .
Why don't you like to talk about it?
I don't want to talk about it because first of all I don't want it to be the central element of my identity as a poet. And secondly, well, it doesn't interest me as

a poet, except when it inadvertently appears in my poetry, the way God may appear, or love may appear, or childhood may appear.—Agha Shahid Ali

Politics r us, but some creative writers aren't comfortable when "the political" appears to trump or influence the "aesthetic." In one pair of quotes above, one writer suggests that exploring gender is an valuable part of creating a (writing) identity while another views gender as a secondary issue, which may or may not arise during composition (Phelan, Shahid Ali). In another pair of quotes, one writer speaks *for* his eclipsed community and another writer speaks *out of* her formative community (Levine, Miner).

Like any group or guild, creative writers have a number of common causes but no absolute consensus. Still, judging from *Poets & Writers* in particular, and the *Writer's Chronicle* to a lesser extent, writers find themselves increasingly obligated and moved to articulate their understandings of how race, class, and gender influence their work. Those who feel there is no need to do this—that the art is all—may focus in this manner because they believe minority positionality is a given: historically, writers have claimed outsider status as rebels, innovators, experimenters, and minority members of certain established coteries and groups by choice. And writing, for many, appeals as a way to champion radical or outsider positions. At the same time, by claiming the radical edge in the "Republic of Letters" (Pease 1990, 110), authors seek to mark themselves as "other," even if this separateness is more a sense of style than substance (bohemian dress and digs and speech and manners—the lesser rebellion of arriving drunk or lecherous or dialectical and *damn*-ing at the reading and insulting the institutional hosts). As a result, in the past and perhaps even more ferociously today, "nationalism is currently being shaped to defend a beleaguered notion of national identity read as white, heterosexual, middle-class, and allegedly threatened by contamination from cultural, linguistic, racial, and sexual differences" (Giroux 1995, 48). For those writers who position themselves not only as aesthetically threatening but also as activists, identity politics include the right to speak—to wage peace and politics as well as poetry—not just the right to learn how to speak.

WHAT *DOES* IT MATTER WHO IS SPEAKING?

The writer who believes that "literary texts are among the most powerful form of cultural discourse, and as such they may attest to, perpetuate, or critique the class divisions prevalent in a given culture at a given period of history" or who understands that her texts may "simultaneously perpetuate and critique the class structure" (Murfin and Ray 1997, 47) understands as well that it does matter who is speaking and that whoever has the stage (the microphone, the authority to write and so to represent) holds certain enviable powers.

In pursuit of authorial power, which powers will writers choose? Political activism or separatism? Are they in support of "others" or *are* they the "other"? Do global communities appear to be a source of cultural pluralism or a scene of contact zones and conflict? Are writers willing to accept and accommodate all other writers in a mélange, believing the whole benefits from all parts, from multivocality? Or does experience tell the seasoned writer that majority and minority will always clash, suggesting that nondominant cultures must always proceed from a regrounding in their own heritage?

Underlying such questions is the larger issue of a writer's worldview, epistemology, and set of intellectual and experiential understandings. Are identity choices made or do they happen, in which case response to events is everything; that is, does writing simply reflect (powerfully, aesthetically) or change (make a difference)? For instance, do all Vietnamese writers have the responsibility to recuperate and revitalize their war-devastated culture? Some would say yes. Charles Johnson describes himself as being "committed to the development of what one might call a genuinely systematic philosophic black American literature, a body of work that explores classical problems and metaphysical questions against the background of black American life" (*Charles Johnson* 1992). But Ray Gonzalez complicates such a position, demanding recuperation for one group while suggesting alignment with other groups: "Latino writing incorporates a great deal of magical realism—though it is not the only style Latinos use—because the culture and the background of many of these writers call for this kind of style. By this I mean that racial, political, and cultural forces in the U.S. fractured Latino artistic sensibilities long ago. In today's slick 'era of the Hispanic,' it is often necessary to write about a world where truth and make-believe clash against one another as they form a more realistic view in a country that, historically, has not been generous to people of color" (Tabor 2001, 36).

John Yau resists cultural stereotyping: "One of the 'codes of authenticity' that Yau has struggled with over the years is the idea of an Asian-American style of writing. 'If you are an Asian American, as I am, many people expect you to write transparent or autobiographical poems,

poems about garlic, soy sauce, ginger etcetera.' In a time when identity politics is the keystone issue for many artists, Yau's concerns turn elsewhere. Instead, he tries—like so many of the abstract artists to whom he's drawn—to circumvent the personal and social codes in search of a purer expression" (Rohrer 2002, 23).

Colson Whitehead recasts the question as the problem: "Well, people talk about pop and commercial African-American fiction—the urban romance, the B-boy novel. And I think that people are always surprised when someone like Paul Beatty or Danzy Senna or me pops up and we're not doing the expected thing, what's been done before, but that's the point of doing this. . . . I guess if I wanted I could write some sort of weird commercial thing . . . well, it wouldn't be weird; it would have to be commercial. But that's not my ambition or aim. I think the white press is always like, Postmodern Black Person? They're more shocked than they should be because there are actually a lot of us who aren't doing what's expected" (Ratiner 1994).

And here's the catch about cultivating a unitary identity—contemporary writers, like all citizens, arise from not one culture but many cultures: many Vietnamese cultures, many Asian American and black American cultures, Hispanic cultures, and European cultures. Hybrids all. And the more hybridity writers experience, the more likely they may be to value and seek to understand what was lost from each formative tributary. In fact, identity politics may be or become the writer's central subject. Garrett Hongo explains: "My project as a poet has been motivated by a search for origins of various kinds, a quest for ethnic and familial roots, cultural identity, and poetic inspiration—all ultimately connected to my need for an active imaginative and spiritual life" (Ling and Cheung 2002).

Identity politics complicates life for those who hold a more monovocal worldview and who seek a more aesthetically oriented identity; or, perhaps, it is the first step on the road to acknowledging complexity in the scene of writing. Consider the student in the workshop who blurts out one frustrating day: "I'm tired of feminists and any 'ists.' I'm a white male and I'm never going to get my fiction placed because only minorities get published these days. I mean, all the journals you look at spotlight this or that special group. Like 'Latin American Jewish Women Writers' or "Gay Writers of Conscience.' Man, I'm just trying to write about alligators and Wakulla County and no one is gonna do a special issue on me."

There is no doubt that at times, movements to include appear based on exclusion, as if the tables have been turned. However, what appear either/or regression is often a step on the journey toward both/and . . . a progression that takes time and commitment. Charles Henry Rowell, founding editor of *Callaloo*, articulates his responsibility to serve the African American community in this manner: "African-American writers, from the time of Phillis Wheatley to today, live in desperate circumstances. We don't have a great number of forums in which to speak. *Callaloo* provides that space for our creative writers, intellectuals, and visual artists. If, like white America, we had hundreds of journals, then you could say that *Callaloo* is trying to do too much. *Callaloo* is a journal of necessity. I don't know if I can repeat that enough. We are a people in desperate need of outlets for our creativity" (Masiki 2003, 25). Here, Rowell argues not for hundreds of journals but for *this* journal. Not all the space but *necessary* spaces.

LOCAL AND GLOBAL

If decisions can be made, no one but the writer can make them. Each has to tally up personal allegiances. And such work takes place in both majority and minority communities. Consider writers who choose political activism. In a review of Carolyn Forché's poetry collection *Angel of History*, her politics and her poetry are discussed together: "For her, the decisive moments of our history are its large-scale calamities: World War II, fascism, the Holocaust, Hiroshima, the Soviet invasion of Czechoslovakia, El Salvador, Chernobyl. All of these events have a ghost-like presence in Forché's poetry. . . . Haunted by the weight of the dead, the volume speaks with a finely elegiac voice that gives it a singular intensity. The characteristic feeling in these poems is one of desolation" (Thompson 1995).

This very haunting concerns others who ask, Who is haunting whom? "The brand 'political poet' was used to both damn and lionize her [Forché's] work. She found herself mired in what she now sees is 'the cyclic debate peculiar to the United States concerning the relationship between poetry and politics. . . . And I felt that the debate wasn't a useful one, that the grounds were reductive and simplistic and unhelpful to anyone who wanted to think about the responsibility of citizens, much less writers. . . . There was no notion that language might be inherently political or perhaps ideologically charged whatever the subject matter and even when the person isn't aware of [it]'" (Ratiner 1994).

For some in the creative writing community, Forché's work is opportunistic even though interviews detail her active, on-site involvement in many of the cultures she writes about. If Forché were an ethnographer, not a poet, similar critiques would arise—particularly regarding the amount and quality of time she has spent "in the field," collecting her data, compiling her notes. For these days postmodern ethnographers are suggesting approaches similar to that advocated by Gayatri Spivak, who "asks that researchers stop trying to know the Other or give voice to the Other . . . and listen, instead, to the plural voices of those Othered, as co-constructors and agents of knowledge" (Fine 1994, 75). Some postmodern ethnographers attempt shared authorship, coauthoring field reports with informants in the effort to co-construct. Such a practice will take longer-to-forever for activist creative writers due to the field's long-standing proscription against coauthoring. While we are not suggesting that Forché coauthor with "The Colonel," it might be worth considering the degree to which she has been able to create poetic polyvocality: the goal of many involved with identity politics. Perhaps this could become one useful evaluative criterion.

When creative writers choose such a route—listening for voices and working toward social justice, no matter how difficult to attain—they may, like Maxine Hong Kingston, do so from the belief that "[a]n artist changes the world by changing consciousness and changing the atmosphere by means of language. So I have to use and invent a beautiful, human, artistic language of peace" (Perry 1993, 173). They may, like Nega Mezlekia, consider writing and writers to have dual functions and multiple responsibilities: "Writing shouldn't be entertaining only. It should be informative as well. Particularly for a person like me who has lived under very, very terrible regimes, he or she has an obligation to bring this to light" (Eiben 2002).

Even writers who cannot be optimistic about the possibilities of creating a socially just world may believe that multivocality continues to trump monovocality and that cross-cultural dialogue is of the highest value. These writers seek to understand rather than to voice for. Sensitivity of this sort could be modeled for novice writers, in part, through workshop exercises. If workshop participants were asked to help peers understand, deepen, complicate, and improve an "alien" voice in a text instead of dismissing it or embracing it out of hand, issues of authorial appropriation might be better understood, resolved, and resisted.

BORN TO WRITE: AESTHETICS VIS-Á-VIS IDENTITY

Hard-working writers may shy away from the degree of theoretical and political commitment overviewed in this entry, given that there is so little time to learn to write well and excel. Or writers may be provoked to ask again, "But what does this have to do with writing? I want to prac-

tice writing, not politics—to be a novelist, not a working-class novelist."
Creative writers in the United States who vie to be recognized for their
literary excellence tend to invest deeply in aestheticism, that familiar and
enduring nineteenth-century movement "that insisted that art need not
be moral to have value" (Murfin and Ray 1997, 4). For these individuals,
a writer's desire to "do art" and to "do good" are often at odds. Consider
another series of quotes, some from the same writers listed previously,
which illustrate this tension:

It's Not Enough

As witness, I know there has always been a political element in my life. I've
always been interested in matters of political conscience and of fairness. There
was a time when I would forgive many poems because I liked their sense of
compassion and humanity, even if the poems were not very good, particularly
when I agreed with their politics. It took me a long time to realize that good
politics don't necessarily mean good poetry.—Agha Shahid Ali

It's Less Important

If you're a writer, you're a writer and if you're any good at all you get beyond
terms like "southern" or "feminist."—Susan Richards Shreve

You don't want to make art about your color, your race, your culture, or your
community. You want to use your community, your race, and your culture to
make a piece of art.—Charles Henry Rowell

How do you feel about being defined as a writer of color or other categorization?
I think it can be a convenient tool at times, but it's finally very boring as a
writer. It's interesting that others talk about it, but when you are writing I think
you should only be committed to how good you can make your poem.—Agha
Shahid Ali

It's Inevitable

Part of the reason I wouldn't call myself a Jewish writer is because I'm not trying deliberately to write Jewish themes. My Jewishness is like the wallpaper in
every room I've been in.—Susan Fromberg Schaeffer

I write because I must. . . . if you write from a black experience, you're writing
from a universal experience as well.—Sonia Sanchez

It's Consequential

Let's just say that though I am a woman, and though much of what I've learned
that I will say here I learned as a consequence of being a woman in my body

and in this culture; nevertheless, I still use the concept of gender as an organizing principle and metaphor for other kinds of marginalization, which I further define not as absolutes but rather as positions along never-fixed continua, stretching not two but many ways from an imaginary center we recognize largely by instinct. Principle, metaphor, position: Gender as a function, which can become inclusive if we are not stingy with our experiences and meanings. . . . Speaking as a woman, what I would say is that it is never enough to know what we know; we also need always to know how we know it, and, most especially, to know what we don't know. To know the knowing, as well as the not.—Katharine Haake

Some writers know their positions and their politics from the moment an image arises, or a character turns around in the mind's eye, or the pen first touches journal and fingers a keyboard. For others, identity evolves more slowly and requires developing the humility to "know the knowing, as well as the not" to which Katharine Haake alludes. Shane Phelan suggests: "If we ask why certain metanarratives function at certain times and places, we find that the answer does not have to do with the progress of a unitary knowledge but rather with shifting structures of meaning, power, and action" (1993, 767).

For a writer, considering politics means asking not only "Will *my* work last?" but also "What other works have lasted and why?" Understanding our positions means asking what we don't know. If the personal is political, then the person's art is likely to be as well. Identity question breeds identity question: Why do class prejudice, sexism, ageism, and racism exist—if they do—in our workshops and classrooms and contests? Why is there so little tolerance for diversity of this sort within a population that claims to value the original, the new, the radical? Why should it be important that the aesthetic value of "art" be so regularly reaffirmed? Why is dialogue regarding politics, theory, and pedagogy often avoided? What are the stakes here? What are your answers?

IMAGE AND METAPHOR

"Show, Don't Tell" is the motto of many a creative writing teacher (and program), and at the heart of that dictum is the primacy of the image, the "mental picture" our mind sees when we read about something that has an analogue in the real world. Interestingly, as Kristie Fleckenstein points out, while we can disconnect image from language—"we do this every night in our dreams"—without language, "we cannot do anything with those dreams except experience them. Imagistic *is* logic lodges us in the moment. To be tugged out of the present, to be known as anything other than life as it is lived, we need the *as if* logic of language" (2003, 32). In short, the "embodied literacy" of an image is more complex than our intuitive grasp of imagery would initially suggest. There is a double logic at work: we "see" an image through the medium of language, yet it is difficult to locate just where that image exists: "An image is not something that we perceive; it is a process that we enact" (24).

Ontological and epistemological complications aside, the image has a long, impressive history throughout world literature. It would be impossible, for example, to conceive of East Asian poetry—of the haiku and senryu and tanka—without the image. In America, the continuing ascendancy of the image (as opposed to the abstraction) can be attributed in part to early-twentieth-century imagist poets like Ezra Pound, H. D., and William Carlos Williams. Of course, even at their most imagistic, these writers themselves never stuck *solely* to the image—language doesn't work that way—but contemporary creative writers still retain their belief that a piece of work isn't quite finished until the reader can see (or smell, taste, hear, and feel) whatever the writer is imagining.

M. H. Abrams identifies three main uses of the word imagery. In its narrowest sense, an image signifies "descriptions of visual objects and scenes" (1981, 79). This definition makes sense insofar as the word "image" refers to something that can only be recognized by the eye. In a much broader sense, imagery "(that is, 'images' taken collectively) is used to signify the objects and qualities of sense perception referred to in a poem or other work of literature, whether by literal description, by allusion, or in the analogues . . . used in its similes and metaphors" (78). In this context, just about any reference—visual, auditory, tactile, olfactory, gustatory, or kinesthetic—that is *not* an abstraction can be called an image.

However, Abrams argues that the most common usage of imagery refers specifically to figurative language, in particular metaphors and similes. As every creative writer knows, a metaphor says that one thing *is* another, while a simile merely suggests that one thing is *like* another. Simile is sometimes considered a poor cousin of metaphor, but for all practical purposes the two figures work the same rhetorical trick, comparing one unlike thing with another. Of course, similes and metaphors are also the basis for clichés, figurative language that has become stale through overuse. To describe the relationship between the thing being referred to and the object of comparison, I. A. Richards coined the terms "tenor" and "vehicle" (1936). The tenor is the subject to which the metaphor is applied, and the vehicle is the metaphor itself. For example, in these lines by Indian poet Manohar Shetty, "The garden / Rake of her eyelashes," eyelashes are the tenor and garden rake is the vehicle.

Metaphor from this vantage is more concerned with style (q.v.) than with conception. Yet because language is such an abstract and protean entity, it's not surprising that we need concrete images to help us get a handle on it (to use an implied metaphor that has since become cliché). As Lakoff and Johnson point out in *Metaphors We Live By* (1980), metaphor isn't only a way to gloss and illustrate experience. Metaphors don't simply reflect the way we look at the world, they can actually *shape* that process, and that shaping is intimately intertwined with how we remember the world: "Our memories are often, or perhaps always, metaphors: we have a particular picture in our minds of a house in our childhood which stands for many years of experience of family life; we sum up the dead in certain intense images from the past" (Anderson 1996, 59). Some linguists believe metaphor is ingrained in our thought processes, and usually we are not aware of the metaphors that direct our thoughts and actions. These basic metaphors permeate our language, Lakoff and Johnson believe, and when they are scrutinized they provide clues about the values and assumptions underlying our words. Meryl Altman argues that the benefit of Lakoff and Johnson's approach "is not just that it is true, as you will discover if you try to write or say something without using any metaphors, but also that it enables us to observe the political operation of a particular metaphor on many levels at once, from the most elevated literary discourse to the most banal conversation, thus underlining the social importance of this inquiry" (1990, 500). Altman goes on to illustrate how the metaphors we use inevitably become a part of the power struggles we engage in.

Metaphors, then, don't just occur *in* creative writing. Many writing teachers find metaphors are essential to talk *about* their teaching philosophies. Indeed, the history of writing instruction is a history of shifting metaphors, and many of the most influential approaches have been metaphorical. The recent history of writing instruction has yielded various attempts to describe the field by designating metaphors that show basic differences in teaching philosophy. As Philip Arrington puts it, "Today, our root-metaphor for composing is 'process,' but we argue about the type of 'process' we are studying. If we examine them carefully, we find our arguments are really about the tropes we use to describe and explain that process" (1986, 326). Pointing out that we need to study carefully "the imagery embedded in our own professional language," Ellen Strenski explores the implications of viewing writing instruction in terms of "the geopolitical model of conquest" or "the religious model of communities." She believes we shouldn't allow ourselves to invest too heavily in one or the other, and that we need to take teaching metaphors seriously: "Metaphors have consequences. They reflect and shape our attitudes and, in turn, determine our behavior" (1989, 137). In a series of articles, Barbara Tomlinson (1988) explores and classifies the range of metaphors used by published writers to explain their work. And Lad Tobin (1989) has argued that composition teachers should analyze student metaphors for writing, engaging students in dialogue about metaphors that direct their composing. Focusing attention on explicit (as opposed to implicit) metaphors by writers, whether generated by professionals or novices, can be a powerful teaching tool. Peter Elbow's use of growing and cooking metaphors in *Writing without Teachers* (1973, 1998) introduced an influential set of analogies for composition and creative writing. Since then, writing textbooks have relied heavily on metaphor, and a number of articles and books, including Wendy Bishop's *Working Words*, have examined, often critically, specific "root" metaphors about writing. So dominant are metaphors in discussions of rhetoric and writing instruction that Wayne Booth, one of the most important thinkers on the subject, jokes, "I have in fact extrapolated with my pocket calculator to the year 2039; at that point there will be more students of metaphor than people" (1978, 47).

MFA (MASTER OF FINE ARTS)

The Master of Fine Arts in creative writing is a studio degree that invites comparison with terminal fine arts degrees in dance, theater, and the visual arts. Consequently, the MFA privileges writers as artists while minimizing their standing as academics. Although nearly all MFA writing programs emphasize participation in workshops (along with enrollment in at least a few literature courses), degree requirements vary widely. Options range from low-residency MFAs, in which most teaching is conducted electronically, through the mail, and via telephone and can be completed in two years, to programs that require sixty or more semester hours of coursework and may necessitate up to four or five years in school. In nearly all cases, though, the final product is a book-length work of poetry, fiction or creative nonfiction, or a full-length play. As is the case with a creative dissertation (q.v.), MFA students typically defend their thesis before a panel of faculty members before the degree is granted.

For many years, in its "Guidelines for Teachers of Writing," the Associated Writing Programs (q.v.) specifically endorsed the MFA as *the* terminal degree and "the appropriate credential for the teacher of creative writing" (Fenza et al. 1999, 317). However, recently the organization changed that endorsement to support both the MFA *and* the PhD with a creative writing emphasis as terminal degrees. If the MFA was once the cornerstone of the creative writing industry, it has begun to look as though its foundation is sinking. Indeed, while the vast majority of creative writing professors in American colleges and universities hold the MFA as their terminal degree, a number of factors have conspired to make these teachers wonder if it may now be too late to save their professional credentials from obsolescence (see "Creative Dissertation" for an alternate view of the situation outlined in this entry).

As D. G. Myers shows in his exhaustive study *The Elephants Teach: Creative Writing since 1880* (1996), American creative writing programs in the early part of the twentieth century benefited from a progressive movement in education that argued that students could become more effective writers when they were engaged in writing that maximized their expressiveness. The valorization of creative writing in both secondary schools and institutions of higher learning bore its most significant fruit at the University of Iowa in the 1930s. Under the directorship of Norman Foerster, the Iowa Writers' Workshop offered the first Master of Fine Arts degree in creative writing, with Paul Engle, later director of the workshop, the first American to receive a graduate degree in creative writing for a book of poems (see "Workshop"). Foerster believed that the writers who made the literature were more than qualified to teach it, and that belief found widespread acceptance from the 1940s on. Ironically, though, the antiacademic bias that has become the MFA's millstone was there from the very beginning. In one speech, Foerster declared that "I would have a writer go to college . . . but I would not have him become what we call an 'academic'" (Myers 1996, 134).

Nevertheless, many writers did go on to become academics. Poets especially, because they could not earn a living wage from their work the way novelists could, flocked to the university, and even a partial list of these writer-teachers makes for an impressive (though gender-biased) list of postwar poets: Randall Jarrell, John Crowe Ransome, John Berryman, Howard Nemerov, John Ciardi, Robert Hayden, Anthony Hecht, Karl Shapiro, Philip Booth, Donald Justice, and many others. As Jed Rasula (1996) points out, the earliest of these writers held MA degrees in literature (the MFA was not yet the dominant degree it would become), but there was an MFA boom in the 1960s and 1970s, propelled by a high demand for creative writing classes, which resulted in an abundance of jobs for writers and a shortage of writers with graduate degrees. In 1967, the growth in creative writing programs was given a professional imprimatur with the foundation of the Associated Writing Programs by R. V. Cassill. In "Theory, Creative Writing, and the Impertinence of History," R. M. Berry sites some rather astonishing figures: "John Barth has estimated that by 1984 Creative Writing programs had turned out over 75,000 literary practitioners . . . and Liam Rector, former director of the Associated Writing Programs, estimated in 1990 that around 3,000 poets and fiction writers were graduating from Creative Writing programs each year. (For comparison, doctoral programs in English average around 800 graduates yearly)" (1994, 57). Through the end of the millennium, most of these graduates would have had MFAs: the ninth edition of *The AWP Official Guide to Writing Programs* published in 1999 lists eighty-three member programs conferring the MFA degree.

Unfortunately, as more and more young writers went from undergraduate to graduate programs in creative writing, scarcity replaced plenty for those who hoped to become teachers. Today, a tenure-track job in creative writing at any reasonably solvent institution of higher education is likely to attract anywhere from several hundred to a thousand applicants, many of whom are more than qualified to fill the position.

One response by English departments to the changed circumstances has been to give administrators what they have wanted all along: PhDs. Programs offering the English degree with a creative dissertation grew almost sixfold in fifteen years: from just five in 1984 to twenty-nine in 1998. Perversely, some of these programs grant both the MFA and the PhD, pitching the MFA as a terminal degree to one group of students while simultaneously selling the PhD with a creative dissertation to another. Indeed, the dearth of academic jobs and the complete "identification of poet with teacher," in Dana Gioia's words (1991, 102), has led some creative writers, even those with MFAs, to give up on the MFA as a terminal degree.

If this resignation gains widespread acceptance—as it appears to be doing—there would, in fact, be several notable advantages. For one, tenured writers with guilty consciences would no longer have to pretend that they were training their future replacements. Programs could openly market the degree to people who weren't quite sure what they wanted to do with their lives and just needed a few years to kick back, hang out, take things easy. (Cynics would say that these are the very people who *are* currently attracted to MFA programs.) This creative-writing-as-vacation approach would be a much easier sell than trying to convince serious students that the MFA is a necessary way station, albeit a very time-con-suming and expensive one, on the road to the PhD. It would help counter the charge of bad faith by those who accuse institutions of marketing the MFA as a terminal degree despite their belief that it is not. Finally, it would relieve proponents of the PhD from their convoluted attempts to denigrate the MFA thesis in comparison with the creative dissertation, even when both are nearly identical book-length works of original cre-ative writing.

Certainly, job candidates who hold the PhD in creative writing would prefer that their degree be given preferential treatment by hiring commit-tees. Similarly, English departments who have invested heavily in adver-tising their options for a creative dissertation have a significant financial stake in the outcome of this debate. Nevertheless, the MFA is not likely to disappear overnight, and when one considers not only the many talented students who still receive MFAs each year but the many experienced teachers with MFAs who have no plans to return to graduate school, it's worth investigating a few ideas that might help at least partially postpone the demise of this terminal degree.

In *Radical Presence: Teaching as Contemplative Practice,* Mary Rose O'Reilley writes, "How can I honor both the intuitive and analytical aspects of my mind, [while] silencing neither?" (1998, 3). MFAs generally do a good job of honoring the former; it is the latter they need to focus on. One of the obvious ways MFAs can increase respect for the degree is by becoming more active scholars who publish not just creative work but also articles and books in literature and rhetoric and cultural studies. Similarly, teaching classes other than creative writing forces MFAs to think more critically about their pedagogical assumptions. While this transition to a new, expanded role may be contentious at larger universities, rare is the faculty member at a small college *in any discipline* who doesn't eventually teach courses for which she has had relatively little graduate school preparation. The institution relies, in large part, on the faculty member's native intelligence and willingness to learn, and neither of these qualities is exclusive to PhDs.

Moreover, since the struggle of MFAs to retain some dignity and power in the early part of the twenty-first century looks very much like a class conflict, unity among degree holders is essential. (The MFA Special Interest Group at the Conference on College Composition and Communication was founded with this goal in mind.) MFAs must respect each other rather than capitulate to the conventional wisdom that the holder of a PhD is in some sense an essentially superior being—an assumption that is particularly galling when it is made by PhDs putatively committed to Marxism, multiculturalism, and other egalitarian ideologies. Stuart Hall is right, "hegemony is maintained when dominant classes 'succeed in framing all competing definitions within their range,'" (1977, 77) so when they are involved in hiring decisions that include equally qualified candidates whose only difference is their degree, MFAs must step forward and refused to be marginalized.

Finally, if there is strength in numbers (as compositionists have learned), creative writing MFAs should connect with MFAs in other departments on campus. They should look for common ground with and mutual support from actors, painters, sculptors, and dancers. At the same time that they expand their credentials as scholars, MFAs must also remember their roots as artists. It is, after all, the "F" in MFA that originally convinced administrators that the degree was terminal.

PEDAGOGY

Pedagogy is the profession, art, and science of teaching. However, for a keyword with such an apparently innocuous definition, pedagogy inspires in many teachers of creative writing a surprising level of fear and loathing. This loathing—perhaps "apathy" is closer to the truth—is rooted to a large degree in American writers' very real *professional* knowledge that most four-year colleges and universities reward publication rather than teaching. As every undergraduate soon learns, faculty members at prestigious institutions are there because their writing has been showered with honors; venerated presses have published their books. Candidates for college creative writing positions don't get the "best" jobs for designing innovative classroom assignments: they are hired because they have entered a book contest and won first prize. From this perspective, of course, there is no need to learn how to teach well. In fact, doing so will only interfere with one's writing time. Ergo, only writers with weak creative publications have to worry about pedagogy.

If the current system of hiring and retaining creative writers makes pedagogy a nasty word for many aspiring poets and novelists, we can find further support for that point of view in the word's etymology. Pedagogy comes from "pedagogue," which is derived from the Greek word *paidagogus,* meaning a boy's tutor. Some scholars claim that a pedagogue was not even a tutor but simply the attendant who led the child to school. A renowned creative writer teaching graduate students at a major university can hardly be expected to embrace a field of study that is linguistically linked with early childhood education. Indeed, over time the word "pedagogue" has taken on increasingly distasteful associations, so that, according to the *Oxford English Dictionary,* the word is now normally used "in a more or less contemptuous or hostile sense, with implication of pedantry, dogmatism, or severity."

When she began writing *Released into Language: Options for Teaching Creative Writing* in the late 1980s, Wendy Bishop soon found that most of her senior colleagues shared this contempt for pedagogy. Bishop had just finished an MFA in creative writing and was turning her attention toward a PhD in rhetoric and composition. Yet as she worked on her dissertation, she discovered that the ideas and methods she was learning about and applying to her beginning composition courses also worked effectively with her beginning creative writing classes, and she soon came to believe that separating creative writing from composition and rhetoric was an unnatural act. After all, she reasoned, in the eighteenth century—to name just one obvious example—writers wrote across genres all the time and without giving the matter a second thought. A work of "literature" could as easily be an essay by Johnson or Swift as a poem by Dryden or Pope. Indeed, Johnson and Swift also wrote poetry; Dryden and Pope wrote prose. Writers certainly kept the boundaries of genre in mind, but they switched genres whenever their primary mode of writing was inadequate for the occasion at hand.

However, in American higher education of the twentieth and early twenty-first centuries, pedagogy and creative writing were seen as, at best, distant cousins. Rather than studying the latest achievements in education or in rhetoric and composition, many current creative writing teachers have, ironically, looked centuries into the past for their models. These instructors see pedagogy as an *art*. In the tradition of Renaissance painters, they have invited apprentices into their studios—the MFA, after all, is a "studio degree." Novelist Nicholas Delbanco situates the master-apprentice relationship all the way back in the Middle Ages, viewing college-level education as a version of the craftsmen's guilds: "After a period of learning, the writer receives a kind of walking paper that permits him to post as a journeyman-laborer and enter the guild; then, ideally, he has the chance of becoming a master craftsman and having people report to him" (1994, 59). In this workshop (q.v.) model, trainees both marvel at their masters' skills and scrutinize and emulate the methods by which the older craftspeople generate their effects. An artist before she is anything else, the teacher relies on her individual genius to teach her students. Rather than formulating a systematic method of instruction that can be applied to all, or most, of her students, she simply follows her muse, imparting insights as they occur to her, before heading home to her "real work." According to Hans Ostrom, the attitude of such writers is "'Out of my way—I have classes to get through and novels to write'" (1994, xiii).

The *science* of pedagogy, however, would argue that these master teachers' assumptions that most of their students ultimately won't measure up may be a self-fulfilling prophecy. According to George Hillock, a teacher's effectiveness is directly related to his belief that his students' work will improve: "Teachers . . . who are not optimistic about their students will have no reason to change. Because [these teachers] so seldom engage in reflective practice, they will have little evidence of any need to change. And because they have low expectations of their students, they will not be surprised when their students fail to learn" (1999, 134). While Hillock is referring primarily to secondary school teachers, he might just as easily be talking about any number of jaded Famous Writers at graduate creative writing programs who believe that—in Hans Ostrom's words—"pedagogy is not considered important enough to conceptualize—to bother with intellectually" (1994, xii). Yet by remaining ignorant of other ways of teaching and adhering to a single method of instruction—close reading of student texts—these workshop-oriented teachers miss out on the opportunity to reach *all* their students. To give just one example, researchers have found that while the workshop method may work well with visual and auditory learners, kinesthetic learners—those whose cognitive functions are best triggered by *doing*—are not well served by simply sitting around in a large circle for anywhere from one to three hours.

Moreover, while this hierarchic model may have functioned effectively centuries ago in class-bound, aristocratic Europe, it is problematic in the democratic and multicultural twenty-first century. One obvious inconvenience is that the master-apprentice system tends to reproduce an image of "genius" held by those in power. Unconsciously or not, masters seek apprentices who are like themselves. In fact, the master's function might be said chiefly to cull out those who do not possess genius. Pedagogy through this lens is survival of the fittest. Those who can't be trained to think and write in the accepted patterns are ultimately rejected. Radical (or critical or liberatory or emancipatory) pedagogy rejects this exclusionist principle and seeks to better the lot of the many rather than just to validate the elite few. Teachers committed to a radical pedagogy address "urgent social problems rooted in race and gender inequality and cultural conflict. . . . [They have] an ambitious aim in enlightening students to recognize the silence of oppression and to reinforce empowerment of individual voices" (Flores 2004).

Liberatory pedagogy, championed by Brazilian educator Paolo Freire in his book *The Pedagogy of the Oppressed* (1970), opposes the "banking" model of education, in which teachers "deposit" knowledge in their students, who are like banks receiving money. At the end of the term, students simply return this knowledge—in the form of essays or exams—with occasionally a small amount of interest into the bargain. Freire detested this relationship because teachers have all the power. Students are discouraged from questioning the information they are given; instead, they regurgitate it (to shift the metaphor) without much thought, and are purged, no longer having anything to do with the knowledge that might have transformed them. With the goal of encouraging radical social change, Freire argued for a method of teaching that would force those being taught to be aware of and, more importantly, critique what they were taught. He believed that this process would allow the powerless to become agents of social change: "the oppressors, who oppress, exploit and rape by virtue of their power, cannot find in this power the strength to liberate either the oppressed or themselves. Only power that springs from the weakness of the oppressed will be sufficiently strong to free both" (26). The Freireian pedagogy led to a change across the entire educational curriculum, but it was especially powerful in English studies. At many institutions of higher learning, a new emphasis on teaching work by writers from historically oppressed groups was matched by an equally aggressive push to hire these writers as classroom teachers. Many established teachers found themselves examining their own prejudice, exposing, as bell hooks says, "the covert conservative political underpinnings shaping the content of material in the classroom, as well as the ways in which ideologies of domination informed the ways thinkers teach and act in the classroom" (2003, 1).

Bishop herself acutely felt this sense of disempowerment in her own graduate education: "To begin with, there was not enough room in the world for great poets of the first rank. Competition was necessarily fierce for the few places in the pantheon for women who were writers (writers who were women?). It was understood: If you make it, you're a poet; if you fail, you're a woman poet" (Bishop and Ostrum 1994, 282). The essentially patriarchal nature of the master-apprentice model led many women creative writers to look for different roles for themselves and alternative methods of teaching their students. Feminist theory incorporates "diverse and sometimes contradictory discursive practices" while still emphasizing "the importance of women's individual and shared experience and their political struggle in the world" (Treichler 1986, 99). In order to harness—rather than to ignore—these contradictory practices, many feminist theorists turned to a hybrid scholarship of teaching, one that, as Jan Zlotnik Schmidt notes, urges "the intertwining of the private and the public; the autobiographical and the theoretical" (1998, 2). Nancy Miller calls this "personal criticism"—"an explicitly autobiographical performance within the act of criticism" (1991, 2). Bishop writes in *Teaching Lives*: "If we accept the job description of writing teacher, then theory and practice, the public and the personal, must form a web, a network, a circle, an interconnected chain, a dialogue, a mutual refrain in our teaching, a tapestry, quilt or momentarily well-constructed whole" (1997, 320). Katherine Haake similarly believes that critical theory by feminist creative writers should be "braided," "multidiscursive," "narrative," "self-conscious," "ironic," and "oblique" (2000, 15).

In Haake's classes, theory plays as important a role as the students' own writing. Students repeatedly examine their work through the lens of critical theory. They begin to question and resist assumptions that they have long taken for granted. Indeed, Haake's students learn that the logo- and phallocentric power structure may be just as dominant in supposedly "liberal" creative writing classrooms as it is elsewhere in American society. Haake writes:

> Having no theory is a dangerous theory because it reinscribes the structures we can't see that nonetheless contain us.
>
> And as always, much of the power of ideology is that it is invisible.
>
> Theory helps make the invisible visible. Creative writers need it, even if it gives them hives. (2000, 240)

As Vincent Leitch observes, out of such thinking "comes a certain strategic stance and practice for pedagogy. Nothing is ordained, natural, unalterable, monumental. Everything is susceptible to critique and transformation" (1986, 53).

Eve Shelnutt, while not as deeply invested in poststructuralist critical theory, runs a creative writing course with no workshops at all. Instead, students spend their time developing an extensive vocabulary that they use to talk about model stories by professional writers. Shelnutt claims that "students certainly need to be conversant with [critical theory's] major themes and be able to accept that it's out there. . . . to ignore and be disdainful and aggressive against those theories is akin to acting as if abstract painting had never existed, or as if we had not music prior to Schoenberg. We would never in music or art take the positions we as writers take against critical theory" (1994, 200).

If creative writing pedagogy has so obviously benefited from critical theory and composition studies, surely it must be a growing academic field. After all, there are so many questions to answer: What is the role of the audience in the composition of a work of literature? Do writers create work primarily for their own satisfaction or to win the approval of their readers? To what extent are authorial voices a fiction? To what degree should creative writers foreground their political passions? their class? gender? sexual orientation? theoretical biases? And on and on. Unfortunately, in most creative writing programs, answering these questions is deemed far less important than honing a writer's publications skills.

Kristen Nichols explains the lack of emphasis on pedagogy this way: "First and foremost, the goal of [a graduate creative writing program] is to educate and equip writers, not teachers." She notes also that "writers who teach in MFA programs often aren't well-versed as teachers themselves. They don't have to be because they are surrounded by students who are also aspiring writers and who are capable of creating and

participating in an effective classroom discussion without very much guidance from a teacher" (2004, 14). As a result, creative writing pedagogy currently remains a small and relatively unvisited academic backwater. Other
than in very rare instances—such as the Certificate in Teaching Creative
Writing offered by Antioch University in Los Angeles—most institutions of
higher learning do not offer graduate instruction in creative writing pedagogy. In the absence of such courses, motivated graduate students who want
to teach are generally left to their own devices to cobble together a theory
of how students learn and how teachers ought to teach. Those who work
as teaching assistants in university composition courses will pick up some
rhetorical theory in their required classes. Those enrolled in literary theory
classes will learn a little more. But they will be swimming upstream.

Nevertheless, despite continued resistance to and distrust of pedagogy,
there is hope. The many emerging creative writers with a passion for
teaching may, pragmatically, keep their focus on their writing. Yet they are
likely, also, to have more interest in pedagogy than their precursors, to
agree with bell hooks that "the classroom with all its limitations remains a
location of possibility": "In that field of possibility we have the opportunity
to labor for freedom, to demand of ourselves and our comrades, an open-
ness of mind and heart that allows us to face reality even as we collectively
imagine ways to move beyond boundaries, to transgress. This is education
as the practice of freedom" (1994, 207).

POETRY

Probably the most significant development in American poetry over the
past fifty years has been the eruption of writing by women and people
of color. "Eruption," "explosion," "outburst"—any of these nouns would
be appropriate, suggesting as they do a force long suppressed suddenly
finding its way into the open air. The twentieth century, for all its hor-
rors, was also a time when previously silenced poets became vocal. Many
of these poets addressed past and current injustices in their poetry; they
challenged, adapted, and adopted the dominant poetic voices imposed on
them by white writers. But their poetry wasn't only about prejudice and discrimination (see "Identity Politics"). The whole range of daily life—both
dramatic and quotidian—found expression among writers being fully

heard for the first time. The *cuentos* passed down to Latino/a writers from parents and grandparents found their way into poetry, as did the myths of Native American poets and the immigration stories of Asian Americans. African American poetry is, as Clarence Major notes, "vast . . . diverse and often brilliant" (1996, xxx). Among the important recent anthologies collecting this work are *The Garden Thrives: Twentieth-Century African-American Poetry* (Major 1996), *Paper Dance: 55 Latino Poets* (Cruz et al. 2000), *Harper's Anthology of Twentieth Century Native American Poetry* (Niatum 1988), and *The Open Boat: Poems from Asian America* (Hongo 1993).

Women poets, likewise, have found new, more attentive audiences. Adrienne Rich led the way in the 1960s and 1970s, as her poetry evolved from the well-mannered verse selected by W. H. Auden for the Yale Series of Younger Poets to the radically charged lyrics of *Leaflets* (1969) and *Diving into the Wreck* (1973). Interested readers should turn to *No More Masks: An Anthology of Twentieth-Century American Women Poets* (Howe 1993), *A Formal Feeling Comes: Poems in Form by Contemporary Women* (Finch 1994), and *Claiming the Spirit Within: A Sourcebook of Women's Poetry* (Sewell 1996), though these books anthologize but a sliver of the outstanding poetry published in the last half century. Equally important are the ever-growing number of volumes in which women poets articulate their aesthetics and their relation to literary history. Noteworthy collections include *Where We Stand* (Bryan 1994), *Dwelling in Possibility* (Prins, Shrieber, and Benstock 1998), and *We Who Love to Be Astonished* (Hinton and Hogue 2001). The voices of women of color have been an especially welcome change to the poetic landscape. Ai, Gwendolyn Brooks (the first African American to win the Pulitzer Prize in poetry), Lorna Dee Cervantes, Wanda Coleman, Rita Dove (the first African American to be chosen America's Poet Laureate), Joy Harjo, Audre Lourde, Naomi Shihab Nye, and Sonia Sanchez are all significant American poets.

"Poetry is mostly hunches," John Ashbery has said, but those hunches are based on more than instinct: they are calculated attempts to create a communication between one person and another. Everyone who has ever written a poem, no matter how ill conceived or cliché-ridden, knows this desire to connect with someone else. Indeed, nonpoets primarily interact with poetry on special occasions. A man writes a poem to his wife for their anniversary. A daughter buys a greeting card for her mother's birthday. For all their sentimentality, these "Hallmark moments" are part of a long tradition of occasional, celebratory poems: epithalamiums for marriage, elegies for funerals, odes for military victories and defeats.

Poetry, from this angle, looks like a made thing. The poet is an architect, an artisan. As the word's etymology suggests, the poet is one who gathers and heaps up ideas and images in an artful way. Indeed, in the 1980s this model seemed particularly appealing to younger poets like Molly Peacock, Phillis Levin, Andrew Hudgins, and Brad Leithauser, who joined the ranks of established formalists such as Mona Van Duyn, Marilyn Hacker, Richard Wilbur, John Hollander, and Anthony Hecht. The younger writers called themselves the New Formalists, and they argued that poems that didn't wrestle with meter and take advantage of at least some of the elements of traditional English prosody weren't really poems at all. These poets invested themselves in villanelles and sonnet sequences. They pontificated, sometimes very eloquently, as in Timothy Steele's *Missing Measures* (1990) and Mark Jarman's *Body and Soul* (2002). They started presses like Story Line and magazines such as *Edge City* and the *New Formalist*. Many believed that the best poems were not only in meter and rhyme, they also told a story. R. S. Gwynn's anthology *New Expansive Poetry* (1999), for instance, argued for the importance of narrative poetry, and several book-length poems appeared that put theory into practice: Vikram Seth's *The Golden Gate* (1986), Frederick Turner's *Genesis* (1988), Gertrude Schnackenberg's *The Throne of Labdacus* (2001).

Granted, the assumption made by some of their detractors that New Formalist poetics inevitably means conservative politics isn't always true. Annie Finch, for instance, advances the idea of "multiformalism," which includes avant-garde traditions. Nevertheless, many New Formalists lean decidedly toward the political right. In May 1991, Dana Gioia published an essay in the *Atlantic Monthly* entitled "Can Poetry Matter?" which seems worth returning to since in 2003 Gioia was named head of the National Endowment for the Arts by George W. Bush. "Poets are like priests in a town of agnostics," Gioia writes (1991, 2), and the simile is instructive. For Gioia, a conservative Catholic, the implication is that poems can be judged against a universal moral code. Moreover, it is not surprising that Gioia, who worked in marketing at the time he wrote his essay, disparages the great migration among American poets to colleges and universities. Yet for all his self-righteous bluster, Gioia does make the excellent point that most "serious" poetry is read only by other poets, and that books of poems are rarely ever given a negative review. Instead, he points out, poetry reviewing is largely a matter of logrolling and mutual back-scratching. And there is something touchingly optimistic about his belief that poetry can and should matter to the world outside of "po-biz," which faintly echoes Shelley's famous belief: "Poets are the unacknowledged legislators of the world."

If Gioia is a persuasive spokesperson for the right, the left is equally well represented by the voluble gadfly Charles Bernstein. While these two white male intellectuals would seem to share a number of similarities, their aesthetics, and their politics, couldn't be more different. With Bruce Andrews, Bernstein coedited the controversial journal L=A=N=G=U=A=G=E and the ensuing collection, The L=A=N=G=U=A=G=E Book (1984). Like Gioia, Bernstein has insisted that poets who don't theorize their positions are doomed to repeat poetry that wasn't worth writing in the first place. For decades now, and from a variety of pulpits, he has harangued, pleaded with, scolded, and cajoled that small portion of the American public that cares about contemporary poetry to reject the "bland blandishments" of "official verse culture." In My Way (1999) Bernstein embraces the possibilities of electronic poetry, a "medium defined by exchange rather than delivery," one that is "interactive and dialogic rather than unidirectional or monologic" (75). He applauds the potential of hypertextual organization "to break teaching, textbooks, and critical writing from their deadly boring fetishization of narrative and expository ordering of information" (72). Bernstein argues that the crime of the avant-garde artist "is not lack of accessibility but a refusal to submit to marketplace agendas; the reductive simplifications of conventional forms of representation; the avoidance of formal thematic complexity; and the fashion ethos of measuring success by sales and value of celebrity" (146). If Bernstein sometimes has chastening words for his allies, he saves his most potent sallies for "self-appointed keepers of the cultural flame" (146), such as Gioia. In one of his more memorable blasts of vitriol, Bernstein writes, "There's more innovation and more cultural acumen in any episode of Ren and Stimpy than in any of the books of our last trio of national poet laureates" (41).

One thing Gioia—in a Hudson Review essay entitled "Disappearing Ink: Poetry at the End of Print Culture" (2003)—and Bernstein—as editor of Close Listening: Poetry and the Performed Word (1998)—have in common is a belief in the increasing importance of oral, or "spokenword," poetry. Naturally, though, their interpretations of this phenomenon are quite different. Because Gioia wants poets to use recognizable rhythm and meter, he cites with approval contemporary rap artists. For Bernstein (and his contributors), returning to orality means listening for new, alternative prosodies. Yet whatever rhythm one listens for in poetry, a poem nearly always benefits from being said aloud. Denise Levertov says, "Writing poetry is a process of discovery, revealing inherent music, the music of correspondences, the music of inscape" (1968). Ideally, in a poem, phrases of words are like phrases of music; poets reading from their work are like musicians interpreting the notes on a page. Moreover, we should remember that if poetry's earliest associations are with music, they are also with drama. The ancient Greek plays were written in verse. The prosody we still use today—trochaic tetrameter, iambic trimeter—comes to us from those comedies and tragedies. And Shakespeare's blank verse not only helps actors remembers their lines, it also gives power to the language, allows it to stutter and dive, sing and soar.

The first flourishing of spokenword poetry in postwar America was during the Beat era, when poets such as Jack Kerouac, Lawrence Ferlinghetti, and Philip Whalen gathered in bars and clubs and coffeehouses to read their work. Kenneth Rexroth often performed accompanied by jazz musicians. It was at the Six Club in San Francisco that Allen Ginsberg wailed out his influential poem "Howl." The energy and experimentation of this era continued into the sixties but waned in the seventies. However, in the eighties, working-class, anti-academic poets like Marc Smith once again tapped into this power source. In places such as Chicago's Green Mill bar and New York's Nuyorican Café, the tradition of poets performing their work—memorizing their lines, reading them dramatically instead of in a singsong monotone—reemerged. Anthologies such as *Aloud! Voices from the Nuyorican Poets Café* (Algarin, Holman, and Blackman 1994), *Bum Rush the Page: A Def Poetry Jam* (Medina, Rivera, and Sanchez 2001), and *Stand Up Poetry* (Webb 2002) showcase performance poetry. *Poetry Slam: The Competitive Art of Performance Poetry* (Glazner 2000) includes articles about how to slam, as well as examples of slam poetry.

Spokenword poets are given a soapbox and often a ready, rowdy audience. Not surprisingly, many poets choose this forum to make political statements. Of course poetry is always political, inasmuch as it preaches a particular point of view, a privileged way of seeing the world; however, its politically outspoken form has been criticized by poets on both the right and the left. The position of those on the right is well summarized by Edwin Muir, who argued that the poet couldn't speak the language of the public, "which is the language of the third party and the onlooker. [The poet] abhors the cliché. He is not concerned with life in its generality, but in its immediacy and its individuality. His object is to see into the life of people, to enter into their feelings and thoughts, good and bad. What can he say to the public, or the public to him?" (1962, 102). While those on the left are typically more sympathetic to political poetry, some believe that the job of advocating is done more efficiently in prose. If Shelley believed that poets were the "unacknowledged legislators of the world," he also believed "[p]oetry lifts the veil from the hidden beauty of the world, and makes familiar objects be as if they are not familiar." One consistent criticism of political poetry is that is does not reach beyond the rational to the imaginative, that it becomes mired in its own arguments.

That said, outside America the political poem seems much easier to write. As Adrienne Rich notes, "the taboo against so-called political poetry in the US . . . was comparable to the taboo against homosexuality. In other words, it wasn't done. And this is, of course, the only country in the world where that has been true. Go to Latin America, to the Middle East, to Asia, to Africa, to Europe, and you find the political poet and a poetry that addresses public affairs and public discourse, conflict, oppression, and resistance. That poetry is seen as normal. And it is honored" (Klein 1999).

In addition to the spokenword anthologies cited above, *Poems for the Nation* (1999), edited by Ginsberg and others, and Carolyn Forché's *Against Forgetting: Twentieth Century Poetry of Witness* (1993) give testimony to the number and variety of poets writing well on political themes. According to Willie Perdomo, "Shouting slogans doesn't do it for me; it doesn't move me. I'd rather paint a picture, take you for a walk and show you shit that affects my community through dialogue, scenes, and images" (n.d.). Perdomo's values clearly originate in the streets, and many would argue that the most effective political poetry today is being written by "conscious" rappers such as Mos Def, Talib Kwali, Common, and the members of the Roots.

If the poetry of rap is appealing to young people, canonical poets like Pope, Tennyson, and Dickinson frequently receive a much less enthusiastic reception. We first *hear* poetry as nursery rhymes, but we first *study* it in school, so it's not surprising that poetry often has negative connotations for the general public. It's boring. It's affected. It's difficult. It's "abstract." In grade schools, poems are memorized, recited in front of the other students, then forgotten. In high school and college, we are meant to dissect and explicate a poem. It doesn't matter if we love it or not. Of course poetry does hold a certain appeal for some students through the luster shed on it by hip-hop and the Beats. Fortunately, creative writing teachers have managed to tap into this vein of word appreciation, and Poets in the Schools programs continue, even in difficult financial times, to promote an early appreciation of poetry.

Poetry is also useful to writing teachers of all sorts because it provides a compact arena for teaching grammar, style, and diction. In *In Praise of Pedagogy* (2000), the authors of this book argue that writing poetry has many values outside those conventionally ascribed to it. Among the many cognitive functions a poem performs are theorizing and investigating positions, highlighting contradictions, and shedding light on new issues. As Art Young writes, "The purpose of poetry across the curriculum . . . is not to teach students to be better poets but to provide opportunities for them to use written language to engage course content in meaningful ways" (2003, 475).

So what, finally, is a poem? The answer is that it can take almost as many forms as one's imagination allows. With the increasing prominence of the prose poem, the standard idea that poetry is that which has a ragged right-hand margin is no longer valid. Coleridge's dictum that it is "the best words in the best order" makes sense, although one could obviously apply that to prose and dramatic writing as well. Keats thought: "If poetry comes not so naturally as leaves to a tree, it had better not come at all." While this may occasionally be true, every poet of any experience knows that revision plays an essential part in the composing process. Charles Olson writes, "From the moment [the poet] ventures into *FIELD COMPOSITION* . . . he can go by no other track than the one poem under hand declares, for itself" (1950, 614). This idea echoes earlier statements by poets as diverse as Wallace Stevens, who said, "Poetry is a pheasant disappearing into the brush," and Robert Frost, who believed: "Like a piece of ice on a hot stove the poem must ride on its own melting." Perhaps it is sufficient to say that in a good poem, even a very long one, every syllable counts. This is not to say that we necessarily count the syllables, but that every moment, every sound, seems somehow necessary. Ultimately, though, no definition of poetry can, or should, satisfy everyone. It is fitting, therefore, to end this provisional assay on the subject with Paul Valery's famous quote: "A poem is never finished, only abandoned."

POSTMODERNISM

Defining postmodernism—in imaginative writing or in any field—is a notoriously difficult endeavor, and there are plenty of elitist guardians at the gate telling us we will never succeed. Susan Wheeler in an essay in the *Antioch Review* is one of the most outspoken. She bemoans the possibility of "successful assimilation" and "trickle-up appropriations," preferring, instead, to remain "resistant" to interpretation (2004, 148–149). Polemicists like Wheeler can make it hard to sympathize with postmodernism until we remember that the volatility of the term is one of its most stable features.

Nevertheless, it *is* possible to make some generalizations. Paul Hoover says simply, "Postmodernism is another term for avant-garde [literature] of the postwar period, 1950 to the present. Postmodernism is either the exhaustion of modernism or its logical extension" (2001, 154). Katherine Haake references a remark by José Ortega y Gasset that "the realist (premodern) writer looks *out* the window to the world, and the modernist writer looks *at* the window and how the world is reflected in and through it." In contrast, "the postmodern writer may be said to look at everything at once: the world outside, the glass, the frame, the window coverings, and the very process of looking" (2000, 272). In *A Primer to Postmodernity*, Joseph Natoli notes a number of viewpoints held in common by postmodernists, including the belief that there is "gap between what we say about ourselves and the world, and the actual intermingling of ourselves and the world" (1997, 17). Postmodernists argue that "without a universal and absolute logic of word/world connection, words get attached to reality in either arbitrary or imposed ways," with the result that "different narratives of reality can be made and therefore people can live in widely different realities"(17 18). As Natoli points out, it is not that postmodernists don't believe in reality, only that they insist reality is necessarily different for everyone who experiences it, that one "cannot extract the prejudices of prior historical accounts and retain only the 'objective' part" (20).

Perhaps the clearest brief summation of the phenomenon can be found in David Lehman's "What Is It? The Question of Postmodernism," which, significantly, first appeared in the *AWP Chronicle* (now the *Writer's Chronicle*), house organ of the creative writing profession. Lehman argues: "More than anything else, postmodernism is an attitude, and that attitude is definitively ironic" (1995, 5). Fragmentation, experimentation, contradiction, and stylistic imitation are the techniques of postmodern artists. Lehman alludes to Marx's famous remark that everything happens twice, "'the first time as tragedy, the second time as farce'" (6), noting that "today the spirit of irony and parody must involve our own sacred objects" (15).

Granted, postmodernism occurs in a historical moment: beginning, by most accounts, sometime after the Second World War with the passing of modernism and continuing into the present (though some would say we now live in a post-postmodern world). Yet postmodernists are generally skeptical of time-determined categories. Hence, postmodernism can claim writers from long ago, and multivoiced, indeterminate, paradoxical Shakespeare is a postmodernist in ways that his contemporary Ben Jonson was not. Laurence Sterne's *Tristram Shandy* is clearly postmodernist, though it was written in the eighteenth century. In our time we might say that Frank Conroy, for instance, is generally not a postmodern novelist, while Thomas Pynchon certainly is. If literary modernism is concerned with breaking, expanding, and combining traditional forms, it also acknowledges the ultimate value of those forms. Postmodernism questions the legacy of European patriarchy altogether. It embraces multiculturalism, oral culture, and the pop cultures of music, film, and television. In Lehman's words, the postmodernist author "tends to blur genres, stealing from all over, conflating kinds of diction, moving from the funny pages to the classics with the speed of a distracted newspaper reader" (1995, 10).

At the heart of postmodernism is the unreliable nature of language. What we think we're saying is never what we actually say. What others hear us saying is never exactly what we intended. If all writing is essentially an act of miscommunication, postmodernists argue that we might as well celebrate, rather than lament, that failure. Since no finite set of grand narratives governs past events, postmodernists renounce the responsibility of conveying Truth with a capital T and begin, instead, to investigate the contradictory, many-voiced nature of small t truths.

The relationship between postmodernism and creative writing has at times been vexed. Lehman's article in the *AWP Chronicle* is plainspoken and commonsensical precisely because, until very recently, most academic creative writers have been so skeptical of the jargon of critical theory. The conventional image of the late-twentieth-century American creative writer is of a belletrist struggling to become part of a canon upon which everyone but a few crazies agrees (see "Author"). Likewise, the paper-cutout postmodernist scorns the conventions and boundaries of institutional learning, is too busy arguing in cafés and breaking rules to worry about curricular reform.

However, if these visions once approximated a kind of truth, they are less and less accurate. Graduate creative writings programs like those at—to name a few—the State University of New York Buffalo, the New School, the School of the Art Institute of Chicago, and the California Institute for the Arts, specialize in turning out postmodern writers. As the latter two institutions indicate, cross-fertilization between writing and other arts makes sense from a postmodernist perspective. The notion that writers should concentrate on and perfect themselves in a single genre, or even a single art form, violates the postmodern love of hybridity and multiplicity. The following list of course titles from Cal Arts gives a sense of what a postmodern graduate education might look like: Irreverent Research, Writing in Pixels, Digital Landscapes, Punk Writing, Queer Books, Globalit, Theorizing the Body, and From the Sublime to the Ridiculous and Other Forms of Non-Sense.

The traditional graduate workshop, in which literary-minded ephebes gather around and learn from a master, is a modernist rather than a postmodernist model. It relies on everyone's consensus that ultimate authority belongs to the teacher; she is the senior member of the group, so her experience and ideas count the most. In contrast, a postmodernist workshop would never allow authority to rest for long in anyone's hands; it would privilege dissent over agreement, aspiring for the democracy of the web (and Web) rather than the hierarchy of the ladder.

Whether they like it or not, American creative writers in the twenty-first century share most of the starting points, if not all the assumptions, of postmodernists. The triumph of global capitalism means that writers work in the shadow of a "market," even if they consciously try to ignore the effects of that market. The preeminence of electronic media ensures that writing for the page will have a much smaller audience than writing for the small or big screen (see also "Electronic Literature"). And even a "realistic" writer inevitably rejects naive mimesis: every serious author soon realizes that what is on the page does not correspond to the complexity of the larger world.

Perhaps postmodernism as it applies to the arts is simply the current word for "avant-garde," for the consciously experimental. If so, its currency is limited. And somewhere in the jungle of critical theory lurks an obscure term that will someday be widely used to describe the general tendencies of the new millennium.

READING

Writers encounter the term "reading" in a confusing set of contexts. Writing students are exhorted *to read*. Anything, everything, and lots:

particularly in the genre they are affiliating with. They are told to *attend live readings.* They are told to *read past masters of their genre* in order to join the tradition. They are taught to undertake *close readings* of texts in order to have a language for discussing other texts in their genre. They are expected to *read and respond* to writing workshop classmates' texts before the next class in order to help fellow writers grow in their craft. They are told that *postmodern theories of reading* have changed how we approach and understand texts and challenge the idea of authorship and authoring, the very act writers are undertaking (see "Author" and "Postmodernism").

When writers read analytically and for stylistic analysis they join their concerns to concerns held by those in composition: they are *reading rhetorically.* Often, too, they *read for advice* since textbooks and how-to trade books offer insight into craft, while professional and trade magazines provide discussions about what's going on in certain writing communities: what's hot and what's not. New writers are inevitably told to *read the journals* they plan to submit their work to, in order to help them begin tailoring their work to particular editorial tastes and publishing communities (see Corey and Slesinger 1990). Since writers' work will never be read by others unless it has certain attributes, they need to read widely to see what those attributes are; in fact, reading is the route to imitation—from routine to inspired. Some writing teachers claim that writing can't be taught but that *writing workshops educate readers* to better appreciate creative works and therefore create a future readership within a world that is often more taken with computer, video, and audio media.

Other teachers are less optimistic about students' ability to read carefully and well. Denis Donoghue writes that "the best way to read English, especially in present circumstances, would be to read it as a second language and a second literature. Most of the defect of our reading and teaching arise from the fact that we are reading and teaching English as though our students were already in command of the language. We assume that they know the language well enough and are qualified enough to move to a study of the literature" (1998, 75–76). Donoghue makes it clear that, in his opinion, assumptions about student competence are unfounded.

Because of the variety of ways we deploy the term reading, it's not surprising that a lot of kernel advice—writerly lore—becomes linked to the word: it generates a lot of baggage. But linking writing knowledge to reading knowledge is essential, as we can see when we look more closely at some of our uses of *reading.*

Students of writing should read in the genre they practice. While this is sound advice, it's not advice that's followed scrupulously by all. Many poets we know read more fiction than poetry. Many prose writers can tell more about the latest crop of Academy Award nominee films than they can about collections of short fiction published in the last year. However, there are more arguments for reading deeply and widely in your genre (and other genres) than reasons to point out the exceptional few who thrive by not doing so.

Any writer wishing to develop fluency in her genre will want to read the writers of the past. T. S. Eliot, in his influential essay "Tradition and the Individual Talent" (1975), argued that all our new writings are influenced by the writings of those that came before us, even as our new work inevitably alters our understanding of those earlier works. Therefore, we use our reading as a way of joining the conversation of past writers, and it is certainly true that those writers who have been canonized through reading lists and course offerings in universities have shaped the tastes of our potential readership. Famous texts shape the texts that follow, and readings of those texts permeate our culture from the classroom to the next *Simpsons* episode. To ignore them is to be continually trying to reinvent the textual wheel. Our supposedly innovative technique strikes someone who has read widely as derivative and clichéd unless we are using it with a knowledge of how it has been used before and then deploy it intentionally in a manner more useful for our own writing aims.

But it is not only past writers who inform us (and many excellent writers of the past who did not attain public notice are regularly being rediscovered and shared with us through historical scholarship). We also go to live readings to hear what our contemporaries are doing and saying. Despite the predominating image of the solitary writer in the garret, writing is actually an intertextual and a very social practice. We are always sharing our texts with other writers and readers of texts. There are schools of writing and communities of writing. And live readings let us do several things. We explore the aural and dramatic potentials of our texts and we come to better understand the reception of our writing. Audience—the silent reader or the appreciative listener—is important to any professional writer. We can hear our text in our inner composing ear and read it aloud in our writing room, but we need the response of readers/listeners to improve our own work, to advance it.

Because of this need to understand audience, we need to become expert readers ourselves: this is less a matter of genre than of overall approach. That is, many writers would argue that, yes, it's important to read in your genre because that is how you join that community, but it's as important to read widely, to understand how all texts are created, received, and circulated. In the late twentieth century, the dominant form of close reading—paying attention to only the words on the page, unattached (as far as possible) to a writer's history or the circumstances of composing—was challenged by a variety of postmodern critical theories: structuralism, deconstruction, New Historicism, feminism, and reader response, to name the most common. Terry Eagleton's *Literary Theory* (1996) provides a useful (though admittedly Marxist) overview of these theories. And David Lodge's *Modern Criticism and Theory* (1999) introduces us to key twentieth-century texts, including those of Barthes and Foucault, mentioned below. Since much of the work of reading and theorizing about reading takes place in university English departments, writers will find it useful to look at Robert Scholes's *Textual Power* (1986), which examines the hierarchies of reading and writing within the academy.

While different critical theories yield different and useful insights for writers, several have had particular impact. Two challenges to authorship are found in Roland Barthes's "The Death of the Author" (2000) and Michel Foucault's "What Is an Author?" (2000). Both essays, often presented together, warn writers to explore the way culture marks and circulates texts, and both highlight the actuality that our words, tropes, and genres are already determined and influenced by the ways these words, tropes, and genres have been used in popular discourse, in the work of previous authors, and in the cultural context from which the writer arises and wherein he or she works. These and other postmodern theorists question the stability of texts, the nature of reality, and the notion of an integrated self. Feminist theory challenges the way the traditionally male-dominated writing market (and universities that house many writers and writing programs) valorize certain voices and asks us to examine the influence of race, class, and gender on the production and circulation of texts. While Toril Moi's *Sexual/Textual Politics* (1985) offers an early and still useful overview of mid-twentieth-century feminist approaches, much work continues to be done in this area. Finally, reader-response theories ask writers to consider more carefully how their works are read by examining readers' differing interpretations of the same texts.

Lest these theories seem divorced from the act of composing that writers best understand, writers who aim to understand theory in action will do well to turn to Patrick Bizzaro's *Responding to Student Poems: Applications of*

Critical Theory (1993). Bizzaro applies theory to student poems and in the process shows writers how to become better readers of their own and others' work. Equally useful is Steven Lynn's "A Passage into Critical Theory" (1990), which looks at a single paragraph through various critical lenses.

When we read rhetorically, we are reading to improve our own technique and to make better writerly decisions. For example: Sakada is working on her poetry thesis, a collection of her own poems. We discuss poetry books and ask ourselves and each other: how does one organize an effective book of sixty-four pages (the traditional length asked for in national poetry book manuscript contests) from the 150 or more poems in various draft states that she has on hand? We decide she should read rhetorically. She collects twenty books of contemporary poetry. She is not reading historical poetry to join the tradition; she is not reading these works to enter the current conversation, looking for trends, techniques, and effective poetic voices. She is looking, instead, at the structure of book making, asking how are effective (because they are published) books constructed? She looks for patterns. She absorbs and she analyzes and starts jotting down observations and possible category systems. She learns much that she can borrow from in supporting her own book-manuscript-in-progress. Sakada finds the poets she is examining have recurring drive words or themes, they repeat (words, themes, sections of poems, types of poems), they mix abstract and narrative poems, they rely on an obvious structure (the death of a family member, phases of the moon, a migration of butterflies, a guiding question), they have a "core" section or a poetic sequence showcased, some work intentionally to build a story while others complete a weave of similar or dissimilar poems. This rhetorical reading is not complete or comprehensive (since the set of poetry books was limited), but it performs a useful function in allowing Sakada to further her own project.

In the same way, writers read literary journals in order to see what the journals are publishing—both for ideas of what they might write themselves and for a sense of whether that journal would be receptive to publishing their own work (see *The International Directory of Little Magazines and Small Presses*). They also read academic and professional publications (see the *Writer's Chronicle* and *Poets and Writers)* for advice on issues of common interest to most professional writers, from how to get an agent to listings of current contests and awards.

It is not really a surprise, then, that there are so many exhortations and adages about reading in the lore of creative writing, since reading is the equal, if sometimes silent, partner in the act of composing: continually we reread to understand what we have written. Just as we read ourselves into our writing community, into the history of writing, and into our writing futures.

REJECTION

Rejection is the dark door at the center of creative writing through which all who hope to survive must pass. Even the most successful writers have been rejected many times, and developing a healthy attitude toward rejection is essential to every writer. "Success is distant and illusory," as Joyce Carol Oates points out, "failure one's loyal companion, one's stimulus for imagining the next book will be better, for, otherwise, why write?" (2003, 73).

Because writing is essentially a communicative act, most beginning creative writers want to share their early efforts with someone else, usually family and friends. Not surprisingly, these efforts are generally met with unqualified approval. A writer's sense of the power of rejection arrives only when someone close to her is courageous enough to say, "That phrase sounds like something I've heard before" or "Maybe you should add a little bit of description here." This first expression of qualified rejection is also the most basic, for it introduces the essential idea that writing can always be improved.

The necessity of rejecting or revising one's early drafts becomes much greater for the writer enrolled in a creative writing course. At this stage, the writer must also learn how to discard advice that he believes will ultimately injure his work: what aspects of a piece of writing can be defended, what deserve to be eliminated, and what need to be modified.

For those writers who decide to share their work with an audience larger than a classroom of fellow students, a great deal of rejection awaits. Perhaps the most basic form of dismissal in the larger arena of creative writing is the rejection letter sent with a returned manuscript. These notices run the gamut from the very brief—a handwritten "No thanks" or a photocopied slip of paper implying that the editors would be happy to never see one's work again—to elaborate apologies and explanations about why, this time, the writer's piece could not be printed. Interestingly, many letters of rejection are longer than letters of acceptance, and a writer who receives the former should consider how much time an editor has invested in commenting on her work. Often, these encouraging letters of rejection ask the writer to submit again and mark the beginning of a writer-editor relationship that ultimately leads to publication. Some writers save their rejection letters in a box, some burn them, some even paper their walls with the things. This last act, a fascinating combination of despair (Everyone hates me!) and chutzpah (But I don't care!), suggests something of the difficult balance a working writer must adopt toward publication. There is even a literary journal, the *Dead Letter Office*, that only accepts manuscripts that have already been rejected (a rejection notice must accompany all submissions).

The lesson here is that there are different levels of rejection, and experienced writers come to distinguish between them. They learn to recognize the important fact that not everyone will be a fan of their work, that race, class, gender, artistic predilections, and whether or not an editor is having a bad day all affect the likelihood of publication. As writer Sue Lick put it in an e-mail to the authors: "I try to tell myself manuscripts are like shoes. If I were selling shoes, I would expect a lot of people to walk by without buying them or even trying them on. Writing is the same way. It usually takes more than one submission to find the publication for which the manuscript fits perfectly" (2003). The smartest writers also use rejection letters as an opportunity to meditate on their writing. Does a pattern of editorial commentary emerge over time? Perhaps editors keep remarking, "Your characters are unconvincing" or "You need to tighten the lines of your poems." If so, how much of this commentary is the editors' inability to recognize a writer's individual style, and how much does the criticism reflect real problems that the writer needs to address?

Of course, rejection in creative writing is not limited to rejection letters. There are few aspects where rejection is not a real possibility. Any serious writer will be rejected for a grant or literary prize (see "Contests"). Fellow writers, both friends and strangers, will inevitably dismiss a particular piece of writing. And if a writer wants to teach creative writing for a living, still more rejection awaits. With hundreds of candidates seeking a single position, competition is fierce, and rejection is far more likely than acceptance even for writers with graduate degrees and significant publications.

Ultimately, it is how one handles rejection that determines whether or not one will continue on as a creative writer. The initial impulse may be to retreat. However, experienced writers learn to disconnect criticism of the work from criticism of the writer: rejection of the work is not equivalent to rejection of one*self.* Poet Michael Dennis Browne lauds the work of psychotherapist Thomas Moore in helping writers overcome their sense of failure. Moore writes: "Ordinary failures in work are an inevitable part of the descent of the spirit into human limitation. Failure is a mystery, not a problem. Of course this means not that we should try to fail, or to take masochistic delight in mistakes, but that we should see the mystery of incarnation at play whenever our work doesn't measure up to our expectations. If we could understand the feelings of inferiority and humbling occasioned by failure as meaningful in their own right, then we might incorporate failure into our work so that it doesn't literally devastate us" (Browne 1993, 48).

Learning to handle rejection gracefully, to *learn* from it, makes us more human. And after all, since all writers get rejected, at least in this one instance we're all in it together.

ROYALTIES AND PERMISSION FEES

A royalty is the payment made to an author for each copy of a work sold by a publisher; depending on their contracts, authors receive varying percentages of the publisher's profit per book. "Royalty calculations can include escalations that attach higher rates to greater numbers of books sold," with authors normally receiving a higher percentage of the take from the more expensive hardbound books. In the early years of the twenty-first century, publishers typically paid 10 percent on the first 5,000 hardback copies and up to 15 percent on anything over 10,000. For trade paperbacks, a figure of 7½ percent for up to 10,000 copies and 10 percent on additional copies was standard. If an author was fortunate enough to have her book published as a mass market paperback, she could expect 6 to 8 percent royalties for the first 150,000 copies, and 8 to 10 percent for sales over 150,000 (Evans and Evans 2003, 101).

Aspiring authors looking at these numbers may wonder why, after they have done all the work of writing a book, their publishers should receive up to 94 percent of the profits. Unless I write nothing but bestsellers, an author may ask, how in the world am I supposed to make a living through my writing? It's a good question—one that most published authors would, unfortunately, have trouble answering.

Of course, most authors beginning a book have high expectations, and, in the early stages, those expectations may be bolstered financially by an enthusiastic editor. If a publisher believes the book has strong sales potential, an author is likely to receive an initial "advance against royalty." This may seem like free money to an unwary author: after all, he is getting paid before he even finishes his book. Surely, there will be great riches awaiting him when the book is actually completed. In fact, an advance "is not a no-strings gift from the publisher. It is deducted from future royalties on the sale of the book. Thus an author may not receive any royalty checks for a year or more" (Embree 2003, 128). The nonpayment of royalties for an extended period after a book's publication can be disheartening. Morris Rosenthal, who has undergone this experience, sees "publishers as little more than law firms with an editorial department in tow." Rosenthal provides the cynic's perspective on why and how authors fail to negotiate for adequate royalties: "Publishers reel in unwary authors with a carrot, the advance, then whack them with a stick, the contract. An acquisitions editor is the employee at the publisher whose job it is to sign authors to write books. Most new authors fail to retain legal counsel before signing their first book contract, and actually depend on the acquisitions editor to tell them what's fair and normal for the publisher to request. This creates an excellent negotiating position for the publisher and a horrible one for the author. Unfortunately, publishers really take advantage" (2005).

As Beth Luey, points out, illusions about the money to be made from royalties are a persistent source of friction between authors and publishers. Yet Luey believes that small and university presses, at least, do not take unfair advantages of the authors they publish:

> An author whose book is priced at $40.00 and whose royalty is 10 percent figures "$4.00 per book, and they're printing 1,500, so I should get $6,000." Unfortunately, the royalty may be paid on net receipts (20 to 40 percent less than gross), at least 100 copies will be given away free for reviews and publicity, and not all the other copies will be sold. When the first royalty check arrives and the author gets, say, $1,500—knowing that the first year is probably the best—disappointment sets in. With disappointment comes suspicion. Where does the rest of the money go, anyway? Authors who do not know what it costs to produce a book and do not understand prices and discounts are apt to think mistakenly that presses are getting rich from their labors. They are not.

University presses do make money on some titles but rarely more than the authors do. (2002, 6)

In a word, most authors will not be able to make a living from their book royalties. As frequenters of gambling casinos know all too well, the house always wins, and most publishing houses effectively cover themselves against losses by insisting on contracts that make sure their own risk and expenses are protected before their authors receive a penny in royalties. Luckily, there are a number of alternative ways to benefit financially from the prestige of being a published author. Most authors with teaching jobs (q.v.) were offered their positions because they have been published. And "many book authors use the books to generate ancillary income from related activities such as speaking, lecturing, consulting and training" (Bly 2000, 12). However, most authors who sit down to write a book so that they can become wealthy and famous are living in a dream.

This is not to say that legitimate publishers do not fulfill their financial responsibilities to their authors. Trade houses and larger university publishers may have an entire unit devoted to the accounting and payment of royalties, and some of these units take great pride in their work. The royalties department at Cambridge University Press, for instance, boasts of the accuracy and clarity of its royalty statements, the punctuality of its payments, and the efficiency of its response to author queries. (Royalties Department 2005)

Royalties are payments made as a result of direct sales of a book. An author may also make money from subsidiary rights if her book is optioned by a film studio, is made into a recorded book, and so on (see "Copyright and Intellectual Property"). Perhaps the most common form of subsidiary right is also the least remunerative for authors: permission fees. These are monies paid to publishers for the right to reprint previously published material, though publishers usually pass on only a fraction of these fees to authors. Creative writers typically receive permission fees when their poems, essays, stories, or novel excerpts are collected in an anthology (q.v.) or textbook. Normally, the editor/publisher of the new work pays a flat rate for the right to reprint the author's piece. Occasionally, editors request the right to use the piece "in all future editions," but most publishers and authors' agents (q.v.) will insist that, as the book moves into subsequent editions, a new permission fee is negotiated and paid. High-profile authors may demand thousands of dollars for the right to reprint their work, but permission fee payments can be as small as $5. One might wonder who would be willing to sell their work for such a paltry sum, but many authors are happy to receive the exposure of having their work reprinted and—if they retain the copyright themselves—are willing to waive permission fees altogether.

Ironically, if authors often complain about receiving too little from permission fees, editors compiling the pieces for an anthology often feel as though they cannot afford to pay those fees. While putting together a collection of stories and novel excerpts, Aaron Shepard found that "in general, the larger the publisher or agency, the higher were the fees, the shorter was the term of license, the longer was the response time and—since I had to remove high-priced selections—the less exposure was received by their authors" (1994, 26). The authors of this book sympathize with Shepard's grievance. The permission fees for David Starkey's textbook *Poetry Writing: Theme and Variations* are deducted from annual sales, with his contract stipulating that all fees be paid off before the author receives any money for his book. Five years after the book's publication, Starkey had yet to receive a royalty check. To avoid this problem, Wendy Bishop relied extensively on friends and colleagues donating their poetry for free when compiling *Thirteen Ways of Looking for a Poem.*

Tracking down the copyright holder in order to pay permission fees can be a nightmare for editors, especially if the work was published many years earlier and/or by an obscure press. Fortunately, in 1999, the Copyright Clearance Center established the Republication Licensing Service, which allows "rights holders to individually set permissions fees, monitor requests and control redistribution medium, all online." Those seeking to buy permissions are able to "get copyright permissions [and] information about available content [and to] monitor the status of their requests quickly and over the Web" (Reid 1999, 79).

SCHMOOZING

"Schmooze" comes from the Yiddish *shmusen,* meaning "to chat," which in turn is derived from the Hebrew *shemu'oth,* which means "rumors." The etymology contains both the harmless aspect of schmoozing—friendly talk—as well as its less appealing side—gossip mongering. The creative writing graduate student at the Associated Writing Programs' annual conference who gushes to the eminent writer, "I *loved* your latest. Can I buy you a drink?" is schmoozing, even if she is entirely sincere in her praise. That same unknown writer who repeats every word of her conversation to entertain an editor who just *may* publish her short story is schmoozing again (see "Conferences, Colonies, and Residencies"). To schmooze is tacitly to declare that you have some inadequacy that you cannot address yourself; you need the help of the person you are schmoozing.

Obviously, schmoozing takes place in all walks of life, and to their credit, most writers seem to feel morally tarnished (though not permanently) by the activity. Nevertheless, literary schmoozing goes on in a number of different guises. There is, for instance, the time-honored gambit in which a writer feigns interest in a publisher's latest offerings merely to have an opportunity to introduce the subject of his own work. Likewise, the editor of a new or obscure magazine may play the sycophant in order to wheedle a contribution from a big-name writer. There is also a kind of cautionary schmooze, in which writers of higher rank cater to someone of lesser renown based on the speculation that while that person is not yet worth a full-scale schmooze, he or she may soon be. Perhaps the most distasteful schmoozing goes on among writers who are putatively friends, but whose real interest in one another is as allies against some other, more noxious rival. It is here, where insincerity is barely masked as goodwill, that the regrettably petty nature of so much of the business plainly emerges.

The great irony is that schmoozing is frequently less effective than a writer might have wished. Granted, there are authors whose chief talent seems to be their ability to work a room, but unless a writer has at least a modicum of talent to back up her cocktail party skills, she probably won't get far. And those few talented writers who don't actively schmooze will probably still get published eventually, even if not as widely or as well as their more socially skillful peers.

Still, attendance at any writers' conference might lead one to believe that the writer with absolutely *no* tendency to schmooze is rare indeed. Even Charles Bukowski, the very emblem of the Anti-Schmoozer, is revealed in his published correspondence to be as adept at flattery, cajolery, and name-dropping as anyone in twentieth-century American letters. Thus, creative writers might as well confess their gift for blarney and take as their motto: *If Bukowski schmoozes, so must we all.*

SCRIPTWRITING

The challenges of the scriptwriter are markedly different from those of the poet, fiction writer, and essayist. Playwriting is one of the oldest forms of creative writing, while screenwriting is among the newest, yet both the playwright and the screenwriter collaborate in a much larger process: control of the final product is out of their hands. Unlike a poem, story, or essay, which can be said to exist once its author has completed writing it, plays and screenplays in their printed form are merely suggestions of what they might become. While it is true that book versions of plays are studied in literature classes and screenplays are studied in screenwriting classes, both plays and screenplays are written with the idea that they will be performed. The "author-function" (to use Foucault's term) of the scriptwriter is clearly constructed and reconstructed by a number of factors outside the writer's command.

Because a scriptwriter depends so much on the cooperation and munificence of others, she must be something of a salesperson. Poets, fiction writers, and essayists may network and schmooze at writers' conferences, but for the most part they simply mail their work off to editors and wait to hear whether it will be accepted or rejected. Scriptwriters, however, and especially screenwriters, are always actively marketing their work, pitching ideas to agents, producers, directors, and other writers. Michael Lent notes that networking is essential in Hollywood because of the "interactive nature" of filmmaking: "There is a logarithmic progression of number of people involved as a movie travels down the development path. The benefits of building a creative community, or at least a marauding hoard of like-minded individuals, are immeasurable" (2004, 157–158).

Scriptwriters must frequently meet face-to-face with their collaborators so their home address is significant. Screen and television writers are expected to live in or around Los Angeles, which is not only a practical advantage, it is viewed as a symbol of a writer's commitment to his profession. "You can write in other places," screenwriter Max Adams admits. "Nobody has to be here to write. And half the time it is better and cheaper to be somewhere else, just to get the writing done." However, she ultimately believes that "the business and personal sides are myriad. And it is very easy in this town to slip out of sight. And in this town, out of sight is, in most cases, out of work. Literally" (2001, 293).

Playwrights, too, benefit from living within driving distance of a thriving community of theater artists. New York, with its three tiers of playhouses (Broadway, Off-Broadway and Off-Off-Broadway), is the center of American playwriting, and serious playwrights move there not just to attend rehearsals of their plays but also to participate in staged readings and workshops of drafts that aren't yet ready for full productions. For those unable (or unwilling) to live in New York, there are also lively regional theater scenes in Los Angeles and Chicago and, to a lesser extent, in the San Francisco Bay area, San Diego, Seattle, Minneapolis–St. Paul, Boston, and Washington, D.C.

One of the manifestations of this emphasis on playwright involvement and professionalism is that writers are expected to have mastered the basics of their craft before approaching an agent or producer. A talented beginning poet may find that one of the first few poems he writes is published by a small literary magazine. A new scriptwriter probably won't be so lucky. Screenwriters are expected to have at least two completed projects in hand (preferably more) before they begin shopping their work around. A television writer would probably have five or six ideas for series episodes other than the one she originally submits to producers. In addition, scripts are expected to be presented in a very specific format with regard to font, spacing, and so on (nearly every book on scriptwriting has examples). A poet who transgresses against conventions of typography and lineation may well be applauded for her inventiveness. A scriptwriter who does these things will not be taken seriously.

PLAYWRITING

While the initial part of the playwriting process may be solitary, everything afterward is collaborative (see "Collaboration"). The playwright must consider the perspective of (most importantly) the director, the producer, the actors, even the stage manager. Typically, playwrights revise dialogue and action based on what happens in rehearsals. They may even continue revising after the play goes into production. Like a poetry reading, a play inspires a response among those who witness it. However, where poets have the luxury of believing in their work even when their readers are baffled or put off by it, playwrights live or die by the reactions of their audiences—and, unfortunately, that reaction is only partially in their control. As Tom Stoppard notes, "the text is only one aspect of an evening at the theater; often the most memorable moments have little to do with the words uttered. It is the totality . . . which is being judged" (1988, 287).

The collaborative process is even more central among theater companies that create their own plays in house. For these groups, the playwright function is distributed across the entire cast, with everyone involved in devising a scenario, creating characters, writing dialogue. In this situation, there is no "playwright" at all, but simply a group of actors intent on generating a stage-worthy event. Toronto's Upstart Crow Theatre Group "believes in and uses the Ensemble Method, whereby we try to foster positive communal interaction amongst a family of Artists and our audiences, and each Artist contributes their talent and energy to all aspects of the production" (2003). Philadelphia's Pig Iron Theatre Company's mission is to "create original performance works which test the boundaries of dance, drama, clown, puppetry, music and text; to experiment with form while staying accessible; to develop a physical, theatrical performance technique that draws from many performance traditions" (n.d.). New Zealand's the clinic produces "multi-media theatre that delves deep into the human psyche and succeeds in blending the real and hyper-real, the familiar and the dreamlike, the magic and the everyday" (n.d.). In all these instances, the piece that is performed onstage would not exist without the efforts of many "writers."

Companies like Upstart Crow and Pig Iron are avant-garde in orientation. In the more traditional realms of the theater, a playwright's most valued talent is the ability to write convincing dialogue. Even plays that convey a great deal of meaning through silence and gesture—such as those by Harold Pinter and Samuel Beckett—ultimately depend on dialogue for their success. And playwrights don't just give characters good lines to say, they must also introduce background and expository material in a fashion that keeps their audiences interested. Playwrights uncover the conflict in a conversation; they make action happen in a small black box. Granted, large commercial theaters have a great deal of technical stagecraft at their command—elaborate costumes, pyrotechnics, impressive lighting effects. Musicals like *The Lion King* are as much about spectacle as they are about story. But most plays are performed in theaters with ninety-nine seats or fewer (theaters with fewer than one hundred seats may perform less expensive non-Equity productions). Properties are modest, and changes of scenery are typically suggested rather than shown. (Anyone who has seen a Shakespeare play performed well knows how seamlessly these imaginative leaps in time and place can be accomplished.)

Because producing all but the most extravagant plays is less expensive than making a movie, playwrights generally find it easier to see their work reach its final phase than do screenwriters. It is far easier to find an artistic director or literary manager of a theater company who will read an unsolicited script than to find a film producer or director who will read an unsought screenplay. (Warning: theater companies usually take longer to respond to a submission than do literary magazines; six months to a year is not uncommon.) Granted, more people will see a small-scale, independent film than even a long-running play. In this respect, the screenwriter's audience is much larger. Yet playwrights are accorded a respect not given to screenwriters. The playwright is generally awarded equal (if not higher) billing with the director and stars of his play. We associate plays with those who wrote them, while we associate films with their directors. And perhaps more than other types of creative writer, the playwright is truly part of a community of like-minded artists. (See the Dramatists Guild of America Web site—www.dramaguild.com—for information about this community.)

Finally, it should be noted that while the ability to write good dialogue is a playwright's chief asset, not all good writers of dialogue become superior dramatists. Charles Dickens was said to be an excellent dramatic reader of his novels, but he never wrote for the theater (although several of his novels have been successfully adapted for the stage in last twenty years). Henry James did write plays, but his theatrical work is judged to be far inferior to his novels. Contemporary creative writers working on their first plays often have difficulty envisioning the differences between a movie screen—where almost anything can happen—and a theater stage. One remedy for this problem is academic study. Earlier playwrights learned their craft by working as apprentices for established companies or by starting their own. That tradition continues, but developing playwrights may also receive undergraduate and graduate training, although there are far fewer graduate programs offering degrees in playwriting than those specializing in fiction and poetry writing. Programs that do offer playwriting MFAs tend, not surprisingly, to be associated with universities that have strong theater programs. Among the best are Yale, New York University, Columbia, and UCLA.

SCREENWRITING

Screenwriting is one of the few activities that offer creative writers the hope of earning a substantial sum of money. The highest-paid screenwriters earn more than a million dollars per script, though normally earnings are much lower. Even when a screenplay is not produced, it may still make its author some money. Many screenplays are "optioned"—a production company pays to have the exclusive option of deciding whether or not to make the film. The majority of these optioned screenplays will never make it to the screen, but screenwriters take consolation in the fact that they have been paid anyway.

Because of the lure of wealth, and the intense competition for the big payday, screenwriters have legitimate concerns about copyright issues and other legal protections of their work. A poet who puts "Copyright by" on his manuscript looks like an amateur; a screenwriter is just being astute. One convenient way of protecting a script is to register it online with the Writers Guild of America (www.wga.org). Both members and nonmembers may take advantage of this service for a very modest fee. The WGA Web site also contains industry news, interviews with and profiles of successful screenwriters, and a host of links to relevant sources. There is always a buzz in the screenwriting world, and the quest to find out what sort of films producers and directors want to make is constant. Screenwriters attend symposiums, seminars, and conferences, where they meet with agents, script analysts, and other screenwriters. Finding a suitable agent is particularly important in such a cutthroat world, where reputations can be made, and destroyed, overnight.

The stakes are high in film production. Movies cost significantly more to make than they did in the past, and studios are less willing to invest in risky projects that might alienate middle- and low-brow movie audiences. Consequently, screenplays tend to be more formulaic than stage plays. Every film fan can name inventive variations on the standard plots, but screenplays typically fall into recognizable genres: romantic comedies, action adventures, science fiction extravaganzas, and the like. Studio heads do want to see a "hook," something to grab an audience's attention, but they also want relatively conventional heroes and heroines and recognizable stories. Moviegoers may not consciously register a screenplay's archetypal blueprint, but they have watched it in action countless times. The "classic" screenplay is two hours long. The first half hour is devoted to the "setup," the introduction of the film's central conflict and subplots. The next hour is devoted to the complication and development of the main confrontation and its accompanying subplots. In the final thirty minutes, the story's conflicts are resolved.

A playwright normally revises her own play, but many authors may be involved in the completion of a screenplay. Indeed, a screenwriter could find herself working in several different capacities. She might write, or collaborate on, an original script. She could be involved in adapting a novel, story, or play for film. Some screenwriters work on assignment as staff writers for producers and directors. Others are brought in as "script doctors" to polish rough drafts, or to bring a missing element—such as action or romance—to a script that a production company otherwise finds acceptable. Like playwrights, screenwriters can receive formal training in the various aspects of their jobs. Among the universities offering established programs in screenwriting are UCLA, USC, New York University, and Columbia.

WRITING FOR TELEVISION

If screenwriting is bound by certain conventions, writing for television is even more closely tied to the need for formulaic writing. Television writers enter a highly collaborative world, where no one voice is likely to dominate. As J. Michael Straczynski writes: "You're required to work with characters created by someone other than yourself, structure your story around commercials and other artificial timing devices, set aside your ego when the producer says, 'Our character wouldn't do that,' and limit yourself in the number of sets and types of situations you can develop into story lines" (1996, 19). Few students enter graduate creative writing programs believing they will end up writing for television. However, the training creative writing graduate students receive is, as Straczynski suggests, applicable to this sort of writing: "the *literati* who turn up their collective noses at the idea of such restrictions on the muse [should remember that] . . . *every* form has its restrictions and its rules. Sonnets, haikus, stage plays . . . you either play by the rules or you don't get to play."

Breaking into television is notoriously difficult, but one way for writers to do so is to submit a script for an episode of a show that is already in production. If the producers admire the writing but cannot use that particular episode, they may invite the writer to add his talents to a larger pool of writers. Some shows work with a staff of writers, but many television programs employ freelancers to write their shows. In addition to network comedy and drama series, there are also made-for-television movies, and with the advent of cable television series, more television writers are needed all the time.

One added benefit for television writers is that the writer-director hierarchy is inverted from the motion picture world. In long-running TV programs, with so much of the vision already established, directors are seen more as technicians who simply get the work done. It is the writers, who must inject original ideas into shopworn characters and situations, who receive the lion's share of the credit, respect, and pay.

OTHER TYPES OF SCRIPTS

Prior to the advent of television, the radio drama had a huge and faithful audience. Now it is all but dead in America, although in Britain it remains a viable format. Public radio occasionally airs such programs, but the work is neither steady nor well paid. Radio and television commercials need script-writers, but these people are normally members of an advertising team. Probably the most lucrative and widely available work for freelance writers is scripting educational and corporate videos. Obviously, writers will be working within very specific guidelines, with goals that they do not dictate themselves. Nevertheless, businesses and schools *do* want videos that will entertain as well as instruct their audiences, so there is perhaps more room for creative expression in these areas than most writers might suppose.

STYLE AND VOICE

"When a reader fancies a particular author," Ben Yagoda claims, "it could be for any of a hundred reasons. . . . But when one writer falls under another's spell, it is generally because of the way the progenitor uses language to forge or reflect an attitude toward the world—that is, it is because of style" (2004, 105). Style, the linguist Peter Verdonk tells us, is "distinctive linguistic expression" (2002, 3). It is, therefore, diction (which words are chosen) and syntax (how those words are put together) and the mood and tone those words create. In fact, every decision a writer makes determines her style, right down to punctuation: using a colon rather than a dash, or a semicolon rather than a period. And style ultimately creates a writer's voice, the "person behind all the *dramatis personae*, including even the first-person narrator persona. We have the sense of a pervasive presence, a determinate intelligence and moral sen-sibility, who has selected, ordered, rendered, and expressed these literary materials in just this way" (Abrams 1981, 132).

Emerson gets at the crucial connection between style and voice in his essay on Goethe: "Talent alone can not make a writer. . . . It makes a great difference to the force of any sentence whether there be a man behind it or no. In the learned journal, in the influential newspaper, I discern no form; only some irresponsible shadow; oftener some mon-eyed corporation, or some dangler who hopes, in the mask and robes of his paragraph, to pass for somebody. But through every clause and part of speech of a right book I meet the eyes of the most determined of men; his force and terror inundate every word; the commas and dashes are alive; so that the writing is athletic and nimble,—can go far and live long" (1850, 756–757).

In a more recent assessment of style and voice, George Steiner said of the essayist Guy Davenport, "A Davenport sentence or short paragraph is instantaneously recognizable" (Schudel 2005, C7). And A. Alvarez con-tends: "Imaginative literature is about listening to a voice . . . unlike any other voice you have ever heard, [one that] is speaking directly to you, communing with you in private, right in your ear and in its own distinctive way" (2005, 17). If we sometimes criticize people for valuing "style over substance," it is difficult to imagine a writer meriting our attention who has not developed something like a recognizable style of her own.

Classical writers divided style into high, low, and middle. Each had its appropriate time and place, but high style had the most prestige. Compositions were written to be read aloud as speeches, and through an effective use of style a speaker could impress, and sway, his auditors. Aspiring Greek and Latin authors worked toward achieving their own style by imitating their masters, a strategy young writers follow to this day. Longinus advises, "[W]e ourselves, when elaborating anything which requires lofty expression and elevated conception, should shape some idea in our minds as to how Homer would have said this very thing, or how it would have been raised to the sublime by Plato or Demosthenes, or by the historian Thucydides" (1899, 86). Of course, some beginning writers worry that if they copy someone else's style, they will never find their own voice, and that fear is valid if the younger writer never moves beyond mere mimicry. But writers can develop their own style by taking what they admire from their idols and combining that with a quality that is essentially their own. Novelist Richard Ford says, "Anyone's style is . . . just a natural incarnation of their intelligence. You can't be someone else's mind. You might learn a trick. But finally it has to heat itself to your own intelligence and make something worthwhile, or it's useless" (Yagoda 2004, 107). And Natalie Goldberg counsels writers not to worry about copying their predecessors: "Writing is a communal act. Contrary to popular belief, a writer is not Prometheus alone on a hill of fire. We are very arrogant to think we alone have a totally original mind. We are carried on the backs of all the writers who came before us" (1986, 79).

As Richard Lanham shows us, the ideals of style ebb and flow from one literary epoch to the next—from high to low, from opaque to transparent, from the elaborate hypotaxis of Henry James to the machine-gunned parataxis of Hemingway. Currently, in much of the writing done for school—both creative and expository—clarity is prized above everything. Yet Lanham reminds us that clarity really only means "'success' in communication; [and] this success almost always means a successful mixture of motives rather than a purity of purpose" (2003, 8). In other words, language, as the deconstructionists have made abundantly "clear," is never as translucent as we want it to be, and no style worth the name ever achieves its effects through a single rhetorical strategy.

For millennia, achieving a distinctive style and voice has been a writer's ultimate goal. Recently, though, writers have begun to distrust conventional ideas of authorship. Roland Barthes has declared "The Death of the Author," revealing to us that what we thought was a solid flesh-and-blood human being is actually a social-historical construct that doesn't exist outside language itself. Examining a sentence by Balzac, Barthes finds it is impossible to pin down just who is talking. Is it the story's protagonist? Balzac the individual? Balzac the writer? Balzac trying to impersonate a woman? "Is it universal wisdom? Romantic psychology? We shall never know, for the good reason that writing is the destruction of every voice, of every point of origin. Writing is that neutral, composite, oblique space where our subject slips away, the negative where all identity is lost, starting with the very identity of the body writing" (1968, 142). Barthes believes that a text is "not a line of words releasing a single 'theological' meaning (the 'message' of the Author-God) but a multidimensional space in which a variety of writings, none of them original, blend and clash" (146).

In response to this bad news for authors, postmodern (q.v.) writers have turned to parody and pastiche—an appropriate technique for our cut-and-paste world. They make fun of style, although in the hands of someone like Mark Leyner, that tactic quickly becomes a style in itself. Their critique of voice as an artificial construct has more weight. After all, identity politics (q.v.) inevitably plays a huge role in who gets to speak, what they are capable of saying, and how what they have to say is heard. Yet if voice is a fictional construct, we nevertheless immediately recognize the "voice" of postmodern writers like Don DeLillo or Charles Bernstein or Donald Barthelme, who defines style as "[b]oth a response to constraint and a seizing of opportunity" (Eder 2004, E.2:35). Indeed, writers who can do many different voices convincingly often receive the most respect. Shakespeare is preeminent here, but contemporary American novelists like Toni Morrison, T. C. Boyle, Louise Erdrich, and Joyce Carol Oates also excel at creating distinctive, individual characters. And they do this, of course, with style.

In any case, we often read writers primarily because we love their style. They may not have many new insights to give us, but the way they deliver what they know keeps us returning for more. Abraham Verghese claims that, typically, "when your mother starts to dislike your writing, that's when you've really found your voice" (Eder 2004, E.2:35). Style from this perspective represents a rite of passage, a coming of age. Yet Dashiel Hammett claimed he stopped writing because he was repeating himself: "It is the beginning of the end when you discover you have style" (Yagoda 2004, 156).

So what's a writer to do? The authors of this book have wrestled with that question: style has been a consistent concern for us. Sometimes we have allowed our individual voices to peep through in unexpected word choices or in idiosyncratic locutions. Once in a while we have even employed dialogue, narrative, and other techniques from creative writing. Our thinking has been that in a book with several different potential audiences, several different styles are warranted. Mostly, though, we have strived for the purportedly transparent voice of current academic scholarship. While in some chapters we have allowed ourselves to grow expansive, in this particular (and potentially colossal) entry, we have generally tried to follow Horace's dictum: "Every word that is unnecessary only pours over the side of the brimming mind" (1903, 73).

SUBMISSIONS

Assuming his work isn't lost in the mail (or in the mailroom), two outcomes await the writer making a submission to a publisher: acceptance or rejection (q.v.). Because the latter outcome is usually the more likely one, we have devoted an entire entry to the process of overcoming the depression and self-doubt associated with a negative response from an editor. The purpose of this entry is to discuss the basics of submissions:

how to decide where to send a piece of creative writing and what to do after making that decision. We'll begin by walking the reader step-by-step through a poetry submission, then point out variations in that process when submitting in the other genres.

POETRY

Imagine this: After much frustration and revision, a talented beginning poet finally has four poems she really, really likes. Each one, she feels, can hold up to and even benefit from repeated rereadings. She's proud of her work, and she wants to share it with the world. What does she do now?

Let's call our new writer Sara and walk her through the submission process. While the details of Sara's search for publication are geared to poetry publication, the general course of action she takes is the same one that is followed by fiction and nonfiction writers.

First of all, Sara should consult a directory of poetry listings to find out which magazines currently print poetry and where they are located. Before the Internet, the two standard sources were *Poet's Market* (Writers Digest Books) and *The Directory of Poetry Publishers* (Dustbooks). While Web listings have made these books less crucial than they once were, both give solid advice about making submissions, and they remain valid ways of checking out potential markets: the listings explain editorial biases, describe the physical appearance of a journal, provide circulation numbers and reporting times, and let the writer know the percentage of manuscripts accepted each year. (The equivalent volumes in the other genres include *The Novel and Short Story Writers Market, The Writer's Market, The International Directory of Little Magazines and Small Presses,* and the *Dramatists Sourcebook.*) The percentage of manuscripts published is particularly helpful for a new writer deciding whether or not to submit to a journal. The *New Yorker* and *Poetry* magazine accept a tiny fraction of 1 percent of the poems that are sent to them. If Sara were to send her work only to first-tier journals such as these, she would probably be in for a world of discouragement. Granted, an acceptance by an exclusive magazine would represent a phenomenal start to one's career as a poet. And new poets may have heard that even writers who have been rejected by a journal many times will give it a try if they have a poem they feel is especially strong and/or that might be particularly appealing to a specific editor. Sara may have also learned that once she develops a solid body of unpublished poems, most poets follow a policy of submitting to journals that are probably out of their reach *and* magazines they believe will publish their poems. Moreover, since a steady diet of rejection is bad for any writer, experienced poets in need of an emotional pick-me-up may occasionally send their work to journals with generous admission standards or to brand-new magazines desperate for submissions.

Sara, however, is a pragmatist. She is just starting out, and she doesn't expect to become famous overnight. After purchasing a copy of *Poet's Market* in her local bookstore, she scours the listings for a journal somewhere between the *Atlantic* and *Lily's Love Letters,* a 5-page corner-stapled newsletter. Sara settles on *Blood Relative,* a relatively new magazine published by a state college in the Midwest. Most print journals now have a Web site, which—in addition to providing current submission guidelines—typically also post at least a few sample pieces from the current and past issues of the journal. Even if a writer is working from a print directory it pays to visit the journal's Web page, so Sara does just this, discovering that the deadline for the upcoming issue is just two weeks away. A statement in italics at the bottom of the Writers Guidelines page saying, "*We're still looking for good poems!*" encourages her. Maybe this is a sign, she thinks, intuiting what most creative writers come to believe, that getting published often depends as much on timing as it does on talent. She is intrigued by the fact that *Blood Relative* has a page entitled "Best of the Rest," which publishes poems on its Web site that don't appear in the print edition of the magazine. As she surfs through other literary journals, she comes to understand that combining print and Web publication is a trend. The *Texas Poetry Journal,* for instance, is a biannual print magazine, but it also posts a weekly "featured poem" that the editors have selected from submissions received during the week. And journals like *CrossConnect,* which are primarily online venues, publish a "best of" print annual.

Following the advice she has received in just about every book she's consulted, Sara writes a short cover letter, introducing herself and stating that the four poems she's enclosing are unpublished and not submitted elsewhere. She places the letter on top of her poems, each of which has been carefully proofread several times, and makes sure that she has her name and address and e-mail address on the upper-right-hand corner of each page. (Some writing guides have recommended that she include her phone number, too, but Sara has decided that's too much personal information to disclose to someone she doesn't know.) She folds the letter and poems in thirds and puts them inside a standard business-size envelope. Then she prints out a stamped, self-address envelope (SASE), folds it in half, and slides it inside the original envelope. Many editors, including those at *Blood Relative*, ask that potential contributors purchase a sample copy of the magazine before submitting. This serves the dual purpose of boosting the magazine's sales and giving the submitter an idea of the type of work published by the magazine. Sara decides to purchase a sample back copy of *BR*; she slips a check for $5 in with her poems and seals the envelope. She knows that her submission weighs two ounces rather than one, so she makes sure to include sufficient postage. Then she takes it down to the mailbox, kisses the envelope for luck, and goes home to wait.

Two weeks later, her sample copy of *Blood Relative* arrives. She reads it through, cover to cover, and feels good about her chances. Each of her four poems, she believes, is as good as anything in this issue of the magazine.

Then she continues waiting to learn the fate of her submission. She waits and waits and waits. And then she waits some more.

Four months pass before she finally hears from *Blood Relative*. One day, though, her SASE appears in her mailbox. She has read that this doesn't necessarily mean she's receiving a rejection: more often than not, editors use a writer's SASE to send a letter of acceptance. Unfortunately, what awaits Sara is a 2" x 3" photocopied form note informing her that while the editors of *Blood Relative* appreciate her submission, they cannot use it as this time. (Could they use it *another* time? she wonders sarcastically.) There is no indication that her poems have been read by a living human being other than the "Sorry" someone has scribbled at the bottom of the note.

Sara sits quietly in her chair for half an hour. She is disappointed, of course, but stunned, too. She feels certain her poems are strong; why can't a bunch of undergraduate "editors" see that? (A thousand miles away, at the same moment, one of those editors, the one who wrote "Sorry" on the note because he blanked and couldn't think of anything more eloquent to say, is remembering a particularly poignant line in one of Sara's poems, a poem he wishes he could have talked his coeditors into publishing.)

After a while, every rejected writer who believes in herself will pull herself together. Sara knows all writers get rejected and that quitting isn't an option if she wants to be published. It is now the middle of June, however, and as she scans once more through the listings of poetry publishers, she realizes that many, if not most, of the journals sponsored by colleges and universities do not read during the summer, since their staffs are on vacation.

For a time, she considers making a simultaneous submission of her lone batch of poems to a number of different journals, knowing this will increase her chance of success and eliminate having to wait so long to hear back from a single journal. She notices that some journals accept, or even encourage, simultaneous submissions, their editors sympathetic to the long wait time writers face. These journals *do* insist that if a poet has her poems accepted elsewhere that she immediately contact them so they may take her poems out of consideration. Sara learned early on that publishing the same poem in two different journals was forbidden. She's even heard rumors from her creative writing teacher that there is a "blacklist" circulating among editors with the names of writers who have tried to double up on a publication without the editors' permission. To avoid situations like this, some journals explicitly forbid double submissions. The *Iowa Review*, for instance, requires writers submitting work to state explicitly that their work is not being considered elsewhere.

Grumpy at the number of print journals that aren't reading during the summer, Sara decides to look at publication in an e-zine. She's read that the rapid development of electronic literature (q.v.) has made online journals more appealing as potential places to publish. Many of these Web sites now have an extremely polished appearance and present the work they accept in an attractive, readable format. Sara finds several comprehensive sites linking to literary journals: Litline (www.litline.org/links) lists print and online journals, small-press book and chapbook (q.v.) publishers, organizations for writers, and miscellaneous links to bookstores, literary agents (q.v.), and grant opportunities (q.v.). The site is a full-on writers' resource (q.v.). The Council of Literary Magazines and Presses (www.clmp.org) also includes links to a variety of resources, and writers sampling its database of member journals can narrow their search down to the magazine's main genres and special interests. WebdelSol.com hosts or links to many of the top Internet literary journals and is another good place to begin exploring. Sara notices that while submissions via e-mail are unwelcome by the majority of print journals (although she has heard this has been slowly changing), nearly all online journals ask that writers submit their work either as attachments or as text pasted directly into the body of the e-mail.

Sara ultimately settles on an electronic journal called *Zap*. According to the About link, its editors are "coffee house denizens" who make their living in the straight world as Web designers, and that technical expertise is evident in the journal's sleek look. Each issue contains work by several photographers and poems by eight to twelve poets, making the overall page count considerably less than that of most print journals. Since *Zap* has no print component, all five back issues are online, allowing Sara to browse without having to pay for a sample copy. The poems are solid, and Sara even recognizes the names of several of the poets. It seems like a good match, so she cuts and pastes her cover letter and her four poems into an e-mail and sends it off to *Zap*. A week later she hears back from the editor. The journal would like to publish all four of Sara's poems. The editor tells Sara that the next issue is going up in two weeks, and sure enough, two weeks later when Sara logs on, there it is.

Sara is now a "published writer," although she won't feel she's truly accomplished her goal until she sees her name in print. On the whole, though, the submission process wasn't nearly as daunting or as mystifying as she'd initially feared.

Sara plans to keep writing, but it will be a long time before she wants to begin trying to publish a book of poems: most publishers suggest that the majority of poems in a book-length manuscript be previously published in magazines. Moreover, Sara can already tell from reading *Poet's Market* and *Poets and Writers Magazine* that is very difficult to get a book of poems published by a reputable publisher. The great majority of poetry collections that are not self-published are published through contests (q.v.) or through network connections made by the poet—in writing groups (q.v.) or at conferences (q.v.). Mostly likely, Sara will want to print a half book, or chapbook (q.v.) first. And when she does arrive at the point when she has fifteen to twenty strong published poems, she will find that the same print and online resources that list poetry magazines also list publishers of chapbooks and full-length collections.

SHORT FICTION AND CREATIVE NONFICTION

A fiction writer submitting a short story or a writer of creative nonfiction submitting an essay will face much the same situation as a poet, with the following exceptions:

- Unless the writer is submitting a short-short story, or a microessay— that is, the piece is less than four double-spaced pages long—normally he should include only a single story or essay in his submission.
- Because they are considerably longer than poems, fewer stories and essays are published in literary magazines, making it all the more important for a potential contributor to become familiar with the journal's biases *before* submitting work.

- With less space for stories and essays, the likelihood of relatively easy publication in a reputable journal—as in the narrative about Sara—also decreases.
- Online journals don't have the space issue of their print counterparts, but since Web readers typically have short attention spans, a story on-screen will probably not receive the same careful attention as it would if it were printed on paper.

THE NOVEL, MEMOIR, STORY AND ESSAY COLLECTIONS, STAGEPLAYS AND SCREENPLAYS

As indicated above, poets seeking book-length publication depend to a large extent on contests. While there *are* contests resulting in the publication of novels and memoirs, writers of these works normally begin by submitting their work to agents (readers should refer to this entry for detailed information about that process).

Short story and essay collections sell fewer copies than novels and memoirs; consequently, they are more difficult to get published. Again, contests may offer the best option: many of these are listed in the bimonthly online classifieds section of *Poets and Writers Magazine* (www.pw.org/mag/classifieds).

Dramatists nearly always seek a production of their play before they even consider publication. A play, after all, doesn't really come alive unless it's on the stage, and in any case, most theatrical publishers won't consider a play unless it's been produced in New York or by a strong regional theater. An agent will prove useful for playwrights, but it is not necessary to have one in order to have a play produced. Many small theaters are actively looking for new plays and are willing to read unagented scripts. Since most theaters have a Web page, playwrights may find it easiest to get in touch with artistic directors via an e-mail, which should include a short description of the play, a brief statement of the playwright's credentials, and a 5 10-page sample—probably the opening scene—from the play itself. Theaters looking for specific types of scripts post calls online at The Playwrights' Noticeboard (www.stageplays.com/markets), The Playwrights Center of San Francisco (playwrightscentersf.org/Resources/), and Playbill (www.playbill.com/jobs/find/).

The entry for scriptwriters (q.v.) outlines the basics for entering that world. Once again, agents are crucial, although screenwriters may take advantage of an increasing number of annual competitions. Among the most prestigious are the Chesterfield, the Nicholl Fellowships, and Sundance. While winners generally do *not* emerge with a signed studio contract, these contests are good at "generating notoriety, providing springboards to careers, and doling out upwards of a million bucks a year in cash and prizes. Many production companies, studios and talent agencies are plugged into these events, so a strong showing can grant instant cachet. Meanwhile, competitions that are tied to festivals create incredible opportunities to meet colleagues and create synergy" (Lent 2004, 209).

TEACHING JOBS

Creative writers have always been teachers, whether they've realized it or not. Perhaps they taught, unaware, through their work, which apprentice writers scrutinized as though studying a textbook on craft. Moreover, for millennia authors have been writing about the art of writing. From Horace to Maxine Hong Kingston, practicing writers have critiqued the style and subjects of others (and sometimes themselves). In the United States in the past fifty years, teaching creative writing has become something of a boom industry. It is probably not hyperbole to say that there are now more active creative writing teachers than there have been in the history of the world. In academic circles, teaching has become synonymous with teaching in the university. This entry will begin there, but—because so many of our keyword entries already address life in this particular institutional setting—we will quickly move on to discuss the many teaching opportunities outside these relatively narrow, and difficult to enter, confines.

What this second category of teaching jobs has in common is the assumption that creative writing is beneficial to people in all walks of life, not just college students. Once a teacher accepts the idea that self-expression can be at least as important as artistic excellence, she comes to realize that every person is a potential writer, every student is a potential teacher. At that point, the undersized province of creative writing as it is generally defined by the Associated Writing Programs (q.v.) opens into an entire world.

UNIVERSITY CREATIVE WRITING PROGRAMS

When students enroll in graduate creative writing programs, they are routinely told not to expect that their degrees will lead to teaching jobs (see "MFA" and "Creative Dissertation"). The market is glutted with qualified teachers, many of them with substantial publications, and more candidates enter each year. It is not uncommon for five hundred or more applicants to seek a single tenure-track job. Yet a great deal about graduate programs leads students to yearn for this sort of work. If nothing else, the excitement of always being around others who love reading and writing is intoxicating.

Granted, even these rare dream jobs have responsibilities. Teaching in graduate programs requires faculty to publish, to teach, to direct creative theses or dissertations. Professors whose focus is undergraduate teaching generally have fewer publishing expectations, but they are likely to have more courses per term, more committee work, and more emphasis placed on the quality of their teaching. Whatever the level of student, though, the duties of a tenure-track faculty member are more than offset by the perks—plenty of time to write, the respect accorded full-time college professors, opportunities to network with publishers and other writers, the sense that one has a position coveted by his peers.

There are three main sources for information about current college and university jobs: the *Chronicle of Higher Education,* the Modern Language Association (MLA) Job Information List, and the Associated Writing Programs Job List. The *Chronicle* list (currently available at chronicle.com/jobs/100/500/2000/) has a significant advantage over the other lists. While all can be accessed online, only the *Chronicle* provides free entry into its database. Online updates occur more frequently in the *Chronicle* and MLA lists than they do in AWP; moreover, the *Chronicle* and MLA databases show positions throughout English studies, while the majority of listings in AWP are creative writing jobs. Of course, the preponderance of creative writing notices makes AWP a good source for those focusing solely on this teaching area, and sometimes potential employers will post jobs on this list and not the others.

Unfortunately, the number of full-time positions is shrinking, and the truth is that very few creative writers with either MFAs or PhDs in creative writing will ever land tenure-track jobs teaching their specialty. The odds are just too heavily stacked against them. Young writers who enter four-year colleges and universities in the new millennium will almost certainly need to have won a prestigious book contest (q.v.); they will need connections and considerable personal charm. Otherwise, chances are that young writing teachers will begin as adjuncts (see this keyword for a full description of the challenges of temporary academic work). So what lies in store for those who have a relentless calling to teach but don't get the breaks? What avenues are there for educators outside the four-year university?

UNIVERSITY AND COLLEGE EXTENSION PROGRAMS

Extension programs draw their students from throughout the community. Because enrollment fees tend to be relatively inexpensive and admissions are open, the range of student skills varies enormously. Some students will already have publications and advanced degrees; others will be writing seriously for the first time in their lives. Payment to instructors varies depending on class enrollment and the prestige and funding of the program. Typically, there is no tenure for instructors, so job security is poor.

However, applicants for jobs in extension programs do not face as much competition for open positions, as teachers are normally hired from the local pool of writers. Moreover, extension programs generally offer far more creative writing courses than do English departments. The Writers' Program at UCLA, for instance, sponsors 550 creative writing courses annually, while the university proper lists only a handful of such classes for its undergraduate and graduate students. At UCLA Extension, "[a]dult learners study with professional screenwriters, fiction writers, playwrights, poets, nonfiction writers, and writers for new media who bring practical experience, theoretical knowledge, and a wide variety of teaching styles and philosophies to their traditional and virtual classrooms" (UCLA Extension n.d.).

UCLA's faculty is well trained, with prestigious publications, but faculty in smaller extension programs need not have spectacular credentials in order to find satisfying employment. Indeed, in less populous areas, extension administrators may be actively seeking qualified creative writing instructors, and someone who holds the MFA degree might find himself unexpectedly in demand.

COMMUNITY COLLEGES

Community colleges typically feature at least one creative writing course among their English department offerings. Normally, this course is multigenre, with units devoted to poetry and fiction and a third section focused on either playwriting or creative nonfiction. Seniority dictates that tenured faculty members will have the first opportunity to teach these classes, but capable and diligent adjuncts are often able to pick up a section of creative writing.

The standard method of community college job hunting is to send out copies of one's curriculum vitae to as many institutions as are within reasonable driving distance. The job applicant indicates that she is able to teach a variety of writing courses, including creative writing. Many creative writers find their way into community colleges by first teaching composition courses, and some composition courses are flexible enough to allow the teaching of creative writing as part of the curriculum. Like extension classes, community college creative writing courses are open to all, so students bring a range of talents with them. Unlike extension programs, community colleges generally pay a fixed rate for each class, regardless of enrollment size.

POETS IN THE SCHOOLS

Poets in the Schools programs began in the 1960s, when the country was flush with cash and high ideals. Improbably, they have survived in many states, with New York and California maintaining the two largest programs. California Poets in the Schools (CPITS), for example, is dedicated to "1) helping students throughout California recognize and celebrate their own creativity, intuition and intellectual curiosity through the creative writing process, and 2) providing students with a multicultural community of trained, published poets who bring their experience and love for their craft into the classroom" (California Poets in the Schools n.d.). The organization claims to have taught more than half a million schoolchildren since 1964, with over one hundred thousand poems written in CPITS workshops every year. The best of those poems are collected annually in local, regional, and statewide anthologies.

Poets in the schools must be enthusiastic and able to connect well with children and teens. They often face students whose knowledge of the subject is limited to a handful of ancient anthology poems, greeting card verse, and song lyrics. Instructors, therefore, must bring considerable knowledge of their subject with them, though generally some further training is required. Normally, a teaching credential is not necessary; instead, new teachers spend time in the classroom with veteran poet-teachers before they are given classes of their own.

CORRESPONDENCE SCHOOLS

While correspondence schools have been the subject of humorous poems by, among others, Elizabeth Bishop and Galway Kinnell, they offer a genuine service to apprentice writers who, for whatever reason, are unable to leave their homes to attend classes. *Writer's Digest* sponsors one of the oldest and most respected correspondence schools, with courses such as Fundamentals of Fiction and Novel Writing Workshop. Students submit assignments via mail, with instructors responding within two weeks to a month. Teachers typically have a solid publications record and some teaching experience, although they do not necessarily hold advanced degrees.

Online creative writing instruction is a variation on traditional correspondence courses (in fact, *Writer's Digest* now offers a selection of these courses). Reputable companies in the field include writingclasses.com, the online division of New York's Gotham Writers' Workshop, and writing-world.com, which features a variety of specialized classes that run from four to eight weeks. Among Writing-World's offerings are How to Write a Nonfiction Book Proposal, Writing the TV Spec Script, and Writing and Selling Erotica. Each week students receive lessons from instructors and respond to new assignments. Fees are more modest here than at *Writer's Digest* and writing-classes.com ($100 per course or less as opposed to $300 and up), but there is less competition for teaching jobs, and consequently opportunities for new teachers are greater. According to instructor Sue Lick, the fact that writing-world.com handles "all the recruiting of students and handling of fees" is a distinct advantage for teachers who are busy pursuing other employment opportunities. "The teachers are paid a large percentage of the fees, so the more students we have the more money we make" (Lick 2003).

WRITING GROUPS

For those who don't mind rounding up their own students and who prefer to work outside an institutional setting, there is always the option of placing an advertisement in the local paper. Such an ad announces that an experienced, published writer will be conducting workshops. If response to the idea of a paid workshop is poor, the group leader can always hold an abbreviated version of the workshop for free, then, assuming participants are satisfied, begin charging a fee.

Once a group is assembled, space becomes a vital issue. Meetings can be held in the group leader's home, although most teachers prefer to safeguard their privacy and meet in comfortable public spaces like coffeehouses. Some guerilla workshop leaders even scout out free times and empty classrooms in the local university and hold their workshops there.

Unfortunately for the teacher hoping to be remunerated for his guidance, a successful writing group may well decide that it can function perfectly well without a paid leader. (Like a flourishing writing class, a thriving writing group is student- rather than teacher-centered.) Yet workshop leaders with charisma, authority, and intellect will find there are always new students seeking instruction, and the advantages of heading one's own writing group are many. Group leaders teach what they want the way they want to. They respond to their students' individual needs directly, without any institutional mediation. The group environment can be as serious or as lighthearted as the leader desires.

POETRY THERAPY

Because the teaching described in the following sections concentrates on students' self-expression and personal enrichment rather than their aesthetic development, it will not appeal to all potential teachers. According to registered poetry therapist Perie Longo, "the focus of poetry for healing is self-expression and growth of the individual whereas the focus of poetry as art is the poem itself" (2005). The National Association for Poetry Therapy (NAPT), which confers professional credentials in the field, divides poetry therapy into two main categories. "Developmental Interactive Bibliotherapy" can be provided by trained teachers without medical or psychiatric credentials. This therapy is given to "children in schools and hospitals, adults in growth and support groups, and older persons in senior centers and nursing homes." The primary goal is to promote individual self-awareness, but the therapy may also be "used as a preventive tool in mental health." Providers of "Clinical Interactive Bibliotherapy" must have medical credentials; they use literature "to promote healing and growth in psychiatric units, community mental health centers, and chemical dependency units" (Poetry Therapy n.d.).

The work is emotionally challenging for both writer and therapist. Writers must confront painful memories if they hope to overcome them. Therapists are deeply involved in this sometimes excruciating process. And yet, as Longo notes, "the therapeutic benefit of poetry [is that] words remain forever for they are sound waves. Wherever we go, they follow us, from room to room, unconsciousness to consciousness, denial to acceptance, sorrow to joy. And hopefully to health" (2005). (For an extended discussion, see "Therapy.")

HOSPITALS

If poetry as therapy is truly beneficial as medicine, then the most obvious location for its healing to occur is in hospitals. The hospital poet-in-residence is a relatively recent phenomenon, so ideas about what the job should and shouldn't entail are ongoing. While a certified or registered poetry therapist would probably be welcome here, often no medical or counseling background is required to obtain such a position. Duties might include sharing and discussing published poems, composing and discussing original work with patients (and occasionally doctors, nurses, and staff), and giving poetry readings. Obviously, teaching methods and readings differ radically depending on the age and medical condition of the patients: children with cancer, for instance, have significantly different needs and skills than AIDS patients.

In nearly every case, however, compiling a printed record of the work created is essential. To this end, most poets-in-residence arrange for the publication of a chapbook (q.v.). As Perie Longo notes, it is important for patients "to fasten their poems down, so that when they move from place to place, they can take their poems with them to provide some continuity." (2005) Clearly, friends and relatives of patients with terminal illnesses will also cherish the work created during this time. Another popular method of "publishing" creative writing is to display it in a "poetry corridor" of the hospital. Such a space allows not just patients but doctors, nurses, and visitors to pause and reflect on the emotional effects of illness (Chatterjee n.d.).

Again, the work is intense. Teachers enter a world where pain and death are common. Fear is a constant presence. Some instructors find the scene overwhelming; the needs of medical patients are far greater—and possibly more intrusive—than those of the casual student. Yet there are few more rewarding experiences than providing someone in a life crisis with the skills to express her fears, to attempt to overcome them.

HOMELESS SHELTERS

Like hospital patients, homeless people live in a world of uncertainty. Unsure of where they will find their next meal, where they will sleep, whom they can trust, the homeless live from day to day, from moment to moment. Creative writing provides them not merely with a means of self-expression but also with a sense of stability. The words they write on the page today will still be there tomorrow.

If the words remain fixed, the writer may not. The transitory nature of their existence makes sustained creative writing instruction with the homeless problematic, to say the least. Homeless children are particularly vulnerable to the setbacks associated with frequent moving. Fortunately, there are institutions such the T. J. Pappas School for homeless children in Phoenix, where creative writing classes, like all the school's courses, are designed to promote "inquiry, positive decision-making, effective communication, cultural appreciation, and life long learning experiences . . . to curtail homelessness" (Pappas School for the Homeless n.d.). Teachers who work with homeless writers will probably want to look for similar institutional settings, places that can provide not just classroom space but services such as food and shelter. Creative writing may sometimes feel like a life-or-death pursuit to its practitioners, but people who are truly in such a struggle must first meet their basic needs before they can begin to think seriously about writing poems and stories.

PRISONS AND JUVENILE DETENTION CENTERS

The downsides of teaching in prisons are obvious. Safety is a legitimate concern for instructors. Pay is generally at the rate for community college adjuncts—low. Some prisoners may enroll in such a class simply as a way of avoiding more onerous duties; they have no intention of taking the assignments, or the teacher, seriously. Moreover, "the primary objective of such institutions is to keep control over the inmates—their bodies, their behaviors and all information about them. The goal of many prison researchers [and teachers] is to illuminate the experience of human beings in the context of the penal institution. How can these tensions co-exist?" (Peltak n.d.). The answer is: Uneasily.

Despite these impediments, teachers who have worked with prisoners extol their desire to write. Incarcerated men and women can initially present challenging behavior problems, but they are also full of gripping stories. In *True Notebooks* (2003), Mark Salzman movingly details the year he spent teaching personal writing in the Los Angeles County Juvenile Detention Facility. Those on "the outside" can barely imagine some of the things prisoners have seen and done. Prisoners' lives are inherently dramatic, full of the raw material of unforgettable creative writing. It is the instructor's task to provide guidance, encouragement, and literary models, to tap the wellspring. To do so, though, they must confront the fact that many prisoners lack basic literacy. The translation of oral into written skills is a major obstacle in the prison creative writing class. (See Judith Tannenbaum's *Disguised as a Poem: My Years Teaching Poetry at San Quentin* (2000) for another full account of the joys and challenges of this endeavor.)

SENIOR CENTERS

People entering the final phase of their lives have seen and heard much; they have many stories to tell. However, creative writers who work with seniors are occasionally frustrated by their unwillingness to write outside traditional boundaries: poems usually rhyme; stories often have sentimental endings. Convention (and cliché) may be hard for poets and fiction writers starting so late in life to conquer. Autobiography, on the other hand, depends on anecdotes that evoke specific people, places, smells, tastes, and sounds—the very qualities a good oral storyteller will already have at his disposal. Teachers will find seniors delighted to share their most memorable events, with other students clamoring for more details. In addition to the advantages it offers student and teacher, "life writing" is also likely to produce valuable family documents.

Senior centers are often cash strapped, so they are reluctant to hire someone who doesn't have significant experience working with their population. The best way to begin interfacing with seniors is to volunteer one's time and expertise. One or two successful gratis workshops that inspire a dedicated following may well result in steady paid work later on.

THEORY

When a smart-ass attacks writing programs, I defend them on the grounds that they, we, teach literature. We are literature's last stand for the simple fact that many university English departments seem to have renounced books (poems, stories, novels, plays) in favor of theorizing about them.—David Lehman (Orem 2001, 16)

Having no theory is a dangerous theory because it reinscribes the structures we can't see that nonetheless contain us. . . . Theory helps make the invisible visible. Creative writers need it even if it gives them hives.—Katherine Haake (2000, 240).

THE ENVELOPE, PLEASE!

In the shabby linoleum halls of the academy that many creative writers currently inhabit, we have lots of definitions of, attitudes toward, and theories about theory. Indeed, no single key term can change the physical face of a writer as much as this one. For most, the immediate response is—if not hives—then a frown, smirk, toss of the head, grimace, body twitch—which indicate attitudes ranging from involuntary rejection to downright revulsion. Like David Lehman, many take the high road, see themselves as writers at the Alamo, united against critics—*we* write it, *they* talk about it (and no one can understand that talk) and even worse, *they* often don't seem to talk at all about what *we* write.

For many, theory is the (arch)enemy of practice, in this case the practice of crafting excellent literary texts. Or perhaps we've (up)dated the OK Corral and (re)turned to a world of battling superheroes at the local academic cinemaplex. Theory is the tool of the reader and the reader/critic, and the critic is eternally opposed to the writer. Writers construct theorists as always already derivative, commentators, reporters or—and worst—imitators (he or she who wishes to be a writer yet has failed and steeps that sorrow in the convoluted opaque antiliterary prose of the academy). Unfortunately, this she or he also appears to have more academic cachet and authority within English department hierarchies, fueling creative writers' sense of battling a foe, fighting against a known evil. David and Goliath. The Wizards of Oz. Theory and theorists are (almost too) easily cast as nemeses.

In a widely circulated article, D. W. Fenza encapsulates what he feels is the generally-held-to-be-true-and-unbridgeable-gulf between writers and their critical readers in this manner: "Scholars, literary theorists, and writers are not compatible in their endeavors or temperaments, and they, necessarily, will be compelled to criticize one another to protect and promote what they believe to be crucial to the enjoyment of literature and its future" (2000). Over the last twenty years (but drawing from a tradition centuries older; see "Reading"), this position has been championed and anatomized in the pages of the AWP journal, which represents the platform of writing programs nationwide (see "Associated Writing Programs"). When the theory that theory is problematic for writers is challenged, this argument is generally raised by the uncombined and mixed forces of maverick creative writers (often those interested in pedagogy), feminist writers, and/or intradisciplinary writers (those who travel comfortably between linguistics and creative writing or composition and creative writing). Notably, most all our discussions continue to be overlooked by those in literature and literary criticism, confirming most writers' sense of alienation when the word comes into town.

However, Katherine Haake argues that creative writers cannot avoid theory in their writing lives even if it does make them uneasy or ill. François Camoin underscores the point by explaining that what most of us assume is theory talk—something done by those other than writers and almost always by the French—Lacan, Derrida, Barthes, Foucault, Cixous—is in fact what we already profess in our own discussions: "Like our critical colleagues, we are faced with texts, and silence is not an option. But we have our own stock of critical terms, familiar and non-threatening. Round and flat characters. Point of view. Narrative persona. Flashbacks. Showing versus telling" (1994, 3). Because we do not name these discussions as theoretical does not excuse us (nor exempt our terms) from the realm of theory. Camoin continues, "The theory (whether we want to call it that or not) is always there, though it's often suppressed, disguised as craft, or common sense, or literary taste or *what-I-have-learned-in-twenty-years-of-being-a-writer.* But finally, it comes down to speaking about how texts mean, what they do, how they exist in the world, how they function"(5).

RASHOMON: (RE)DEFINING TERMS

Here, then, are two new ways to look at theory and theory talk. For the record and simplified, Beth Daniell offers this explanation of the two terms as used by Stanley Fish: "Applying a theory to a particular text . . . in order to explain that text, is theory. Arguing that theory *x* is more useful than theory *y* is theory talk" (1994, 132). First, theory talk is not disinterested. The degree to which we assume theory to be impartial helps construct a status quo. The degree to which we believe theory is a tool for speculation and interrogation helps question the status quo. Overall, a movement from modernism to postmodernism (q.v.) requires a similar move from understanding that our theories represent fixed realities and values to an understanding that our realities and our values are constructed. Theory in the second case now helps us to understand such constructions.

Instead of the writer viewing theory as an aggravated attack on artistic freedom, theory/theories offer ways of thinking about who we are as authors in cultures: "We have been taught that theory, neutral and a-rhetorical, determines knowledge. Yet we discover that theory is determined by and protects beliefs"(Daniell 1994, 131).

Those who have interests not only in producing (creative) writing but also in teaching their art, craft, and most valued (literary) genres find theory a tool for improving their writing and their teaching: "Instead of coming before practice, [as compositionists Knoblauch and Brannon argue] then, theory comes out of practice—theory helps us explain what we are already doing" (Harris 1994, 147). In fact, as writers accept their responsibilities as teachers (call it, even, the craft of teaching), they are including in their world the need to evaluate literary texts—those constructed by their students. Not to mention the fact that they have always needed to evaluate the effectiveness of their own texts by becoming better readers of them on the long, winding, narrow, yellow brick road to becoming better writers.

A brief review of the complicated term is in order, one that looks and looks again at the way theory performs in the sciences compared to the way it performs in the fine arts, as well as how theory performed half a century ago compared to the way(s) it might perform today. Consider the following arguable points.

- In the fine arts, theory is different than theory in the sciences, yet, for historical reasons, we often apply a science-based understanding to a fine arts-based life.
- Theory can be assumed to be fixed or change-oriented—that is, interpretive and predictive.
- Theory cannot be proved. Theory is contingent. (Theories fail. Theories illuminate.) No one owns theory. Theory is political and rhetorical.

First, most of us have a general idea of what we mean by theory that goes something like this. A theory is a reasoned guess. It's based on observations. Based on those observations, we generate a hypothesis that—given the same conditions—this or that will always (or for those more postmodern—generally) be true. Say, for a creative writer, the reasoned guess is that writers need readers. We observe that those who read widely write more fluently and flexibly. We study the history of writing and see that well-respected writers note their influences, those writers whom they have read. We find that we often use memory of what we've read to help us out of a writing corner. We find that our writing students who have read most widely write best. We firm up our theory, we argue strongly and widely that writers are or should be readers.

Others have a theory that genius and talent matters more than influence and wide acquaintance with reading. They point out to us that many writers (they name some) talk about intentionally avoiding influence, not reading other writers while they write so as not to have that author's prose rhythm influence their own, that writers like (they name them) say they don't read widely. And so brews a theory battle: one that writers who prefer to avoid theory walk away from. But can they? And should they? Or, why should they?

In the sciences, the first set of theorists are instantly discredited because "[i]n scientific circles . . . *theory* is distinguished from *hypothesis*, the latter being an educated guess subject to verification through experimentation, the former being a hypothesis that has so far withstood the test of time and experimentation and, consequently, is viewed as a given or a fact. Scientists hypothesize without data, but never theorize without it" (Daniell 1994, 140). Scientific theorizing, Daniell reminds us,

> is supposed to move us beyond politics, beyond questions of power; theory, we have been taught, is the way to attain neutrality. . . . The best scientific theories have been thought not only to include all phenomena accounted for by any previous theory but also to explain anomalies that earlier theories failed to account for.
>
> Theorists in the social sciences and the humanities tried to adopt this model, only to find that their theories don't do a very good job of predicting. . . . theories in these fields serve a more interpretive than predictive function. . . . That is, a given interpretive theory may explain the anomalies that a previous theory failed to account for, but it rarely, if ever, explains all the phenomena accounted for by previous theories. (128–129)

And as British philosopher A. J. Ayer has noted, "There never comes a point where a theory can be said to be true. The most that one can claim for any theory is that it has shared the successes of all its rivals and that it has passed at least one test which they have failed" (qtd. in Daniell 1994).

Theorists about theory, then, definers of the same, suggest that our attitude toward the word can change, that there are various ways to look at theory. If we use the scientific or descriptive lens, the second set of theorists may claim our allegiance. If we use an interpretive and predictive lens, the first set of theorists may better serve.

More simply, if we have been raised in a culture that valorizes the scientific approach to meaning making, we tend to import those assumptions about theory to areas where those assumptions don't serve us well. Instead, we might think of other ways theory can and does work. For example, after studying the work of writing researchers Albert Kitzhaber and James Britton, Joseph Harris offers another way of thinking about these seemingly antithetical approaches (the scientific and the interpretive):

And so while Kitzhaber looked to theory for a map of the subject to be studied, for a set of principles that would organize what we need to know about how texts are composed and interpreted, Britton took a more rhetorical or performative view of it as a means to an end, a form of reflection on action whose aim is to change teaching in direct and immediate ways. . . . *the constative view asks whether a certain theory is true or false. It is concerned with theory as knowledge. The performative view looks to the possible effects of holding a theory.* It deals with theory as persuasion. We can of course look at any theory, just as we can analyze any utterance, for how it functions both as a constative statement and as a performative act—for what it says and what it does. We can ask, that is, not only what a theory has to say about the nature of composing or interpreting but also what changes it would have us make in our work as teachers and intellectuals. (1994, 142–143; emphasis added)

When we approach or define theory by asking how it does or might work for writers, we arrive at the third set of observations, outlined above: theory cannot be proved. Theory is contingent. Theories fail. Theories illuminate. No one owns theory. Theory is both political and rhetorical. We are, like it or not, hives or not, theorists.

So what's a creative writer to do?

A LITTLE DAB'LL DO YOU VS. WORLD ENOUGH AND TIME FOR THEORY

Some writers benefit from the systematic study of theory. Others eschew it . . . but at their own risk. Our theory claims that, even if she is not closely following these discussions, the not-sold-on-theory writer would still benefit from a working acquaintance, a little dab of theory, for the following practical reasons:

- Theory is political, particularly in the hierarchies of English departments where many writers now house themselves. To feel angry about or indifferent to theory, to lack a bit of theory knowledge and theory talk is to make oneself vulnerable and defensive. To do the reverse is to participate in what is—for now—the lingua franca of these departments.
- Theory is rhetorical and there are any number of genre arguments in contemporary writing programs; knowing which genres have currency for which reasons can matter because "Who owns creative nonfiction?" is revving up to be the next big theoretical debate in these locales (see "Creative Nonfiction").

- Theory is practical *and* performative (at least in some of its political and rhetorical manifestations), for there are any number of moments (the cover letter, the grants application, the plea for national arts funding) when writers have a need to articulate their practices, their beliefs, their field, their genre, and so on.

While this much of an acquaintance with theory will suffice for many creative writers, both inside and outside the academy, for others, theory can lead into and out of better writing.

- Practice into theory and theory into practice is the normal ebb and flow of excellent teaching. Teachers evaluate student texts and need to have understandings of/ability to articulate their theories of reading, their values and beliefs, their judgments. Teaching is the fastest route into theory, for without theories, teaching practices cannot be tested and improved; curriculums cannot be defended or improved. Any interaction with credentialing (MFA or PhD, undergrad and graduate writing major requirements, and so on) is a result of political and rhetorical representations of theory.
- Theory is a tool for thinking and innovation. There is no experimentation without convention. There is nothing to rebel against without a community to approach or retreat from. Without theories of writing and writers, there are no genre innovations, movements, and schools of writing. Without theory, we could even claim there is no community, no need for writers and readers to meet.
- Theory can be serious but theory can also be play when a writer is not on the run, on the defensive, battling a nemesis. Theory is language and language is the grubstake of writing. Some writers are avid linguists, are word mavens, are fascinated with the deep study of theory. Others take the exploratory approach, valuing the epigraph, the idea, the gesture toward a new facet of practice in a new language for thinking about art and event.

The play of theory may be the newest idea in this entry for many creative writers. For such an approach, we'd suggest beginning with the self-admittedly idiosyncratic initiation to critical terms offered by Katherine Haake in the last chapter in *What Our Speech Disrupts* (2000). Her discussion of sign, difference, supplementarity, and others terms join story terms like narrate and focalization. Her exercises here and in *Metro* are combinatorial play with language, for the writer, by the writer. She "strips" theory into language exercises that both illuminate it and make it strange—to those who would own it, to those who would avoid it. In so doing, her aims are both rhetorical and political. She theorizes a "radical pedagogy of inclusion that sees the creative writing classroom as an intra- and interdisciplinary site where basic questions of language and discourse can lead to transformed notions of how we know and experience not just our writing but ourselves" (18).

Let's return to the thorny problem once again, What does theory— Haake's theory, Foucault's theory, New Critical theory, practicing writers' beliefs (even those who say they don't have or need theory)—have to offer creative writers, and what might be some of the attitudes and relationships writers take toward theory and theory talk?

MAKE USE

We take our final subhead from a poem so titled by Raymond Carver in which he suggests that writers/readers/humans look around them and make use of all they observe and experience. We would suggest that theory is for all of us—it is democratic if we make it so. We need to demystify it and decide on degree of investment. Further, those who see theory as the language of opportunity will find added value as they explore its avenues and applications.

Beth Daniell, whom we've drawn on usefully here, helps us end this entry with her theory of theories. In the spirit of serious play, we strip and turn her words into a practical checklist. She argues: "Once we understand that theory is rhetorical and political, then our project as intellectuals goes beyond merely formulating theories or applying them. . . . We need to ask":

- How valid and how rigorous is the research that supports this theory?
- What phenomena does this theory fail to take into account? That is, where does it "leak"?
- Can we state the limitations of the theory, so that we do not claim more for it than it can do, so that we can caution others that this theory works in this domain but not in that one?
- What are the assumptions, both stated and unstated, on which the theory rests? But also:

- What is the hard core of unstated beliefs underlying the theory?
- Whose interests are being served?
- Is the theory consistent with what we say we want to do?
- What are the social and ethical implications of this theory?
- Does it serve our stated beliefs about knowledge, language learning, and the value of human beings?
- Or does it challenge them?
- Are we better off with the theory than we are without it? (1994, 131)

Daniell's questions help us theorize; that is, they can help us consider long-standing claims more systematically: The MFA (rather than the PhD) is the most appropriate terminal degree for creative writing programs. Critical theory has little/has a great deal to offer creative writers. Creative writers are harmed/hurt by (choose: employment in English departments, teaching, the study of theory). Creative writing/writers should/should not be political. National funding for the arts is essential/problematic. Publishing is a crapshoot. The novel is dead. Workshops produce McWriters.

And so our theories grow and go.

THERAPY (AND THERAPEUTIC)

Many writers describe their will to write as springing from a complex mixture of intellectual concerns and activities that support their fascination with language, their desire to investigate or understand thought, their commitment to self-knowledge (spiced by general or even unrelenting human curiosity), their drive to communicate (particularly for the introverts among us) or to develop a speaking platform (particularly for the dispossessed). Many authors also point to the affective dimensions of their craft, admitting that writing is also therapeutic process and a necessary constituent of their daily lives. Jeffrey Berman and Jonathan Schiff lay out the connections between writing and talking "cures," emphasizing that while there are differences there are also many and important similarities, since both

> encourage people to express their problems, find constructive solutions to them, and thus achieve control over their lives. Talking and writing are

therapeutic regardless of the explanatory system that is used and regardless of whether anyone hears or reads one's words. As [researcher] James Pennebaker [1990] has demonstrated, while writing about traumatic experiences is often painful, writing leads to short-term and long-term improvements in both physical and psychological health. Whether one believes that writing leads to the discovery of truths by which to live or the construction of these truths, what is most important is that by writing about our life stories, we are able to compare them with others' and broaden our point of view. If knowledge is power, then there is no better way to empower ourselves than through reading and writing. (2000, 308–309).

Historically, creative writers have been viewed as and have attested to being prone to depression and affective disorders (see "Creativity") and also regularly attest to their twinned sense of being marginalized and having a calling (see "Author" and Simonton [1999, 96] for a chart of "Alleged Psychopathology among Eminent Creators"). Productive writers take the attributes of risk taking, intensity or overexcitabilty, naiveté, intuition and perception, and transmit them into productivity. Jane Piirto suggests personality configurations exist among writers that would lead them to strive for the sorts of empowerment through writing outlined by Berman and Schiff above. Piirto found the following of the creative writers in her sample:

> Highly verbal, highly conceptual, highly opinionated, often nonconforming, frank, highly driven writers are prone to self-abusive and self-destructive behavior even as they are enriching the lives of their readers. But this is not always the case, and there are many writers whose lives are not lived so tragically, or who have, as Styron said, "struggled through." The high incidence of depression would seem to be an indication of the intense sensitivity with which creative people apprehend the world. It is as if the senses were tuned louder, stronger, higher, and so the task becomes to communicate the experience of both pain and joy.
>
> The creative person's products become consumable commodities for the public, but these very products are the stuff of life for the creative person. (2002, 75–76)

Not surprisingly, then, in interviews or in writings about writing, authors regularly attest to the therapeutic aspects of their craft, which they find are many and varied. Some see writing as a spiritual journey. "It's very profound self-analysis. It's like meditation," explains Erica Jong (Piirto 2002, 187). For others, writing aids in a process of reclamation or self-empowerment, part of a healing process, medical or spiritual. Gary Snyder suggests writing is "a healing act . . . it means healing psychological distress, integrating people in the Jungian sense, their inner discontinuities harmonized . . . to be healed is to be sane, and to be sane is to be very energetic, rather than tranquilized."

At the same time, writing offers the hope of connecting the (re)(integrated)self to the world. Patricia Goedicke explains, "I write to keep myself honest. I write for pleasure, for rolling words around in the mouth. I write for poetry's great, healing ability to move us beyond ourselves" (Piirto 2002, 185). And writing protects the individual by allowing the writer to deal with chaos. "Maybe the reason for writing anything down, letters, diaries, poems or a grocery list is to keep what is from dissolving," explains Lynn Lifshin. "I've shelves full of diaries," she says, "sometimes they seem more like a moat around what is happening than a bridge" (188). Writing is regularly described as a tool in the search for integration and a talismanic act of self-protection and expression. "I keep writing to understand my own life, and express the truth as I see it around me" (187), explains Linda Hasselstrom.

In addition, published authors readily acknowledge their need to deal with intense psychological traumas. Early loss of parents. Physical and sexual abuse. Depression. Alcoholism. All are dealt with, transcended, and/or drawn upon. Willa Cather acknowledges the power of early life experience, believing that a writer "may acquire a great many interesting and vivid impressions in his mature years, but his thematic material he acquires under fifteen years of age" (Cather, 1921). And Milan Kundera sees the self as an inevitable subject: "But isn't it true that an author can write only about himself?" (Murray 1990, 19).

Not only does writing help authors process the events of their younger years, it also helps them grapple with the continuing and developing affective challenges of their lives. Writing helps the survivor testify to personal and global trauma, war and dislocation. Early loss teaches how to deal with later loss. In writers' explanations, we hear the echo of the Book of Job's "I alone am escaped to tell thee," and when we examine a definition of trauma, we realize why these experiences must be processed. "Trauma is enacted in a liminal state, outside the bounds of 'normal' human experience, and the subject is radically ungrounded. Accurate representations of trauma can never be achieved without recreating the event since, by its very definition, trauma lies beyond the bounds of 'normal' conception" (Tal 1996, 15). In fact, it might be argued that the work of the writer or artist is to provide versions of such regroundings. And for readers, creative writers function at times as scapegoats, holy interpreters, and cultural healers.

Poets have acknowledged this testamentary function by designing forms for the ritual sharing of loss and grief (the aubade, the dawn song of lovers parting; the elegy, the memorial on the death of an individual). Confessional poets. Political witness. Memoir. In the late twentieth and early twenty-first centuries, at least, it has become increasingly obvious that writing helps individuals process and make meaning from the dark nights of their lives. In this way Isabel Allende survives the unimaginable, the death of her daughter, by returning to the written word: "But as soon as I started writing, I stopped taking medication and I could deal with the pain. I could set boundaries to the pain. I could see that this pain is called death; it's called love; it's called my daughter died. I could finally say the words aloud and I could deal with it. . . . By writing, everything became clear; it had its own space" (Piirto 2002, 183). Kenzaburo Oe, who has a son, Hikari, who was born with a brain hernia, finds that therapeutic writing returned him to the world, changed: "If Hikari hadn't been born, I think I would have given up writing or committed suicide. There I was, a famous young writer and I couldn't continue with my work. I started out an existentialist. I had to learn to hope" (157–158).

Writing, it would appear, helps set the house (of the psyche) in order, even if only temporarily. It helps humans create temporary order out of a bewildering array of lived experience, it's a speculative tool for spiritual investigation, and it's a lens that focuses the flame of catharsis. Why, then, are writers often equally eager to distance themselves from connections between writing and therapy? While a writer as prolific and successful as Stephen King might be willing to admit, "Writing is necessary for my sanity. I can externalize my fears and insecurities and night terrors on paper, which is what people pay shrinks a small fortune to do." For others, this is an admission not to be shared. If too confessional, if driven primarily by therapeutic aims, if sentiment overpowers craft, writers (possibly rightly) worry that their work will seen as "mere therapy," and therefore not valuable art. That is, it will be admired for *pathos* and not for the power of the word, *logos*. Greek rhetoricians realized that effective writers drew on emotions, words, and a speaker's presence, *ethos*, to shape the constructed artifact (in their case, speech). Taste changes, and that includes our expectation for how much sentiment and emotion are allowed into the brew of a successful text. Our belief that excellent writing exhibits a particular degree or sort of sentiment, presence, or intellectual wordplay has much to do with the communities of readers we affiliate with as writers (see "Postmodernism," "Theory," and "Reading"). For some, Charles Dickens is sensationalist; for others, not so much. But of course Dickens himself might have found something enervating and unsatisfying in the experimental novelists of our times.

Certainly there can be many a slip between the cup and the lip in moving between writing as personally valuable therapy of the sort practiced by unpublished authors and promoted by health care professionals (see the *Journal of Poetry Therapy*) to the shaping of public art of examination, witness, and testimony. *The Bell Jar, One Flew over the Cuckoo's Nest*, and *Girl, Interrupted* perform different textual work than do the therapist's notes, the patient's unsent letters or journal, or the sufferer's e-mail to his spouse.

While many writers would claim that all writing sinks its roots in the nutrients of the therapeutic process, there are others who would sharply disagree and who distrust the "merely" or "primarily" personal impulse in art, finding it messy and seemingly ungovernable. The problem seems to come when we forget that not all therapeutic writing is or should be public writing. Equally, we forget that in policing sentiment and emotion in writing we are probably doing so because we are disturbed by its disruptive, carnivalesque potentials. Aims and audiences matter crucially in this discussion.

"Happy families are all alike; every unhappy family is unhappy in its own way." If all happy writings (like all happy families) are so undistinguished, and all writing based in trauma, like the unhappy Oblonsky family in Tolstoy's *Anna Karenina*, is of much greater authorial interest, then it is no surprise that writers ply the profitable territories of strife, death, and love.

However, for the writer in the academy, the writing and therapy connection gains another layer of complexity when one considers the classroom as a site of sharing. Writing may be a therapeutic process, but a writing class, most agree, is not and should not be a course in personal therapy. Ann Murphy reminds us that "the analogy between the two professions [psychotherapy and teaching] is not symmetrical: analysis . . . may be a 'pedagogical experience,' but teaching is not a purely psychoanalytical one" (1989, 179). Because of this, it's important to distinguish between terms. "Therapy . . . is a change-process that takes place with another person (in our culture, a person who has undergone rigorous training, controlled and prescribed for the specific fields within the profession). Processes can be therapeutic; they can make you feel healthy and facilitate change, but the processes themselves are not 'therapy.' Thus, 'therapeutic process seems to be the more appropriate term for what happens in a writing class'" (Reid and Lord, qtd. in Bishop 1997, 144).

Certainly some writers choose to disclose "the facts" of their lives, but we should be wary about assuming that disclosure equals truth. Instead, we should understand that the result of writing as a therapeutic process is the public rendering of a version, like any other constructed version of reality. John Edgar Wideman offers a useful caution to those who equate confession or the exploration of trauma or even apparently artless testimonial writing as indisputable evidence that the author is sharing his inner soul: "When I write," explains Wideman, "I don't open up my life for people to see; I open up what I want people to see. Writing is both revealing and an act of concealment. It is deciding to construct a public persona. It is often a preemptive strike. One might write because one doesn't want people to know one's life." Understanding that the personal made public is a crafted version may help teachers of writing deal with a pedagogical life spent in intense emotional terrain.

Many teachers focus on the process and on the product, refusing to treat the resulting construction as an unrevisable memorial to Truth, or fact. They are equally careful to respect the person behind the project. Identity politics and postmodernism (qq.v.) have complicated our understandings of the personal in the writing classroom and are discussed in useful depth by Michelle Payne in *Bodily Discourses*. While published authors, viewed professionally, have a body of texts and traditions that legitimize the personal subject, student writers are caught in institutional hierarchies of powers that seek to regularize their behavior in ways that suggest emotions and investigations of the personal are aberrant and solely individual. Payne suggests that "it is important that we, as writing teachers, stop seeing emotion, pain, and trauma as threatening, anti-intellectual, and solipsistic, and instead begin to ask how we might, like therapists, feminists theorists, and philosophers, begin to recognize them as ways of knowing" (2002, 31). In teaching writing, we are moving from the days of *don't* to the days of *might* toward the days of *should*. For instance,

> As Pennebaker [1990] and others have shown, most people are helped by speaking or writing to another of their experiences even if the "other" is not a trained therapist. . . . Felman and Laub argue in their book *Testimony* that personal and cultural recovery from trauma requires a conversation between the victim and a witness, that indeed the witness is an utter necessity to complete

the cycle of truth telling. If we shy away from offering our students the opportunity to tell their truths, we may be preventing them from learning what control they can have over their own lives. The more violent and threatening our culture becomes, the more we need to acknowledge the effects of trauma on our students. Those of us whose professional lives are defined by the classroom need to be aware that every pair of eyes facing us has probably borne witness to some difficult moments that can affect learning. (MacCurdy 2000, 197)

However, for many writers, the fact that they are sensitive investigators of and recorders of human history is exactly what sets them apart from other individuals, even when these individuals are their students. Writers, they know, go beyond therapeutic personal journaling and group therapy training to construct the written record. Lynn Freed speaks to the tacit worry many writers share that making too strong a connection between writing and therapy will trivialize their art and result in the sense that anyone can open up a vein and bleed sentiment onto a page. For Freed, the task facing the writer is to "avoid the awful curse of sentimentality and nostalgia," which "clouds the truth with threadbare images, useless abstractions" (2005, 24).

Our stories can't simply be "told"; they must be shaped. In the workshop (q.v.), the focus is on the tools and techniques of craft. While writers have long expressed their personalities in the bar and at the late-night gatherings at the conference, they have been trained to focus on the text, just the text, Ma'am, in their own version of New Critical rigor. Most of the last century, writers went to school with images of the master writer-novice relationship filling their heads (and the Oedipal and Elektra baggage some of these images engender). They continue to be trained to seek to join the tradition, which means emulating masters and modeling via imitation and emulation (anyone who attends the AWP convention knows the writer arrives dressed differently than the MLA attendee, and emulation can and does move from dress to lifestyle).

Creative writing teachers in that sense are different from certain of their counterparts in composition who may not view themselves as writers nor view the subject of writing in a similarly personal manner. Composition teachers, have, in fact, tended in recent years to move from personal pedagogies toward social pedagogies (see "Theory"), even as some in the field suggest that there is an artificial divide created by such distinctions (see Payne 2002). Inevitably, *student* writers draw on the same wellsprings as any individual making meaning through text making. Because of this,

Lad Tobin (1991) argues for exploring the connections between health professions and the professions of writing instruction, and Robert Brooke (1987) and Eric Torgerson (1988) suggest that the teaching relationship is about transference (students becoming deeply interested in the teacher's self) and countertransference (teachers becoming deeply interested in the student's self), which may involve teachers and students in emotional relationships with ethical dimensions. "You cannot lay pen to paper, you cannot write a poem, without the desire to communicate . . . we're all in this together. It's our own blood that we're writing with, using this ink. That's all right. This is our little secret," explains Alicia Ostriker. When the creative writer's "little secret" is being extended to thousands of college students across the country via required writing classes—which are currently being taught so well that those moments of transference as well as the image of creative writer are leading students to an elective creative writing course in a subsequent term—discussions about the therapeutic aspects of the endeavor are sure to arise.

We should be wary of the tradition that suggests that when an expert mines the psyche, trauma is a "normal" subject, but when a novice explores the same territory, she's indulging in abnormal behavior and producing a text fated to exhibit the hallmarks of naiveté, indulgence, and aesthetic murder. When a student enters the writing classroom, we can predict that student brings along with him a history of complicated life experiences; they can't be left at the door, and the testimony of successful writers suggests that they shouldn't be. "Psychiatrist Alice Miller wrote that creativity results when there is trauma with warmth present; destructiveness is the result when there is no warmth present" (Piirto 2002, 155). The pedagogy that doesn't treat trauma with warmth (of certain sorts) is contributing to a culture of destructiveness. Tilly Warnock finds that "[t]here is no guarantee, of course, that reading and writing make people act more wisely. But, writing and reading, by expanding our experience and repertoire of strategies, can provide additional possibilities from which we may choose in order to live and act effectively in specific contexts" (2000, 51). And Mark Bratcher argues: "For cultural workers—teachers, critics, and others—who want their work to serve the end of positive social change, a psychoanalytic writing pedagogy offers the opportunity to undermine the psychological roots of many social problems, such as intolerance and various forms of self-destructive behavior" (1999, 2).

Creative writers have long learned to harness the power of the personal in their own lives and writing and have the chance to amplify those insights as they work with young writers. This does not demand a course in counseling (though that could never hurt), but it does suggest that writers bring their own sensitivity about these issues to the pedagogical scene. Michelle Payne emphasizes that "we don't need to reinforce the violence that has destroyed someone else's humanity by banning that person's story from the classroom or rallying around our roles as gatekeepers of the rational class" (2002, 128), arguing instead that writing teachers need to be willing to listen to stories and texts, to help writers shape what they find there within supportive yet professional classroom communities. Mark Bratcher directs us toward language, claiming that "[i]t would be much more prudent for them [teachers] to follow Lacan's advice to analysts and, instead of trying to divine students' needs and desires by means of their own empathetic and intuitive powers, focus like Lacanian analysis on students' language and help them recognize and grapple with the desire embodied in their own utterances" (1999, 182).

Language and the desire embodied in utterance. Writing as a therapeutic process. We have admired the bravery with which the poet writes about loss, the memoirist writes about abuse, the novelist writes about violence and dependency. We have turned to those works that investigate the unhappy (and sometimes even the happy) family and in so doing join in a literary conversation of reintegration and, some feel, redemption. We have turned to the work of peers for solace. We grapple with our pasts and find our futures. We have revealed and concealed. Evidently, we, as well as our students, craft our work from and with our lives.

TRANSLATION

Anyone who has taken a foreign language class and attempted to translate either from the source language into English or vice versa knows the difficulties translators face. Even fluent bilingual speakers may have trouble with an accurate rendering in writing, and those who are learning a new language from scratch struggle mightily with grammar and vocabulary, syntax and tone. One can illustrate just how much meaning and nuance are lost in any translation by using a popular computer program like AltaVista's Babel Fish (world.altavista.com/). Here is what the previous sentence looks after being translated from English to French and back to English again: "One can illustrate just how much significance and nuance are lost in the translation by using a programme of great diffusion of translation per computer like fish of Babel d'AltaVista." A careful reader should be able to tease out the sense of the source message in the confusing second half of the sentence. But then again, maybe not. At any rate, computers are clearly a long way from being the answer for translators, and if translating a fairly straightforward sentence of prose is fraught with difficulty, translating a complex work of literature is that much more daunting.

Susan Bassnett and André Lefevere divide the history of literary translation into three main models. The Horace model is pragmatic and based on expediency. The Roman poet was purportedly an astute businessman, delivering to his customers a quick and reliable—if not especially subtle—product. A translator in this model can be trusted in both the source and the target language, but ultimately negotiation between the two languages is "always slanted toward the privileged language, and . . . the negotiation does not take place on absolutely equal terms" (1998, 4). The Jerome model, styled after Saint Jerome's translation of the Bible, was "characterized by the presence of a central, sacred text, that of the Bible, which must be translated with the utmost fidelity" (2). While this model prevailed for centuries, it was eventually replaced by the Schleiermacher model, named for the German translator Friedrich Schleiermacher. He believed that "the reader should be able to guess the Spanish behind a translation from Spanish, and the Greek behind a translation from Greek. If all translations read and sound alike . . . the identity of the source text has been lost" (8). Cultural sensitivity, attempting to honor *both* the source and target languages, is at the heart of this model.

Lefevere and Bassnett see the future of translation studies as continuing to focus still more on the historical and cultural circumstances in which the work was created, a goal with which Gayatri Spivak would be sympathetic. Spivak maintains that "the translator from a Third World language should be sufficiently in touch with what is going on in literary production in that language to be capable of distinguishing between good and bad writing. . . . She must be able to confront the idea that what seems resistant in the space of English may be reactionary in the space of the original language" (1992, 404). And it is not just the *translator's* responsibility to understand the work's culture of origin. According to Kwame Anthony Appiah, the teacher—and by implication, all readers—must do so as well: "utterances are the products of actions, which like all actions, are undertaken for reasons. Understanding the reasons characteristic of other cultures and . . . other times is part of what our teaching is about" (1993, 427). Of course, in the postcolonial world, there are no simple exchanges between the former colonizers and their former subject peoples. Because translators of third world literature "can shift allegiances . . . they are, therefore, not to be trusted" (Cronin 2000, 39). And while many writers from third world and/or politically repressed countries welcome the opportunity to have their work read abroad, some scholars worry that translating work from these countries into European languages is ultimately exploitive rather than liberating.

Even setting the focus on cultural awareness aside—and it is probably impossible to do so—literary translators inevitably face numerous technical problems. Translating metrical poetry is perhaps the most forbidding task. Lefevere mentions a number of the tricks employed by translators trying to be true to the exact rhythm of the original: truncating words, using "sense equivalents," resorting "to words that do not really belong in the target language but are understood by most of its readers," using archaisms and "ready-made utterances," "expressing one . . . notion in the source text with two closely related words in the translation," and—the translator's great bane—padding (1975, 38–39). As all these expediencies suggest, replicating the meter and rhyme of the original poem has the potential to do more damage than good.

Exasperated by the many obstacles of rendering formal verse into a target language, some translators essentially give up, arguing that is virtually impossible to reproduce a poem in a new language. These translators acknowledge the impediments up front and strive for a "humble fidelity" to the literal meaning of the work. Based on his own attempts to translate Pushkin's novel-in-verse *Eugene Onegin*, Vladimir Nabokov came to the following conclusions: "I want translations with copious footnotes, footnotes reached up like skyscrapers to the top of this or that page so as to leave only the gleam of one textual line between commentary and eternity. I want such footnotes and the absolutely literal sense, with no emasculation and no padding—I want such sense and such notes for all the poetry in other tongues that still languishes in 'poetical' versions, begrimed and beslimed by rhyme" (1955, 83). Ironically, Nabokov's translation of *Onegin* has been widely panned for being *too* literal, for failing to attempt to capture the music of the original.

Perhaps, as Bassnett argues, the very world "'translation' is vague and unhelpful," and has been for a long time. Bassnett claims that "quibbling about determining the difference between 'adaptations' and 'versions' and 'imitations'" is an unfortunate, and relatively recent, occurrence: "The medieval world had a far more open attitude to translation and writers do not seem to have operated with a binary opposition between translation and original, but with a cline along which the meaning of those terms passes though many different shades. Indeed, as has been so often demonstrated, the concept of the original is a product of Enlightenment thinking. It is a modern invention, belonging to a materialist age, and carries with it all kinds of commercial implications about translation, originality and textual ownership" (Bassnett and Lefevere 1998, 38).

Once a work of literature exists in a new language, is it a new creation or simply a secondhand version of the original? As suggested above, the aesthetic answer to that question isn't likely to be decided anytime soon. The "commercial implications," however, are easier to track down, since translations bring copyright and royalty (qq.v.) issues into play. Laws vary from country to country, depending on where the original and the translation are published. European-based translators tend to have their work well-protected and well-remunerated. In contrast, Breon Mitchell warns American translators against working though the "flat-fee system," in which the copyright belongs to the person who hired the translator: "In this case, you lose your moral and legal rights. . . . It's very important to avoid the work-for-hire syndrome, and instead to insist on payment in advance against royalties, which gives you an ongoing legal interest in [the translation]" (Homel and Simon 1988, 79).

Despite the many difficulties inherent in translating works of literature, translation will likely remain a key feature of the literary landscape for some time to come. Indeed, creative writers with a facility for second languages may find translation an avenue to publication, payment, and even name recognition. After all, translators "are, at present, responsible for the general reception and survival of works of literature among non-professional readers, who constitute the great majority of readers in our global culture, to at least the same, if not to a greater extent than the [translated] writers themselves" (Lefevere 1992, 1). Moreover, translating a poem "is one way of learning what delicate clockwork causes the poem to keep accurate faith with music, meaning and time" (Hirshfield 1997, 79).

While other countries are increasingly becoming bi- and tri- and quadrilingual, many Americans remain stubbornly monolingual: the popularity of "English-only" statutes in states throughout the country demonstrates just how entrenched our fear of The Other is. Yet curious creative writers will continue wanting to know what is being written outside their home country, outside the language that, at times, may seem more like a prison house than a means of communication and understanding.

Two-Year Colleges

Most of the research on creative writing focuses on students enrolled in either four-year colleges and universities or graduate programs. In sharp contrast, there is very little material about teaching creative writing at the community college level, although most two-year college English departments offer creative writing courses. Because there is so much basic research yet to do, two-year colleges are a potentially rich source for future investigation. This entry will be limited to an examination of four significant aspects of community college creative writing courses: staffing, resources, student population, and student motivations and goals.

STAFFING

A large research university, especially one that supports a graduate creative writing program, can hire an entire creative writing department. Such programs may have individual writers who specialize not only in poetry, drama, and fiction but also in literary journalism, nature writing, screenwriting, and so on. And within the confines of individual genres, individual faculty members will have differing aesthetics. Students, in short, receive a range of approaches to writing creatively. Even a small liberal arts college generally has one member of the English faculty whose primary responsibility is teaching creative writing. That person may well have resources to periodically bring visiting writers to campus and perhaps to sponsor a writing conference. In the four-year college, creative writing has a real and varied presence: it is a viable entity with a face, or faces, to make it substantial and human.

Community colleges, on the other hand, don't normally have a surfeit of creative writing teachers. Indeed, faculty who teach the courses may not self-identify primarily as creative writers, and typically there are only one or two such courses offered each semester. Therefore, the creative writing teacher must not only introduce students to her own particular ideas and attitudes, she must also fairly represent the sorts of writing that she herself does not do or does not like. Moreover, if an instructor is part-time and she has no full-time colleagues who are creative writers, she clearly faces challenges in establishing creative writing as a significant part of the curriculum. Part of her mission will be to remind other members of her department how important it is for *all* students to have the opportunity to write creatively, even if, as Ed Davis acknowledges in "Our Corner of the Sky," "courses at community colleges may not grow much beyond what we have now" (Waggoner 2001, 68).

RESOURCES

As every elementary and secondary schoolteacher knows too well, class size dictates course design. In four-year institutions, introductory creative writing courses range from fifteen to twenty-five students. Instructors of these courses tend to take certain things for granted. They may, for instance, assume that every student will be able to have every significant assignment workshopped by the entire class. However, in the two-year college, it is not uncommon for a writing course to have thirty or forty students. There simply isn't enough time (or resources) to critique every person's short story as a full class. It's unrealistic to think that students who are sometimes just barely making ends meet can afford to make thirty photocopies of a 10-page story. At most copy shops that's $24—the day's food budget for many two-year college students. Community college teachers also quickly learn how crucial it is to select textbooks wisely; they take no expense for granted.

Of course a well-stocked library can supplement required classroom texts, but two-year college library collections are nearly always much smaller than those of universities. Granted, this may mean more in theory than in practice. Most four-year college students don't read extensively outside their assigned syllabi; however, they *do* have the option to do so, to delve deeper into a single author, to read around, to browse. Even a mediocre research library allows students the important insight that T. S. Eliot was not the last American poet, that the art of the novel did not die with Ernest Hemingway.

If modest library holdings mean students won't be able to read and review volumes of contemporary poetry and fiction, they also mean students will have limited access to literary periodicals. Research libraries can subscribe to a range of journals, showcasing writers from different schools and different geographies. Community college periodical collections focus more on general-interest magazines than discipline-specific journals. These libraries can only afford a few, if any, literary journals—a circumstance that tends to foreshorten students' ideas of what it is possible to write. Yes, the *New Yorker* and *Poetry* magazine contain quality creative writing, but they give students the idea that entry to the world of publication is through a very narrow door, indeed.

Two-year college students don't expect their institutions to have the same resources as land-grant research universities, but they *do* expect something like the education they would get at a four-year school. Not every student is so cash-strapped that he can't afford a textbook—although at some community colleges this is a real problem—but instructors should remember that a wealth of canonical and contemporary literature is now online. Since Web access on campus is not a problem at most community colleges, teachers may either supplement or replace their textbooks by creating a course home page with appropriate links. The quality of literary Webzines has improved markedly over the past five years, and most reputable print journals now include at least some full-text poems, stories, and essays on their Web sites. The literary journals on webdelsol.com alone could easily make for a semester's worth of exciting multicultural, multigenre reading for a financially stressed class.

STUDENT POPULATION

In most places, the two-year college population is far more diverse than in the four-year college. In these courses (to cite an example of one of our recent classes), the international student from Korea sits next to the Anglo student from the 'burbs who sits next to the Latina student from the barrio. The student who can't afford the textbook is sitting next to the student whose parents just bought him a new BMW. The student who's been struggling with a learning disability for the past six years as she tries to earn her AA sits next to the retired businesswoman with an MBA from UCLA. Incidentally, students enrolling in community college creative writing classes with BAs already in hand are not uncommon. These students normally come to class with positive attitudes and solid leadership experience, and they often have considerable experience as writers, even if they've only shared their writing with friends and family.

This diversity of student population provides both the greatest rewards and the greatest challenges for the two-year college creative writing teacher. The rewards are obvious. For every struggling writer there is one who shows flashes of brilliance. Class members learn that perspectives vary with race, culture, age, class, and sexual orientation. Because it is more flexible than expository prose, creative writing allows English as a Second

Language (ESL) students to more fully engage in their first-language discourse patterns. All students can abandon the stiff formality they associate with academic prose and embrace the role of *vates* or raconteur: they can, in short, find their own voices.

The challenges come in the form of designing assignments that are stimulating to the brightest students yet manageable for slower learners. Experienced instructors recommend breaking into small groups whenever possible so that stronger writers can help the less skilled. However, even in the unlikely event that most students are writing at approximately the same level, their reading background will probably be less extensive than that of their peers at the university. The majority of students in a four-year college creative writing course are English majors. Even if they're not, they're likely to have taken a literature course or two. The same assumption cannot be made about two-year college students, who have probably read less in canonical English literature, though they may be much better read in genre fiction like horror and sci-fi. Ultimately, as Steve Abbott notes, "it's less what two-year schools have to offer than *who* they offer it to" (Waggoner 2001, 60).

MOTIVATIONS AND GOALS

If there are so many differences between two- and four-year colleges, should community college instructors expect the same from their students as their colleagues at the university? The answer is yes, especially if their courses will earn transfer credit. Fortunately, the level of engagement of most two-year students justifies this rigor. Although it may seem counterintuitive, many community college students are more serious than their four-year peers. One reason is that two-year college students are less likely to take a creative writing course as an elective. Those who intend to transfer to a four-year college—the vast majority, that is—have less flexibility in their schedules than students already enrolled in the university. In general, they take the courses they *need* rather than the courses they *want*. Therefore, students who do take creative writing as an elective tend to be more committed—they truly want to improve as writers. And of course students who already have their bachelor's degrees—who come in for a three-hour night class after a full day of work—are clearly enrolled in the course because they're there to become writers.

There *is* usually a small contingent that enrolls in the course on a whim, but the workload tends to drive them off. Once they realize their instructor has real goals for them as writers—that they need to write, read, and come to class—students who don't want to make a serious commitment simply drop the class.

CONCLUSION

Perhaps the most important thing to remember about the community college creative writing classroom is how essential it is to the community itself. Above all, it is a true bargain. As Ed Davis says in "Our Corner of the Sky," "We're kind of like a well-kept secret and people haven't caught on that they can have a creative writing teacher of quality for less than a hundred bucks" (Waggoner 2001, 68). In many parts of the country, there aren't many other affordable options for aspiring writers who aren't full-time students at a university.

Prior to the publication of books like *Released into Language* (Bishop 1998), *Creative Writing in America* (Moxley 1989), and *Colors of a Different Horse* (Bishop and Ostrom 1994), four-year college and graduate school creative writing professors suffered from a dearth of pertinent research. Two-year college instructors are currently in a similar predicament. Whether they've secretly wanted to be writers for thirty years, or just been told by their English teachers that they've got some talent, community college students *do* want to learn. The important work of finding effective ways to serve this vulnerable population is largely still to come.

VANITY PRESS

According to the National Endowment for the Arts (NEA) guidelines for fellowship for creative writers, a vanity press publication is defined as one that does any of the following: "requires individual writers to pay for part or all of the publication costs; asks writers to buy or sell copies of the publication; publishes the work of anyone who subscribes to the publication or joins the organization through membership fees; publishes the work of anyone who buys an advertisement in the publication; or publishes work without competitive selection" (U.S. Office of Management and Budget 1999, 5–6).

Of course, if the NEA were to enforce this policy strictly, there would be very few fellowship applicants. Rare is the magazine, even the most prestigious, that doesn't encourage its contributors to subscribe and/or purchase extra copies. Many quite prestigious journals indicate in their submission guidelines that subscribers receive preferential treatment; the *Hudson Review,* for instance, reads unsolicited poetry from nonsubscribers only for four months of the year, while subscribers may submit at any time. And "competitive selection" is clearly a term fraught with ambiguity. In short, it's not as easy as one might believe to pinpoint just what a "vanity press" is.

The problem of defining this keyword is compounded by historical circumstances. Writers have been complaining about the equivalent of vanity press publications almost since the beginning of writing itself, with the poets of classical Greece and Rome particularly adept at satirizing those who paid to have their own work distributed. Moreover, from Gutenberg to the inception of the circulating libraries in the early nineteenth century, most books were what would now be called self-publications. If an author was wealthy enough, he—almost always it was a he—paid a printer to bring out his book, which he then passed out to friends, family members, and anyone else he thought might be interested and/or able to promote his career. Not surprisingly, with wealth rather than talent as a fundamental means of access to publication, far more bad work than good reached print.

Yet, ultimately, the current pariah status of vanity press publications is the direct result of the professionalization of creative writing. With book publication and/or extensive publications in literary journals a requirement for candidates seeking academic jobs, the need becomes pronounced to distinguish between writers who have paid someone to print their work and those whose writing has met with the approbation of an editor or editors. Because patiently putting together a record of "legitimate" publications is the equivalent of "paying one's dues" as a blues musician, the taboo against vanity press publications helps academic hiring committees screen out writers who haven't taken the approved route to success. Similarly, magazine editors and book publishers, who may receive many thousands of submissions a year, can do some initial screening simply by checking to see whether a writer has published a previous book with a "reputable" publisher. The effect for academic creative writers can be synergistic. Should a job candidate, for instance, be one of those rare individuals fortunate enough to have her books published by a trade publisher, she is likely to receive maximum respect from both hiring committees and literary publishers. Likewise, publication by a university press, or through one of the countless contests, will also serve as validation for her poetry or fiction.

However, one may wonder whether—given the hundreds of submissions to most book contests and the frequent accusations of logrolling against judges (see "Contests")—the prejudice against vanity press publications is justified. No doubt there are irregularities in the creative writing business: one hand constantly washes another. Still, we can be pretty certain that for every Walt Whitman—an unknown writer with the courage to bring his boldly innovative work directly to an audience who hasn't yet recognized his brilliance—there are a countless Whit Waltmans—unknown writers whose work is careless and self-indulgent, primarily of interest only to themselves. If the bias against those whose work has been published by vanity presses excludes the occasional good writer, the legions of authors clamoring for recognition probably make this tendency inevitable.

Finally, we ought to differentiate between publishing with a vanity press and self-publication. Although the two terms are often used interchangeably, there *is* a notable difference. The self-published writer pays to have her book made by a book-making company. She shops around for the lowest price and the best-quality product and has no illusions that the publisher will promote her work. Instead, she actively markets the book herself, and if she does a good job she may eventually even see a profit. (See *The Complete Guide to Self-Publishing* [Ross and Ross 2002] for details.) In contrast, publication with a vanity press is more than a simple exchange of money for product. Vanity presses often make vague promises of fame that the publisher has no ability to keep, and their profit margins are unconscionably fat: they lure writers into spending far more money than is necessary to produce the book. As an added insult, rather than delivering all copies to the writer, the press may retain a portion of the print run itself, then charge the writer even more for those copies of the book when, inevitably, it fails to sell.

Perhaps the best-known vanity press scam is the advertisement placed in newspapers and teen and homemaking magazines encouraging new and unpublished writers to submit their work to an anthology of poetry. Cash prizes are promised—and may even be paid—but the real money is made by accepting everyone who submits a poem. The publishers pay no money and no contributor's copy (q.v.), but they do charge writers for the book in which their work appears. Using thin paper and cramming many authors onto a single page, these volumes, of a thousand pages plus, can run more than $100; unsuspecting authors are bilked of even more money if they are seduced into purchasing elaborate bindings or multiple copies of the book for family and friends. In such cases, the preacher does truly warn, "Vanitias Vanitatum," for these vulturelike publishers feed on the author's own overweening desire to see his name in print.

WORKSHOP

Loosely defined, the workshop model of artistic development is probably as old as art itself. Historians believe that ancient Egyptian sculpture and wall paintings, for instance, were the result of a communal effort involving both skilled artisans and those in training. Certainly, the medieval craft guilds exerted an influence on apprentice-master relations in the arts, and Renaissance painters often employed underlings who would complete the uninteresting background work for a master painter, just as Renaissance playwrights occasionally relied on apprentices to help finish their plays.

In the context of twentieth-century American literature, however, the word "workshop" has come to have a fairly specific meaning. Although D. G. Myers argues in "Educating Writers: The Beginnings of 'Creative Writing' in the American University" (1989) that the pedagogical practices we now take for granted have their roots in Harvard's late-nineteenth-century freshman composition courses, the more obvious source of the writing workshop is the University of Iowa's creative writing program. Begun in 1930 by Norman Foerster, the program awarded its first MFA to Paul Engle (later head of the program) and gradually expanded, eventually producing a dozen Pulitzer Prize winners and three U.S. Poet Laureates. Among the prominent writers who have graduated from the Iowa Writers' Workshop are Robert Bly, Raymond Carver, Rita Dove, Andre Dubus, John Irving, Donald Justice, Tracy Kidder, Philip Levine, Flannery O'Connor, Jane Smiley, William Stafford, Wallace Stegner, Mark Strand, and Margaret Walker. With success breeding success, and the Iowa graduates themselves becoming college professors, the hegemony of the workshop model was quickly established, its naturalness as the dominant form of pedagogy becoming a matter of common sense.

Over time, several shared qualities have emerged in most American creative writing workshops. Typically, the student whose work is under discussion will pass his story, play, poem, or essay out the class period before it is to be workshopped (the noun has long since also become a verb). The other students read and comment on the draft at home, then the piece is discussed in class. In order to avoid sessions that amount to nothing more than an extended self-defense of the work, the author is normally asked not to speak while discussion of his manuscript is in progress. After the workshop, students return their marked copies to further guide the writer's revisions. Anyone who has ever had the full attention of fifteen or twenty fellow writers trained on her work knows it can be a harrowing process. As Jan Ramjerdi writes, "What most characterizes the workshops, distinguishing them from academic classrooms, is their *intensity,* deriving, I think, from the fact that *more is at stake in the workshop than in the academic classroom.* . . . [T]here is no object of study that filters, directs, constrains, and distances responses as there is in academic classes" (Ramjerdi and Garber 1994, 14).

If the workshop personalizes literary criticism, it also implies that writing is a craft. Yet creative writing instructors tend to take this idea for granted and remain unaware of the significance it has for their pedagogy. Most importantly, the workshop model suggests that writing, like carpentry, *can be* both learned and taught. While the qualities that make a master carpenter—a feel for wood, a knowledge of the appropriate tools, precision, perceptiveness, and so on—may be as elusive as those that make a master writer, the assumption is that just about anyone can become functional in the craft. And, indeed, that is what has happened in creative writing—to the chagrin of those editors who complain of a deluge of mind-numbingly uniform work, of McPoems and McStories. Nevertheless, the workshop *has* led to an unprecedented democratization of imaginative writing in America. Now that nearly every American high school and community college offers at least one creative writing class, access to basic instruction in the art is widely available.

Still, not all assessments of the writing workshop are positive. From a pragmatic point of view, there is the cost and inconvenience of distributing manuscripts, which can be particularly problematic in community colleges (see "Two-Year Colleges"). Many two-year (and some four-year) college students simply cannot afford the $20–40 it requires to photocopy a short story. And while sending work via e-mail circumvents financial issues, not everyone has Internet access, attachments may not open or they may be infected with viruses, and it is surprisingly difficult to get a full class of students to remember to print out manuscripts and bring them to class.

Moreover, once the workshop begins, students often find it difficult to sort through the sometimes wildly varying responses from their peers. If Jim raves about the characterization of the protagonist while Joan finds it absolutely spiritless, does the author entirely ignore one or the other respondent, or does she split the difference and try to accommodate both? Moreover, because the author is effectively silenced during the discussion of her piece, the potentially dialogic nature of the workshop is muted, while the New Critical assumption that the work should speak for itself is reinforced (see Roskelly 1998). Too, there is the question of the instructor's role in the workshop. Does she use her superior wisdom and experience to firmly guide the classroom give-and-take, thereby undercutting the authority of student comments, or does she adopt a less directive position and place herself in the role of fellow writer and "co-learner," possibly allowing patently bad advice to go unaddressed?

In part because of conundrums like these, in the late 1980s and throughout the 1990s the heavy reliance on workshops by creative writing faculty came under increasing scrutiny. In three edited collections—Joseph Moxley's *Creative Writing in America: Theory and Pedagogy* (1989), Wendy Bishop and Hans Ostrom's *Colors of a Different Horse: Rethinking Creative Writing Theory and Pedagogy* (1994), and David Starkey's *Teaching Writing Creatively* (1998)—contributors again and again point to the absence of any sustained theoretical approach in creative writing classes (see "Theory"). Ostrom sees instructor laziness, as much as anything else, as the reason for the workshop's popularity: "Most probably, those who retreat from theory and pedagogy are likely to fall back on the workshop in its simplest form: 'going over' poems and stories in a big circle, holding forth from time to time, pretending to have read the material carefully, breaking up squabbles like a hall monitor, marking time" (xiv). Some critics contend that the workshop should be replaced with instruction in literature, while others complain that ideological assumptions about what constitutes "good" writing are rarely questioned in the workshop because good writing is essentially whatever the instructor and the class say it is.

Obviously, the writing workshop has become an increasingly contested site in English studies. While advocates claim the workshop's emphasis on consensus and compromise is helping to build a national literature notable for its moral sense and ability to consider multiple points of view, detractors believe a herd mentality predominates, that all individuality is being lost. Yet whichever point of view eventually triumphs, there can no doubt that, for the foreseeable future, the writing workshop will continue to provide the most prevalent form of feedback to young creative writers.

WRITERS' RESOURCES

If we define a writer's resource as a place where one can find "information on the art, craft and business of writing" (Pack 1998, 24), then *Keywords in Creative Writing* is itself intended to be one of the best available writers' resources. Many of the entries in this book answer specific questions creative writers are likely to have about the profession (the reference list alone provides a wealth of articles, books, and Web sites to explore). "Conferences, Colonies, and Residencies," for instance, discusses how to connect with master writers, editors, and publishers and how to find the time and place to write. "Grants" considers avenues writers can pursue to receive funding. "Contests" examines the world of literary prizes and publications. "Writing Groups" makes suggestions for ways to link up with other writers. "Associated Writing Programs" looks at the umbrella organization for creative writing programs in American and Canadian colleges and universities. "Teaching Jobs" gives advice on finding jobs teaching creative writing. And on and on throughout the volume.

Outside of *Keywords* itself, there are a number of books that writers can consult. Almost every publisher with a line of composition textbooks also sells "handbooks," many of them with variations on the words "writers" and "resource" in their titles. These guides give advice on every aspect of writing: from how to draft an essay to how to construct a paragraph to the fine points of grammar. While creative writers will occasionally consult handbooks to make sure their work is "correct," they are unlikely to look to these books as sources of inspiration. A superior fund of information is offered by creative writing textbooks. Among the books the authors of *Keywords* have found particularly instructive are the following: in poetry (q.v.), *Writing Poetry* by Barbara Drake (1994) and *Writing Poems* by Robert Wallace and Michelle Boisseau (2003) (we also like our own textbooks, *Thirteen Ways of Looking for a Poem* by Wendy Bishop [1999] and *Poetry Writing: Theme and Variations* by David Starkey [2000]); in fiction (q.v.), *Writing Fiction* by Janet Burroway (2002); in creative nonfiction (q.v.), *The Fourth Genre* by Robert Root and Michael Steinberg (2004); for multiple genres, *Three Genres* by

Stephen Minot (2003) and *The College Handbook of Creative Writing* by Robert DeMaria (1999) and *Working Words* by Wendy Bishop (1991). There are literally hundreds more, and anyone who teaches or takes a course in creative writing will soon generate a list of favorites. Among the general books for creative writers that have guided, revived, and inspired us, we include *Bird by Bird* by Anne Lamott, *Writing Down the Bones* (1986), *Wild Mind* (1990) by Natalie Goldberg, and *On Writing* (2000) by Stephen King.

One "resource" writers should avoid is agents, editors (qq.v.), and "book doctors" who charge excessive fees for doing their work. (See also "Vanity Press.") Editorial consultant Jerry Gross points to the following indications that someone claiming to be a resource for writers is actually a scam artist:

- An editor who says you can't get published unless you hire a book doctor. He or she insists that publishers demand that a manuscript be professionally edited before they will consider it for publication, or that agents won't take on a client unless the writer first has it professionally edited.
- An editor who guarantees, or strongly implies, that the editing will get you accepted by an agent and that the agent will definitely be able to sell your book.
- An editor who has a "financial arrangement" with the person or company who referred him to you—meaning he kicks back part of his fee to the referring agent or company.
- An editor who does not guarantee that he will edit your manuscript personally, or who tells you he will subcontract your manuscript but won't tell you who will edit it, nor provide you with that editor's background, samples of that editor's work or references. Nor does he give you the right to accept or refuse the editor he suggests.
- An editor who won't provide references from authors or agents he's worked with.
- An editor who won't give you samples of his editing and/or critiques.
- A letter of agreement or contract that does not specify all the costs you will incur, what the editor will do for each of his fees, the schedule of payment and due date for delivery of the edited manuscript.
- An editor who wants the entire fee before he begins any work. (Davis 2002, 34)

Getting published by a legitimate press or literary magazine isn't easy, and beginning writers should be wary of shortcuts and quick fixes. Caveat emptor applies in creative writing as much as it does anywhere else: If it looks too good to be true, it probably is.

Simply keeping abreast of the field is a good way to become a resource oneself. Several well-established magazines offer useful advice for writers in print and, to a lesser degree, online. *Writer's Digest Magazine* (www.writersdigest.com) and the *Writer* (www.writermag.com) are geared toward freelance nonfiction writers, but they sometimes provide helpful tips for literary creative writers. Zuzu's Petals (www.zuzu.com) has one of the best resources pages for online writing and writers. *Poets and Writers Magazine* (www.pw.org) is the first place many literary writers turn to find out what editors and publishers are interested in and who's saying what about whom. While very few *P & W* print articles appear on their Web site, the online version does contain updated listings for grants and awards and publication opportunities. Of course, the ultimate resource for twenty-first-century writers is probably the Internet itself. Type a query into Google, and you're likely to come back with information that's at least as current as anything in this entry.

WRITING GROUPS

Writing is often a solitary occupation. Granted, our race, gender, and class will shape the things we are likely to say, and the literature we create struggles to find voice amid the deafening din of all the writers who have come before us. Yet when a writer sits down at her computer, she is alone. Even if she writes in the bustle and hubbub of a coffeehouse, once she begins to compose, she is—in very obvious ways—on her own. All writers know how frightening it can be to face this isolated (and isolating) process, and writing groups offer one way of confronting the solitude.

Support groups for writers have existed whenever and wherever more than one writer inhabits the same general vicinity. Anne Ruggles Gere points out that what we now call "'writing groups' . . . have existed for more than two hundred years, but the continuing 'discovery' of them demonstrates the extent to which they have remained on the edge of educational consciousness" (1987, 52). In large measure, this marginalization can be attributed to ideas that are centuries old. The myth of the solitary writer would indicate that—as Gere points out—when writers mature and come more fully into their skills, they are less likely to want or need the support of writing groups. Gere notes that this attitude comes to us from eighteenth-century notions of individual achievement and genius, and it was compounded by the romantic myth of the solitary author, which has persisted since the early nineteenth century. In this model, the author always works alone, drawing on inspiration from either unseen external forces—God, the muses—or from some deep wellspring within himself. Other people exist primarily as an audience for the *completed* work; they rarely have anything to do with creating it.

However, with the rise of feminism and composition studies, college and high school writing instructors have begun scrutinizing and questioning the romantic myth of authorship (see also "Author" and "Collaboration"). Lisa Ede and Andrea Lunsford show that those participating in "dialogic groups," rather than in hierarchical environments, "generally value the creative tension inherent in multivoiced and multivalent ventures" (1990, 133). Teacher-writers who have themselves experienced the desire to come together and share work with one another, who have received and offered constructive criticism, who have been consoled in defeat and congratulated in victory are constantly looking for ways to reproduce the dynamic of all-volunteer groups in their classrooms. When they are successful, the "nature and place of these . . . involuntary writing groups extend classroom boundaries, making the boundaries even more fluid, broadening the sites where writers interact" (6). And of course that broadening of boundaries, the sense that the extraordinary and unexpected are just around the corner, brings writers pleasure. Hephzibah Roskelly writes: "Groups are tailor made for playing. The group can assign roles, set up rules, act out situations, consider possibilities, and arrive at solutions—and have fun—as they talk together" (2003, 50).

One of the most persistent fears of inexperienced writers is that the group will overpower their individuality, but poet Barry Spacks believes that writers who fear being jerked hither and thither by the conflicting "reactions and prescriptions" of their peers should relax: "Those ideas that do not speak to your essence simply slide away, but now and then a brilliant 'save' will occur as you profit from seeing your work as if you'd taken on new sets of eyes. And there's also the side-product of mind-sharpening that comes from trying to articulate a complex response. And sometimes the hoped-for confirmation that you're really on to something"(2004).

Nevertheless, the belief that groups tend to homogenize the style and subject of their members are not unfounded. Poet Paul Willis recalls being told by Robert Hass, "Writing groups tend to revise toward clarity and away from strangeness." Willis goes on to say: "That has felt true to me. The danger is the loss of a distinctive voice, of an essential non-rational quality. On the other hand, if we need to know what is 'too' strange in our writing, a writing group is a good place to find out" (2004). Longtime writing group leader Perie Longo adds: "Writing groups are a bit like snakes, full of beauty or sting. They can move you to unprecedented heights, if they have the right make up—challenge you to look closer and improve what is there. But they can also poison your work, if opinions are too dominant. In commentary, sensitivity is key. The voice of each poet needs to be respected. But groups can help you shed the skin of each poem, help it move where it needs to go" (2004).

Writers can be difficult at times, and groups must be prepared to adapt and compromise. If writers sometimes crave the approbation of their peers, at other times they can be frustratingly solitary. If at times they make good use of criticism from their colleagues, at other times this criticism may make them want to scream or to give up writing altogether. If writers can commiserate well with others suffering fates they themselves have experienced, they can also be hopelessly egotistical and mean.

Simply *forming* a writing group that meets outside of a school setting requires diligence and ingenuity. Chris Golde suggests a writing group be put together with the following criteria in mind:

- Groups are best organized along different lines and themes . . . . Having a shared bond is an important basis for building intellectual trust.
- The participants should have a similar commitment to the group.
- A long-term commitment to the group is important.
- The number of participants should be limited, with the size of the group geared to the frequency of presentation.
- A group convener helps: someone to reserve a space, remind people who is on, etc. (1996)

We've found that in poetry groups having two or three more members in the group than is absolutely desirable is a good safety measure. Someone is always out of town or at work on something else, and there is no more discouraging meeting for a writing group than one where there are only two or three participants. On those rare occasions when everyone is able to make it to the meeting, less work will be accomplished, but there is a satisfaction in having everyone together. However, when members are all working on longer projects—essays, short stories, novel chapters, plays—a group with as few as three participants can function effectively. As long as the work is distributed ahead of time so that everyone can read it before arriving, members should be able to receive valuable and extensive feedback in a relatively short time span.

For many writers, especially those living far from urban centers, locating other writers who want to come together seems daunting. Tina Marie Smith recommends looking for fellow writers in the workplace. She claims four advantages for such groups: (1) everyone is already there, ready to meet; (2) companies often have a large and pleasant meeting space that can be used after work; (3) the writers in the group will share a common bond and level of professionalism; and (4) the networking done among writers in the group may also benefit the company for which they work (Smith 2003, 22–23).

If seeking group members at work fails, writers can always try the Internet. Fortunately, writers can take advantage online of the equivalent of posting notices in the local newspaper or on the notice boards of area coffee shops or bookstores. The Web site forwriters.com lists both national and local writing groups, as does the Yahoo! directory for Creative Writing Workshops (dir.yahoo.com/Arts/Humanities/Literature/Creative_Writing/Workshops/). In Britain, writers may turn to the National Association of Writers' Groups (www.nawg.co.uk/).

Online writing groups solve two of the biggest problems facing most writers when they want to meet with one another: time and space. Mary Pat Mahoney laments that after "I put eight hours on the job, ferry my sons to after-school activities, prepare dinner, and attempt to make a dent in the pile of laundry . . . I can usually squeeze in two hours of writing, if I don't fall asleep first! There's barely enough time to write, let alone get together with my fellow writers for a critique session. That's why I was so excited to start an on-line writing group" (2003, 67). Deepa Kandaswamy belongs to a writing group with members in India, Britain, Australia, Hong Kong, Canada, and the United States. Clearly, members cannot convene face-to-face for their meetings. Nevertheless, Kandaswamy finds the group functions effectively, provided participants interact the way they would with friends. He believes members need "individual attention;

pats on the back; prompt responses; a little empathy; and honest, intelligent, and gentle critiques" (2003, 95).

Once the group has formed, work is far from over. A writing group is not a perpetual motion machine: it needs constant, if usually minor, attention on the part of *all* of its members. Spacks warns that unwary groups can devolve from a locus for serious criticism to "the kaffeeklatsch, offering mainly a chance to socialize" (2004). Jeffrey Golub proposes a number of strategies for making participant interaction successful. He suggests group members practice the following skills during meetings:

- Ask appropriate questions as well as answer them.
- Contribute and respond, but do not dominate the discussion.
- Help the group reach agreement.
- Recognize the significance of nonverbal communication.
- Draw the group back to the topic.
- Check perceptions about and clarify the meanings of statements and ideas.
- Seek people's opinions, especially those who have not been talking. (2000, 86)

Even when groups are running smoothly, however, writers who come to rely too extensively on their group—whether it meets online or in person—inevitably face disappointments. Not everyone's advice will be equally useful, and advice may too often take the form of encouragement rather than close critical scrutiny. Tara Harper cautions: "If you are looking for a writing group to fulfill your need for professional-quality editing, you had better think about this a bit. How many professional editors do you know who hang out in writing groups just so that they can give away their time and skills for free?" (2000).

Nevertheless, both the authors of this book have benefited for decades from sharing our work in groups that have consisted of friends, colleagues, and even former students. And we are not alone. Ken Autrey points out: "Some writers, such as Ray Bradbury, have participated in a writing group for much of their careers, believing that they continue to need stimulation and critical commentary from other accomplished voices" (2004). Barry Spacks believes that "putting new poems to the test of comment by peers [is] a central device in the toolbox of poetry-work" (2004). Above all, writing groups will continue to "offer a means for individuals, both in and outside of school, to enter literate communities" (Gere 1987, 121).

REFERENCES

Abels, Caroline. 1999. Lee Gutkind Hails the Artistry to Creative Nonfiction, but Others Approach It with Distrust. *Pittsburgh Post-Gazette Magazine,* 26 December. www.post-gazette.com/magazine/19991226creative6.asp.

About Intellectual Property. n.d. World Intellectual Property Organization. www.wipo.int/about-ip/en/.

Abra, Jock. 1988. *Assaulting Parnassus: Theoretical Views of Creativity.* Lanham, MD: University Press of America.

Abrams, M. H. 1981. Genre. In *A Glossary of Literary Terms.* 4th ed. New York: Holt, Rinehart and Winston.

Abuhamdeh, Sami, and Mihaly Csikszentmihalyi. 2004. The Artistic Personality: A Systems Perspective. In Sternberg Grigorenko, and Singer, 2004.

Acocella, Joan. 2004. Blocked: Why Do Writers Stop Writing? *New Yorker,* 14–21 June, 110–129.

Adams, Hazard, ed. 1971. *Critical Theory since Plato.* San Diego: Harcourt.

Adams, Max. 2001. *The Screenwriter's Survival Guide, or, Guerilla Meeting Tactics and Other Acts of War.* New York: Warner.

Algarin, Miguel, Bob Holman, and Nicole Blackman, eds. 1994. *Aloud! Voices from the Nuyorican Poets Café.* New York: Owlet.

Altman, Meryl. 1990. How Not to Do Things with *Metaphors We Live By. College English* 52.5:495–506.

Alvarez, A. 2005. *The Writer's Voice.* New York: Norton.

Amabile, Teresa M., and Elizabeth Tighe. 1993. Questions of Creativity. In *Creativity,* edited by John Brockman. New York: Touchstone.

Anderson, Charles M., and Marian M. MacCurdy, eds. 2000. *Writing and Healing: Toward Informed Practice.* Urbana, IL: NCTE.

Anderson, Chris. 1990. Late Night Thoughts on Writing and Teaching Essays. *Pretext* 11.1 2:85–93.

Anderson, William. 1996. *The Face of Glory: Creativity, Consciousness, and Civilization.* Hanover, NH: University Press of New England.

Andrews, Bruce, and Charles Bernstein, eds. 1984. *The L=A=N=G=U=A=G=E Book.* Carbondale: Southern Illinois University Press.

Appiah, Kwame Anthony. 1993. Thick Translation. In Venuti 2000.

Arana, Marie, ed. 2003. *The Writing Life: Writers on How They Think and Work.* New York: Public Affairs.

Aronson, Marc. The Evolution of the American Editor. In Grass 1993.

Arrington, Phillip K. 1986. Tropes of the Composing Process. *College English* 48.4:325–338.

Association of Authors' Representatives. www.aar-online.org/about.html.

Atkins, G. Douglas. 1994. Envisioning the Stranger's Heart. *College English* 56.6:629–641.

Autrey, Ken. 2004. E-mail to David Starkey, 22 August.

Bakhtin, Mikhail. 1975. *The Dialogic Imagination: Four Essays.* Edited by Michael Holquist et al. Translated by Kenneth Bostrom. Austin: University of Texas Press, 1982.

Barthes, Roland. 1968. The Death of the Author. In *Modern Criticism and Theory: A Reader,* 2nd ed., edited by David Lodge with Nigel Wood. New York: Longman, 2000.

Bassnett, Susan, and André Lefevere. 1998. *Constructing Cultures: Essays on Literary Translation.* Clevedon, UK: Multilingual Matters.

Baxter, Charles. 1997. *Burning Down the House.* St. Paul, MN: Graywolf.

Bazerman, Charles. 2002. Genre and Identity: Citizenship in the Age of the Internet and the Age of Global Capitalism. In *The Rhetoric and Ideology of Genre,* edited by Richard Coe, Lorelei Lingard, and Tatiana Teslenko. Cresskill, NJ: Hampton Press.

Berman, Jeffrey, and Jonathan Schiff. 2000. Writing about Suicide. In Anderson and MacCurdy 2000.

Bernstein, Charles, ed. 1998. *Close Listening: Poetry and the Performed Word.* Oxford: Oxford University Press.

———. 1999. *My Way: Speeches and Poems.* Chicago: University of Chicago Press.

Berry, R. M. 1994. Theory, Creative Writing, and the Impertinence of History. In Bishop and Ostrom 1994.

Best, Stephen. 2004. *The Fugitive's Properties: Law and the Poetics of Possession.* Chicago: University of Chicago Press.

Bianco-Mathis, Virginia, and Neal Chalofsky. 1996. *The Adjunct Faculty Handbook.* Thousand Oaks, CA: Sage.

Birkerts, Sven. 1996. The Fate of the Book. In *Tolstoy's Dictaphone: Technology and the Muse,* edited by Birkerts. St. Paul, MN: Graywolf.

Bishop, Wendy. 1991. *Working Words.* New York: McGraw-Hill.

———. 1997. *Teaching Lives: Essays and Stories.* Logan: Utah State University Press.

———. 1998. *Released into Language: Options for Teaching Creative Writing.* 2nd ed. Portland, ME: Calendar Islands.

———. 1999. *Thirteen Ways of Looking for a Poem.* New York: Longman.

———. 2003. Suddenly Sexy: Creative Nonfiction Rear-ends Composition. *College English* 65.3:257–275.

Bishop, Wendy, and Hans Ostrom, eds. 1994. *Colors of a Different Horse: Rethinking Creative Writing Theory and Pedagogy.* Urbana, IL: NCTE.

Bishop, Wendy, and David Starkey, eds. 2000. *In Praise of Pedagogy.* Portsmouth, NH: Boynton/Cook.

Bizzaro, Patrick. 1993. *Responding to Student Poems: Applications of Critical Theory.* Urbana, IL: NCTE.

Bizzell, Patricia, and Bruce Herzberg, eds. 1990. *The Rhetorical Tradition: Readings from Classical Times to the Present.* New York: St. Martins.

———. 1996. *The Bedford Bibliography for Teachers of Writing.* 4th ed. New York: Bedford.

Blew, Mary Clearman. 1993. The Art of Memoir. In *The True Subject: Writers on Life and Craft,* edited by Kurt Brown. St. Paul, MN: Graywolf.

Bloom, Lynn Z. 2003. Living to Tell the Tale: The Complicated Ethics of Creative Nonfiction. *College English* 65.3:276–298.

Bly, Robert W. 2000. *How to Get Your Book Published.* White Plains, NY: Roblin.

Boden, Margaret A. 2004. *The Creative Mind: Myths and Mechanisms.* 2nd ed. London: Routledge.

Boice, Robert. 1985. Psychotherapies for Writing Blocks. In Rose 1985.

———. 1996. *Procrastination and Blocking: A Novel, Practical Approach.* Westport, CT: Praeger.

Book Publishing. 2000. In *The Columbia Encyclopedia.* New York: Columbia University Press.

Booth, Wayne. 1961. *The Rhetoric of Fiction.* Chicago: University of Chicago Press.

———. 1978. Metaphor as Rhetoric: The Problem of Evaluation. In *On Metaphor,* edited by Sheldon Sacks. Chicago: University of Chicago Press.

Bousquet, Marc, Tony Scott, and Leo Parascondola, eds. 2004. *Tenured Bosses and Disposable Teachers: Writing Instruction in the Managed University.* Carbondale: Southern Illinois University Press.

Bowers, Neil. 1997. *Words for the Taking: The Hunt for a Plagiarist.* New York: Norton.

Branon, Lil. 1988. Nothing but the Truth. In *Writers on Writing,* edited by Tom Waldrep. New York: Random House.

Bratcher, Mark. 1999. *The Writing Cure: Psychoanalysis, Composition, and the Aims of Education.* Carbondale: Southern Illinois University Press.

Brodkey, Linda. 1987. Modernism and the Scenes(s) of Writing. *College English* 49.4:396–418.

Brooke, Robert. 1987. Lacan, Transference, and Writing Instruction. *College English* 49:679–91.

———. 1988. Modeling a Writer's Identity: Reading and Imitation in the Writing Classroom. *College Composition and Communication* 39:23–41.

Browne, Michael Dennis. 1993. Failure. In *The True Subject: Writers on Life and Craft,* edited by Kurt Brown. St. Paul, MN: Graywolf.

Browning, Bev. 2001. *Grant Writing for Dummies.* New York: Wiley.

Bruffee, Kenneth A. 1984. Collaborative Learning and the "Conversation of Mankind." *College English* 46:635–652.

Bryan, Sharon, ed. 1994. *Where We Stand: Women Poets on Literary Tradition.* New York: Norton.

Burroway, Janet. 2002. *Writing Fiction,* 6th ed. New York: Longman.

California Poets in the Schools. n.d. www.cpits.org/.

Camoin, François. 1994. The Workshop and Its Discontents. In Bishop and Ostrom 1994.

Campbell, Karlyn Kohrs, and Kathleen Hall Jamieson. 1990. *Deeds Done in Words: Presidential Rhetoric and the Genres of Governance.* Chicago: University of Chicago Press.

Carroll, B. Jill. 2003. *How to Survive as an Adjunct Lecturer.* San Diego: Aventine.

———. 2004. *Machiavelli for Adjuncts: Six Lessons in Power for the Disempowered.* San Diego: Aventine.

Cassidy, Christine. 1996. On Publishing: Granted. *Lambda Book Report* 5.4:17.

Cather, Willa. 1921. Willa Cather in Person. The Willa Cather Archive. libtextcenter.unl. edu/cather/writings/bohlke/interviews/1921e.html.

Chandler, Daniel. 2000. Introduction to Genre Theory. Aberystwyth University Media and Communications Studies. www.aber.ac.uk/media/Documents/intgenre/intgenre1.html.

Charles Johnson. 1992. Dir. Matteo Bellinelli. Videocassette.

Chatterjee, Debjani. n.d. Sheffield Children's Hospital. The Poetry Society. www.poetrysociety.org.uk/places/sheff.htm.

Checkoway, Julie, ed. 1999. *Creating Fiction.* Cincinnati: Story Press.

the clinic. n.d. What We Do. www.theclinic.co.nz/.

Coe, Richard, Lorelei Lingard, and Tatiana Teslenko, eds. 2002. *The Rhetoric and Ideology of Genre.* Cresskill, NJ: Hampton Press.

Conroy, Thom. 2001. Writing Possibilities: Email and the Creative Writing Classroom. *Journal of Cooperation & Collaboration in College Teaching* 10.2:61–67.

Corey, Stephen, and Warren Slesinger, eds. 1990. *Spreading the Word: Editors on Poetry.* Columbia, SC: Bench Press.

Cronin, Michael. 2000. History, Translation, Postcolonialism. In *Changing the Terms: Translating in the Postcolonial Era,* edited by Sherry Simon and Paul St.-Pierre. Ottawa: University of Ottawa Press.

Cruz, Victor Hernandez, Leroy Quintana, and Virgil Suarez, eds. 2000. *Paper Dance: 55 Latino Poets.* New York: Persea Books.

Csikszentmihalyi, Mihaly. 1990. *Flow: The Psychology of Optimal Experience.* New York: Harper.

Curtis, Richard. 2001. The Flight to Quantity: Will the Internet Ruin It For Everybody? In Dickerson 2001.

Daly, John R. 1985. Writing Apprehension. In Rose 1985.

Daniell, Beth. 1994. Theory, Theory Talk, and Composition. In *Writing Theory and Critical Theory,* edited by John Clifford and John Schilb. New York: MLA.

Davis, Charles R. 2002. Watch Out for Scams. *Writer* 115.2:34.

Delbanco, Nicholas. 1994. Interview with Alexander Neubauer. In Neubauer 1994.

DeMaria, Robert. 1997. *The College Handbook of Creative Writing.* Boston: Heinle.

Demers, Elizabeth. 2004a. Breaking into Publishing. *Chronicle of Higher Education.* chronicle.com/jobs/2004/11/2004111201c.htm.

————. 2004b. Getting a Real Job in Publishing. *Chronicle of Higher Education.* chronicle. com/jobs/2004/04/2004041301c.htm.

Devitt, Amy J. 2004. *Writing Genres.* Carbondale: Southern Illinois University Press.

Dickerson, Donya. 2001. *2001 Guide to Literary Agents.* Cincinnati, OH: Writers Digest.

Directory of Poetry Publishers. n.d. Dustbooks. www.dustbooks.com/poetpub.htm.

Donoghue, Denis. 1998. *The Practice of Reading.* New Haven: Yale University Press.

Drake, Barbara. 1994. *Writing Poetry.* Boston: Heinle.

Eagleton, Terry. 1996. *Literary Theory.* 2nd ed. Minneapolis: University of Minnesota Press.

Ede, Lisa, and Andrea Lunsford. 1990. *Singular Texts/Plural Authors: Perspectives on Collaborative Writing.* Carbondale: Southern Illinois University Press.

Eder, Richard. 2004. Ride into Battle, Writers, Astride Style's Glorious Steed. *New York Times,* 23 July, E.2:35.

Editors Association of Canada. 1991. So You Want to Be an Editor? www.editors.ca/pubs/ so.htm.

Eiben, Threse. 2002. Out of Ethiopia: An Interview with Nega Mezlekia. *Poets and Writers* 30:267–33. www.pw.org/mag/eiben.htm.

Elbow, Peter. 1973. *Writing without Teachers.* New York: Oxford University Press.

————. 1998. *Writing without Teachers.* 2nd ed. New York: Oxford University Press.

Eliot, T. S. 1975. Tradition and the Individual Talent. In *Selected Prose of T. S. Eliot,* edited by Frank Kermode. New York: Harcourt.

Embree, Mary. 2003. *The Author's Toolkit: A Step-by-Step Guide to Writing and Publishing Your Book.* New York: Allworth.

Emerson, Ralph Waldo. 1850. *Essays and Lectures.* New York: Library of America, 1983.

Evans, Tonya Marie, and Susan Borden Evans. 2003. *Literary Law Guide for Authors.* Philadelphia: FYOS Entertainment.

Faigley, Lester. 1986. Competing Theories of Process. *College English* 48:527–542.

Fenza, D. W. 2000. Creative Writing & Its Discontents. *Writers Chronicle* (March–April). www. awpwriter.org/magazine/writers/fenza1.htm.

Fenza, D. W., et al., eds. 1999. *The AWP Official Guide to Writing Programs.* 9th ed. Paradise, CA: Dustbooks.

Finch, Annie, ed. 1994. *A Formal Feeling Comes: Poems in Form by Contemporary Women.* Ashland, OR: Story Line Press.

Fine, Michelle. 1994. Working the Hyphens: Reinventing Self and Other in Qualitative Research. In *Handbook of Qualitative Research,* edited by Norman K. Denzin and Yvonna S. Lincoln. London: Sage.

Fleckenstein, Kristie S. 2003. *Embodied Literacies: Imageword and a Poetics of Teaching.* Carbondale: Southern Illinois University Press.

Flores, Becky. 2004. "Sheep in Wolf's Clothing: The Paradox of Critical Pedagogy." *Radical Pedagogy* 6.1. <radicalpedagogy.icaap.org/content/issue6_1/flores.html>.

Foer, Franklin. 1997. Book Publishing. MSN Slate. slate.msn.com/id/1082/.

Forché, Carolyn, ed. 1993. *Against Forgetting: Twentieth Century Poetry of Witness.* New York: Norton.

Foucault, Michel. 1969. What Is an Author? In *Modern Criticism and Theory: A Reader,* 2nd ed., edited by David Lodge with Nigel Wood. New York: Longman, 2000.

Freed, Lynn. 2005. *Reading, Writing, and Leaving Home: Life on the Page.* Orlando: Harcourt.

Freire, Paolo. 1970. *Pedagogy of the Oppressed.* New York: Continuum.

Fulton, Len, ed. 1999. *The International Directory of Little Magazines and Small Presses.* Vol. 35. Paradise, CA: Dustbooks.

Gamalinda, Eric. 2002. Poems Are Never Finished: A Final Interview with Agha Shahid Ali. *Poets and Writers* 30.2:44–51, 75.

Gardner, John. 1984. *The Art of Fiction.* New York: Knopf.

Garrett, George. 1999. Going to See the Elephant: Our Duty as Storytellers. In Checkoway 1999.

Gere, Anne Ruggles. 1987. *Writing Groups: History, Theory, and Implications.* Carbondale: Southern Illinois University Press.

Geyh, Paula, Fred Leebron, and Andrew Levy, eds. 1998. Introduction to *Postmodern American Fiction: A Norton Anthology.* New York: Norton.

Ginsberg, Allen, Andy Clausen, and Eliot Katz, eds. 1999. *Poems for the Nation: A Collection of Contemporary Political Poems.* New York: Seven Stories Press.

Gioia, Dana. 1991. Can Poetry Matter? *Atlantic* 267.5:94–106.

———. 2003. Disappearing Ink: Poetry at the End of Print Culture. *Hudson Review* 56.1.

Giroux, Henry A. 1995. National Identity and the Politics of Multiculturalism. *College Literature* 22.2:41–56.

Glazner, Gary Mex, eds. 2000. *Poetry Slam: The Competitive Art of Performance Poetry.* San Francisco: Manic D Press.

Goldberg, Natalie. 1986. *Writing Down the Bones.* Boston: Shambhala.

———.1990. *Wild Mind: Living the Writer's Life.* New York: Bantam.

Golde, Chris M. 1996. Tips for Successful Writing Groups. Association for the Study of Higher Education. www.soemadison.wisc.edu/edadmin/faculty/facultyextras/write-groups.html.

Goldstein, Paul. 2003. *Copyright's Highway: From Gutenberg to the Celestial Jukebox.* 2nd ed. Stanford: Stanford University Press.

Golub, Jeffrey. 2000. *Making Learning Happen: Strategies for an Interactive Classroom.* Portsmouth, NH: Boynton/Cook.

Gradin, Sherrie L. 1995. *Romancing Rhetorics: Social Expressivist Perspectives on the Teaching of Writing.* Portsmouth, NH: Boynton/Cook.

Graves, Donald. 1985. Blocking and the Young Writer. In Rose 1985.

Greer, Barry Roberts, ed. 1994. *Paper Graders: Notes from the Academic Underclass.* Corvalis, OR: Cairn Press.

Gross, Gerald, ed. 1993. *Editors on Editing: What Writers Need to Know about What Editors Do.* 3rd ed. New York: Grove.

Gutkind, Lee. 1993. What's in This Name—And What's Not. creativenonfiction.org/the-journal/articles/issue01/01editor.htm.

———. 1995. The Five Rs of Creative Nonfiction. creativenonfiction.org/thejournal/articles/issue06/06editor.htm.

Gwynn, R. S., ed. 1999. *New Expansive Poetry.* New York: Consortium.

Haake, Katherine. 2000. *What Our Speech Disrupts: Feminism and Creative Writing Studies.* Urbana, IL: NCTE.

Hall, Stuart. 1977. Culture, the Media and the "Ideological Effect." In *Mass Communication and Society.* Ed. James Curran et al. Thousand Oaks, CA: Sage.

Harper, Tara K. 2000. Writing Groups and Critiques. www.tarakharper.com/k_crit.htm.

Harris, Joseph. 1994. The Rhetoric of Theory. In *Writing Theory and Critical Theory*, edited by John Clifford and John Schilb. New York: MLA.

———. 1997. *A Teaching Subject: Composition since 1966.* Upper Saddle River, NJ: Prentice Hall.

Harvey, Gordon. 1994. Presence in the Essay. *College English* 56.6:642–654.

Hass, Robert. 2001. Introduction to *The Best American Poetry, 2001*, edited by Robert Hass. New York: Scribner.

Heard, Georgia. 1995. *Writing Toward Home: Tales and Lessons to Find Your Way.* Portsmouth, NH: Boynton/Cook.

Heilker, Paul, and Peter Vandenberg. 1996. *Keywords in Composition Studies.* Portsmouth, NH: Boynton/Cook.

Herman, Jeff. 2003. *Guide to Book Publishers, Editors, and Literary Agents, 2004.* Waukesha, WI: Writer Books.

Hesse, Douglas. 2003. The Place of Creative Nonfiction. *College English* 65.3:237–241.

Hillock, George. 1999. *Ways of Thinking, Ways of Teaching.* New York: Teachers College Press.

Hinton, Laura, and Cynthia Hogue, eds. 2001. *We Who Love to Be Astonished: Experimental Women's Writing and Performance Poetics.* Tuscaloosa: University of Alabama Press.

Hirshfield, Jane. 1997. *Nine Gates: Entering the Mind of Poetry.* New York: HarperPerennial.

Holden, Constance. 1994. Madness and Creativity Revisited. *Science* 266.5190:1483.

Homel, David, and Sherry Simon, eds. 1988. *Mapping Literature: The Art and Politics of Translation.* Montreal: Véhicule Press.

Hongo, Garret, ed. 1993. *The Open Boat: Poems from Asian America.* New York: Anchor.

hooks, bell. 1994. *Teaching to Transgress: Education as the Practice of Freedom.* New York: Routledge.

———. 2003. *Teaching Community: A Pedagogy of Hope.* New York: Routledge.

Hoover, Paul. 1994. Introduction to *Postmodern American Poetry: A Norton Anthology,* edited by Paul Hoover. New York: Norton.

———. 2001. A Score for Undetermined Moments. In *Fables of Representation.* Ann Arbor: University of Michigan Press.

Horace. 1903. Art of Poetry. Trans. E. C. Wickham. In Adams 1971.

Howe, Florence. 1993. *No More Masks: An Anthology of Twentieth-Century American Women Poets.* New York: HarperCollins.

Howe, Michael J. A. 1999. *Genius Explained.* Cambridge: Cambridge University Press.

Hugo, Richard. 1979. *The Triggering Town: Lectures and Essays on Poetry and Writing.* New York: Norton.

Hunter, Susan, and Ray Wallace, eds. 1995. *The Place of Grammar in Writing Instruction: Past, Present, Future.* Portsmouth, NH: Boynton/Cook.

Hurston, Zora Neale. 1947. What White Publishers Won't Print. In *African American Literary Theory: A Reader,* edited by Winston Napier. New York: New York University Press, 2000.

International Directory of Little Magazine and Small Presses. n.d. Dustbooks. www.dustbooks.com/lilmag.htm.

Jarman, Mark. 2002. *Body and Soul: Essays on Poetry.* Ann Arbor: University of Michigan Press.

Jones, Russell Celyn. 1995–96. Teaching Creative Writing. *Richmond Review.* www.richmondreview.co.uk/features/jones.html.

Kandaswamy, Deepa. 2003. Recipe for Maintaining an On-Line Writing Group. In Rosenthal 2003.

Karsh, Ellen, and Arlen Sue Fox. 2003. *The Only Grant-Writing Book You'll Ever Need.* New York: Carroll & Graf.

Kiefson, Ruth. 2004. The Politics and Economics of the Super-Exploitation of Adjuncts. In Bousquet, Scott and Parascondola 2004.

King, Stephen. 2000. *On Writing: A Memior of the Craft.* New York: Pocket.

Kirkpatrick, David. 2000. Random House to Establish Exclusively Digital Unit. *New York Times,* 31 July, C1.

Klein, Michael. 1999. A Rich Life: Adrienne Rich on Poetry, Politics, and Personal Revelation. *Boston Phoenix.* www.bostonphoenix.com/archive/1in10/99/06/RICH.html.

Knox-Quinn, Carolyn. 1990. Collaboration in the Writing Classroom: An Interview with Ken Kesey. *College Composition and Communication* 41.3:309–317.

Lakoff, George, and Mark Johnson. 1980. *Metaphors We Live By.* Chicago: University of Chicago Press.

Lamott, Anne. 1995. *Bird by Bird: Some Instructions on Writing and Life.* New York: Anchor.

Landow, George. 1992. *Hypertext.* Baltimore: Johns Hopkins University Press.

Lanham, Richard. 2003. *Analyzing Prose.* 2nd ed. London: Continuum.

Larsen, Michael, and Elizabeth Pomada. 2003. 3 Ways to Make Yourself Irresistible to Any Agent or Publisher. www.larsen-pomada.com/perspective1.html.

Larson, Reed. 1985. Emotional Scenarios in the Writing Process: An Examination of Young Writers' Affective Experience. In Rose 1985.

Lefevere, André. 1975. *Translating Poetry: Seven Strategies and a Blueprint.* Amsterdam: Van Gorcum.

————. 1992. *Translation, Rewriting, and the Manipulation of Literary Fame.* London: Routledge.

Lehman, David. 1995. What Is It? The Question of Postmodernism. In *The Big Question.* Ann Arbor: University of Michigan Press.

Leitch, Vincent B. 1986. Deconstruction and Pedagogy. In Nelson 1986.

Lent, Michael. 2004. *Breakfast with Sharks: A Screenwriter's Guide.* New York: Three Rivers.

Levertov, Denise. 1968. Origins of a Poem. *Michigan Quarterly Review* 7.4. www.studiocleo. com/librarie/levertov/prose.html.

Lick, Sue. 2003. E-mail to David Starkey, 19 January.

Ling, Amy, and King-Kok Cheung. 2002. Garrett Kaoru Hongo. In *Heath Anthology of American Literature,* 4th ed., edited by Paul Lauter. college.hmco.com/english/lauter/ heath/4e/students/author_pages/contemporary/hongo_ga.html.

Lodge, David, ed. 1999. *Modern Criticism and Theory: A Reader.* 2nd ed. New York: Addison-Wesley.

Longinus.1899. On the Sublime. Trans. W. R. Roberts. In Adams 1971.

Longo, Perie. 2004. E-mail to David Starkey, 24 August.

————. 2005. Poetry as Therapy. www.spcsb.org/advoc/poetrytx.html.

Lopate, Phillip, ed. 1994. Introduction to *The Art of the Personal Essay: An Anthology from the Classical Era to the Present.* New York: Anchor.

Lovas, John. 2001. How Did We Get in This Fix? A Personal Account of the Shift to a Part-Time Faculty in a Leading Two-Year College District. In *Moving Mountains: Transforming the Role of Contingent Faculty in Composition Studies and Higher Education.,* edited by Eileen Schell and Patricia Lambert Stock. Urbana, IL: NCTE.

Lucero-Trujillo, Marcela Christine. 1980. The Dilemma of the Modern Chicana Artist and Critic. In Madison 1994.

Luey, Beth. 2002. *Handbook for Academic Authors.* 4th ed. Cambridge: Cambridge University Press.

Lutzker, Arnold P. 2003. *Content Rights for Creative Professionals: Copyrights and Trademarks in a Digital Age.* 2nd ed. Oxford: Focal Press.

Lynn, Steven. 1990. A Passage into Critical Theory. *College English* 52.3:258–71.

The MacArthur Fellows Program. 2004. www.macfound.org/programs/fel/fel_overview.htm.

MacCurdy, Marion M. 2000. From Trauma to Writing: A Theoretical Model for Practical Use. In Anderson and MacCurdy 2000.

Madison, D. Soyini, ed. 1994. *The Woman That I Am.* New York: St. Martin's.

Mahoney, Mary Pat. 2003. On-Line and in Touch: Organizing a Writing Group in Cyberspace. In Rosenthal 2003.

Major, Clarence, ed. 1996. Introduction to *The Garden Thrives: Twentieth-Century African-American Poetry.* New York: HarperPerennial.

Malinowitz, Harriet. 2003. Business, Pleasure, and the Personal Essay. *College English* 65.3:305–322.

Masiki, Trent. 2003. Aesthetically Speaking: The Emergence and Survival of *Callaloo. Poets and Writers* 31.1:25–29.

McWilliams, John. 2002. Poetry and Presence. *Middlebury Magazine On-line,* 30 December. www.middlebury.edu/~publish/middmag/features/pack/pack1.html.

Medina, Tony, Louis Reyes Rivera, and Sonia Sanchez, eds. 2001. *Bum Rush the Page: A Def Poetry Jam.* New York: Three Rivers.

Milkweed Press. n.d. Mission Statement. www.milkweed.org/2_0.html.

Miller, Jean Baker. 1976. Creativity with a Place to Go. In *Women, Creativity, and the Arts,* edited by Diane Apostolos-Cappadona and Lucinda Ebersole. New York: Continuum.

Miller, Nancy K. 1991. *Getting Personal: Feminist Occasions and Other Autobiographical Acts.* New York: Routledge.

Milliot, Jim. 2003. Top Five Trade Houses Take 45% of Market Share. *Publishers Weekly,* 16 June. www.keepmedia.com/pubs/PublishersWeekly/2003/06/16/270336?extID=10026.

Minot, Stephen. 2003. *Three Genres.* 7th ed. Upper Saddle River, NJ: Prentice Hall.

Moi, Toril. 1985. *Sexual/Textual Politics: Feminist Literary Theory.* London: Methuen.

Moore, Dinty W. 2004. E-mail to David Starkey, 3 August.

Moxley, Joseph, ed. 1989. *Creative Writing in America: Theory and Pedagogy.* Urbana, IL: NCTE.

Muir, Edwin. 1962. The Public and the Poet. In *The Estate of Poetry.* St. Paul, MN: Graywolf.

Murfin, Ross, and Supryia M. Ray. 1997. *The Bedford Glossary of Critical and Literary Terms.* New York: Bedford.

Murphy, Ann. 1989. Transference and Resistance in the Basic Writing Classroom: Problematics and Praxis. *College Composition and Communication* 40:175–187.

Murray, Donald. 1985. The Essential Delay: When Writer's Block Isn't. In Rose 1985.

———. 1990. *Shoptalk: Learning to Write with Writers.* Portsmouth, NH: Boynton/Cook, 1990.

Myers, D. G. 1989. "Educating Writers: The Beginnings of 'Creative Writing' in the American University." PhD diss., Northwestern University.

———. 1996. *The Elephants Teach: Creative Writing since 1880.* Englewood Cliffs, NJ: Prentice-Hall.

Nabokov, Vladimir. 1955. Problems of Translation: *Onegin* in English. In Venuti 2000.

Natoli, Joseph. 1997. *A Primer to Postmodernity.* Oxford: Blackwell.

Nelson, Cary, ed. 1986. *Theory in the Classroom.* Urbana: University of Illinois Press.

Nelson, Cary, and Michael Berube. 1994. Graduate Education Is Losing Its Moral Base. *Chronicle of Higher Education,* 23 March. chronicle.com/free/v40/i29/29b00101.htm.

Nelson, Cary, and Stephen Watt. 1999. *Academic Keywords.* New York: Routledge.

Nettle, Daniel. 2001. *Strong Imagination: Madness, Creativity, and Human Nature.* Oxford: Oxford University Press.

Neubauer, Alexander, ed. 1994. *Conversations on Writing Fiction: Interviews with 13 Distinguished Teachers of Fiction Writing in America.* New York: HarperPerennial.

Newkirk, Thomas, ed. 1993. *Nuts and Bolts: A Practical Guide to Teaching College Composition.* Portsmouth, NH: Greenwood-Heinemann.

Niatum, Duane. 1988. *Harper's Anthology of Twentieth-Century Native American Poetry.* San Francisco: HarperSanFranciso.

Nichols, Kristen. 2004. Beyond Being Miffed: An MFA Grad Takes a Realistic Look at the Place of Pedagogy. Unpublished essay.

North, Stephen. 1987. *The Making of Knowledge in Composition: Portrait of an Emerging Field.* Portsmouth, NH: Boynton/Cook.

———. 2000. *Refiguring the Ph.D. in English Studies: Writing, Doctoral Education, and SUNY-Albany's Fusion-Based Curriculum.* Urbana, IL: NCTE.

Novel and Short Story Writer's Market. 2004. Writers Digest Books. Cincinnati: F & W Publishers.

Oates, Joyce Carol. 1980. On Editing the *Ontario Review.* In *The Art of Literary Publishing: Editors on Their Craft,* edited by Bill Henderson. Yonkers, NY: Pushcart.

———. 2003. *The Faith of a Writer.* New York: HarperCollins.

Olson, Charles. 1950. Projective Verse. In *Postmodern American Poetry,* edited by Paul Hoover. New York: Norton.

O'Reilley, Mary Rose. 1998. *Radical Presence: Teaching as Contemplative Practice.* Portsmouth, NH: Boynton/Cook.

Orem, Laura Pinto. 2001. An Interview with David Lehman. *Writer's Chronicle* 34.3:12–16.

Ostrom, Hans. 1994. Of Radishes and Shadows, Theory and Pedagogy. In Bishop and Ostrom 1994.

Pack, Thomas. 1998. So, You Want to Be a Writer. *Link-up* 15.3:24.

Pappas School for the Homeless. n.d. www.tjpappasschool.org/.

Pease, Donald A. 1990. Author. In *Critical Terms for Literary Study,* edited by Frank Lentriccia and Thomas McLaughlin. Chicago: University of Chicago Press.

Peltak, Jennifer. n.d. Communication in Prisons: Taking Action through Teaching, Scholarship, and Activism. National Communication Association Convention. 9 January. www.natcom.org/Convention/2002/PreCons/prisons.htm.

Pennebaker, James. 1990. *Opening Up: The Healing Power of Confiding to Others*. New York: Morrow.

Perdomo, Willie. n.d. Where a Nickel Costs a Quarter: Willie Perdomo Gets Political. What You Need to Know About. poetry.about.com/library/weekly/aa052301a.htm.

Perry, Donne. 1993. *Backtalk: Women Writers Speak Out*. New Brunswick, NJ: Rutgers University Press.

Petracca, Michael. 1999. An Interview with Barry Gifford. In *The Graceful Lie: A Method for Making Fiction*, edited by Michael Petracca. Upper Saddle River, NJ: Prentice-Hall.

Pig Iron Theatre Company. n.d. Mission. www.pigiron.org/mission.html.

Phelan, Shane. 1993. (Be)coming Out: Lesbian Identity and Politics. *Signs* 18(4): 765–90.

Philip Roth Residence in Creative Writing. 2005. www.bucknell.edu/Academics/Resources/Stadler_Center/The_Philip_Roth_Residence_in_Creative_Writing.html.

Piirto, Jane. 2002. *My Teeming Brain: Understanding Creative Writers*. Creskill, NJ: Hampton Press.

Plucker, Jonathan A., and Ronald A. Beghetto. 2004. Why Creativity Is Domain General, Why It Looks Domain Specific, and Why the Distinction Does Not Matter. In Sternberg Grigorenko, and Singer 2004.

Poetry Therapy. n.d. National Coalition of Creative Arts Therapies Associations. www.nccata.com/poetry.html.

Poets and Writers Magazine. 72 Spring Street. New York, NY 10012. www.pw.org.

Powers, Richard, and Bradford Morrow. 2000. A Dialogue. In American Fiction: States of the Art. Special issue, *Conjunctions* 34:171–188.

Pratt, Linda Ray. 1997. Disposable Faculty: Part-Time Exploitation as Management Strategy. In *Will Teach for Food: Academic Labor in Crisis*, edited by Cary Nelson. Minneapolis: University of Minnesota Press.

Prins, Yopie, Maeera Shrieber, and Shari Benstock, eds. 1998. *Dwelling in Possibility: Women Poets and Critics on Poetry*. Ithaca: Cornell University Press.

Public Domain and Copyright How-to. 2002. Project Gutenberg. promo.net/pg/vol/pd.html.

Rabiner, Susan, and Alfred Fortunato. 2002. *Thinking Like Your Editor: How to Write Great Serious Nonfiction—And Get It Published*. New York: Norton.

Rabinowitz, Peter. 1988. Canons and Close Readings. In *Falling into Theory: Conflicting Views on Reading Literature*, edited by David H. Richter. Boston: Bedford, 1994.

Ramjerdi Jan, and Eugene Garber. 1994. In Bishop and Ostrom 1994.

Rasula, Jed. 1996. *The American Poetry Wax Museum: Reality Effects, 1940–1990*. Urbana, IL: NCTE.

Ratiner, Steve. 1994. Carolyn Forche: The Poetry of Witness. Interview excerpt from *Giving Their Word—Conversations with Contemporary Poets. Christian Science Monitor*. www.csmonitor.com/atcsmonitor/specials/poetry/p-forche.html.

Reid, Calvin. 1999. CCC Debuts Online Republication Service. *Publishers Weekly* 246.29:79.

Richards, I. A. 1936. *The Philosophy of Rhetoric*. New York: Oxford University Press.

Ríos, Alberto. 1999. Eleven Style Considerations You Can't Live Without. In Checkoway 1999.

Roen, Duane, Stuart C. Brown, and Theresa Enos. 1999. *Living Rhetoric and Composition: Stories of the Discipline*. Mahwah, NJ: Erlbaum.

Rogers, Carl. R. 1961. *On Becoming a Person*. Boston: Houghton.

Rohrer, Matthew. 2002. Where Art and Poetry Collide: A Profile of John Yau. *Poets and Writers* 30.3:25–31.

Romano, Tom. 2000. *Blending Genre, Altering Style: Writing Multigenre Papers*. Portsmouth, NH: Boynton/Cook.

Root, Robert L. Jr. 2003. Naming Nonfiction (a Polyptych). *College English* 65.3:242–256.

Root, Robert, and Michael Steinberg, eds. 2004. *The Fourth Genre.* 3rd ed. New York: Longman.

Rorty, Richard. 1979. *Philosophy and the Mirror of Nature.* Princeton: Princeton University Press.

Rose, Mike, ed. 1985. *When a Writer Can't Write.* New York: Guilford.

———. 1990. *Lives on the Boundary.* New York: Penguin.

Rosenthal, Lisa. 2003. *The Writing Group Book.* Chicago: Chicago Review Press.

Rosenthal, Morris. 2005. Book Contracts. www.fonerbooks.com/contract.htm.

Roskelly, Hephzibah. 1998. Broken Circles and Curious Triangles: Rethinking the Writers' Workshop. In *Teaching Writing Creatively,* edited by David Starkey. Portsmouth, NH: Boynton/Cook.

———. 2003. *Breaking (into) the Circle: Group Work for Change in the English Classroom.* Portsmouth, NH: Boynton/Cook.

Ross, Tom, and Marilyn Ross. 2002. *The Complete Guide to Self-Publishing.* 4th ed. Cincinnati: Writer's Digest.

Royalties Department. 2005. Cambridge University Press. authornet.cambridge.org/information/royalties/.

Ruland, Richard, and Malcolm Bradbury. 1991. *From Puritanism to Postmodernism: A History of American Literature.* New York: Penguin.

Salzman, Mark. 2003. *True Notebooks.* New York: Knopf.

Satterfield, Ben. 1994. Kick 'Em While They're Down. In Greer 1994.

Schell, Eileen. 1997. *Gypsy Academics and Mother Teachers.* Portsmouth, NH: Boynton/Cook.

Schell, Eileen, and Patricia Lambert Stock, eds. 2001. *Moving Mountains: Transforming the Role of Contingent Faculty in Composition Studies and Higher Education.* Urbana, IL: NCTE.

———. 2004. Toward a New Labor Movement in Higher Education: Contingent Labor and Organizing for Change. In Bousquet, Scott, and Parascondola 2004.

Schmidt, Jan Zlotnik, ed. 1998. Introduction to *Women / Writing / Teaching.* Albany: SUNY Press.

Schnackenberg, Gertrude. 2001. *The Throne of Labdacus.* New York: Farrar, Straus & Giroux.

Scholes, Robert. 1986. *Textual Power: Literary Theory and the Teaching of English.* New Haven: Yale University Press.

Schudel, Matt. 2005. Guy Davenport Dies; Writer Had Distinctive Voice. *Washington Post,* 9 January, C7.

Schuster, M. Lincoln. 1962. An Open Letter to a Would-be Editor. In Gross 1993.

Science Fiction and Fantasy Writers of America. 2005. Warnings and Cautions for Writers— Literary Agents. 20 July. www.sfwa.org/beware/agents.html.

Seidman, Michael. 1993. The Editor and the Author at the Writers' Conference: Why They Go, What They Do. In Gross 1993.

Sewell, Marilyn. 1996. *Claiming the Spirit Within: A Sourcebook of Women's Poetry.* Boston: Beacon Press.

Seth, Vikram. 1986. *The Golden Gate.* New York: Random House.

Shapard, Robert, and James Thomas, eds. 1986. *Sudden Fiction.* Salt Lake City: Peregrine Smith.

Shelnutt, Eve. 1994. Interview with Alexander Neubauer. In Neubauer 1994.

Shepard, Aaron. 1994. Pity the Poor Anthologist. *Publishers Weekly* 241.7:26.

Simonton, Dean Keith. 1999. *Origins of Genius: Darwinian Perspectives on Creativity.* New York: Oxford University Press.

———. 2004. Creativity as a Constrained Stochastic Process. In Sternberg, Grigorenko, and Singer 2004.

Sims, Norman. 1995. The Art of Literary Journalism. In *Literary Journalism,* edited by Norman Sims and Mark Kramer. New York: Ballantine.

Smith, John B. 1994. *Collective Intelligence in Computer-Based Collaboration.* Hillsdale, NJ: Erlbaum.

Smith, Tina Marie. 2003. The Workplace Writing Group. In Rosenthal 2003.

Smith, Valerie. 1989. Black Feminist Theory and the Representation of the Other. In Madison 1994.

Sours, Nancy. 2004. Review of *Steal This University: The Rise of the Corporate University and Academic Labor Movement,* edited by Benjamin Johnson et al. Forum: Newsletter of the Committee on Contingent, Adjunct and Part-Time Faculty. *CCC* 56.1:A6–10.

Spacks, Barry. 2004. E-mail to David Starkey, 20 August.

Spivak, Gayatri Chakravorty. 1992. The Politics of Translation. In Venuti 2000.

St. John, David. 1990. On Editing. In Corey and Schlesinger 1990.

Stafford, William. 1987. *You Must Revise Your Life.* Ann Arbor: University of Michigan Press.

Stafford, William, and Marvin Bell. 1983. *Segues: A Correspondence in Poetry.* Boston: Godine.

Starkey, David. 1994. The MFA Graduate as Composition Instructor. In Bishop and Ostrom 1994.

———, ed. 1998. *Teaching Writing Creatively.* Portsmouth, NH: Boynton/Cook.

———. 2000. *Poetry Writing: Theme and Variations.* New York: McGraw-Hill.

Steele, Timothy. 1990. *Missing Measures: Modern Poetry and the Revolt against Meter.* Fayetteville: University of Arkansas Press.

Stern, Jerome. 1991. *Making Shapely Fiction.* New York: Norton.

Sternberg, Robert J., Elena L. Grigorenko, and Jerome L. Singer, eds. 2004. *Creativity: From Potential to Realization.* Washington, DC: American Psychological Association.

Sternberg, Robert J., James C. Kaufman, and Jean E. Pretz. 2002. *The Creativity Conundrum: A Propulsion Model of Kinds of Creative Contributions.* New York: Psychology Press.

Stewart, Robert. 1990. Choosing Poems for Publication: The Dynamics of Wit. In Corey and Schlesinger 1990.

Stoppard, Tom. 1988. Interview with Shusha Guppy. In *The Paris Review Playwrights at Work,* edited by George Plimpton. New York: Modern Library, 2000.

Straczynski, J. Michael. 1996. *The Complete Book of* Scriptwriting. Cincinnati: Writers Digest.

Strenski, Ellen. 1989. Disciplines and Communities, "Armies" and "Monasteries," and the Teaching of Composition. *Rhetoric Review* 8.1:137–145.

Tabor, Maria Garcia. 2001. Toward a Larger, Listening World: An Interview with Ray Gonzalez. *Poets and Writers* 29.6:35–39.

Tal, Kali. 1995. *Worlds of Hurt: Reading the Literatures of Trauma.* Cambridge: Cambridge University Press.

Tannenbaum, Judith. 2000. *Disguised as a Poem: My Years Teaching Poetry at San Quentin.* Boston: Northeastern University Press.

Tenenbaum, Jeffrey. 2002. The Difference between Nonprofit and Tax-Exempt Status. Ohio Health Information Management Association. 31 May. www.ohima.org/orientation/Nonprofitvstaxexempt.html.

Thompson, Jon. 1995. A Turn Toward the Past: Review of *The Angel of History,* by Carolyn Forché. *Postmodern Culture* 5.2. muse.jhu.edu/journals/postmodern_culture/v005/5.2r_thompson.html.

Thralls, Charlotte. 1992. Bakhtin, Collaborative Partners, and Published Discourse: A Collaborative View of Composing. In *New Visions of Collaborative Writing,* edited by Janis Forman. Portsmouth, NH: Boynton/Cook.

Tizon, Tomas Alex. 2005. In Search of Poetic Justice. *Los Angeles Times,* 17 June, A1, A33.

Tobin, Lad. 1989. Bridging Gaps: Analyzing Our Students' Metaphors for Composing. *CCC* 40.4:444–458.

———. 1991. Reading Students, Reading Ourselves: Revising the Teacher's Role in the Writing Class. *College English* 53:333–348.

———. 1993. *Writing Relationships: What Really Happens in the Composition Class.* Portsmouth, NH: Boynton/Cook.

Tomlinson, Barbara. 1988. Tuning, Tying, and Training Texts: Metaphors for Revision. *Written Communication* 5.1:58–81.

Tompkins, Jane. 1980. *Reader-Response Criticism: From Formalism to Post-Structuralism.* Baltimore: Johns Hopkins University Press.

Torgersen, Eric. 1988. Loving (Hating) the Messenger: Transference and Teaching. *AWP Newsletter,* 1, 12, 14–15.

Treichler, Paula. 1986. Teaching Feminist Theory. In Nelson 1986.

Trimmer, Joseph, ed. 1997. *Narration as Knowledge: Tales of the Teaching Life.* Portsmouth, NH: Boynton/Cook.

Turkle, Sherry. 1995. *Life on the Screen: Identity in the Age of the Internet.* New York: Touchstone.

Turner, Frederick. 1988. *Genesis: An Epic Poem.* New York: Saybrook.

Tuttle, Jon. 2004. E-mail to David Starkey, 9 August.

UCLA Extension: Writers' Program. 2003. www.uclaextension.org.

University of Pittsburgh Department of English. 2005. Creative Nonfiction Requirements. 27 June. www.english.pitt.edu/graduate/.

Upstart Crow Theatre Group. 2003. About Us. www.upstartcrow.ca/aboutus.html.

U.S. Office of Management and Budget. 1999. National Endowment for the Arts. *Application Guidelines for Literature Fellowships, FY 2000/2001.* Washington: OMB.

Venuti, Lawrence, ed. 2000. *The Translation Studies Reader.* London: Routledge.

Verdonk, Peter. 2002. *Stylistics.* Oxford: Oxford University Press.

Villanueva, Victor, ed. 1997. *Cross-Talk in Comp Theory: A Reader.* Urbana, IL: NCTE.

Waggoner, Tim. 2001. Our Corner of the Sky: Two-Year College Creative Writing. *Teaching English in the Two-Year College* 29.1:57–68.

Walker, Scott. 1993. Editing for a Small Press. In Gross 1993.

Wallace, M. Elizabeth. 1994. Lower Than the Low One on the Totem Pole. In Greer 1994.

Wallace, Robert, and Michelle Boisseau. 2003. *Writing Poems.* 6th ed. New York: Longman.

Warnock, Tilly. 2000. Language and Literature as "Equipment for Living": Revision as a Life Skill. In Anderson and MacCurdy 2000.

Watchel, Eleanor. 1992. An Interview with Cynthia Ozick. In *Writers & Company,* edited by Eleanor Watchel. San Diego: Harcourt Brace, 1993.

Webb, Charles Harper, ed. 2002. *Stand Up Poetry: An Expanded Anthology.* Iowa City: University of Iowa Press.

Wheeler, Susan. 2004. Reading, Raiding, and Anodyne Eclecticism: Word without World. *Antioch Review* 62.1:148–155.

Williams, Alan. 1993. What Is an Editor? In Gross 1993.

Williams, Bronwyn T. 2003. Never Let the Truth Stand in the Way of a Good Story: A Work for Three Voices. *College English* 65.3:290–304.

Williams, Raymond. 1976. *Keywords: A Vocabulary of Culture and Society.* Oxford: Oxford University Press.

Willis, Paul. 2004. E-mail to David Starkey, 27 August.

Woll, Thomas. 2002. *Publishing for Profit: Successful Bottom-Line Management for Book Publishers.* 2nd ed. Chicago: Chicago Review Press.

Wolff, Tobias. 1994. Introduction to *The Vintage Book of Contemporary American Short Stories,* edited by Tobias Wolff. New York: Vintage.

World Intellectual Property Organization. 2004. www.wipo.int/about-ip/en/world_ip/2004/index.html.

Wright, Anne, ed. 1986. *The Delicacy and Strength of Lace: Letters between Leslie Marmon Silko and James Wright.* St. Paul, MN: Graywolf.

Writer's Chronicle. Associated Writing Programs, Tallwood House, MSN 1E3, George Mason University, Fairfax, VA 22030. awpwriter.org.

Writers Market. Writers Digest Books. F & W Publishers. 4700 E. Galbraith Road. Cincinnati, OH 45236.

Writers on Writing. 2004. *New York Times* online supplement, 20 April. www.tigerseye.ca/tigerwatch/articles/Writers%20on%20Writing%20NYTimes.pdf.

Yagoda, Ben. 2004. *The Sound on the Page: Style and Voice in Writing.* New York: Harper Resource.

Yancey, Kathleen Blake. 2004. Made Not Only in Words: Composition in a New Key. *CCCC* 56.2:297–328.

Young, Art. 2003. Writing across and against the Curriculum. *CCC* 54.3:472–485.

Young, Art, and Toby Fulwiler, eds. 1995. *When Writing Teachers Teach Literature: Bringing Writing to Reading.* Portsmouth, NH: Boynton/Cook.

Yuasa, Nobuyuki, trans. 1975. Introduction to Basho's *The Narrow Road to the Deep North and Other Travel Sketches.* New York: Penguin.